Everything Has Karma

Learning to Embrace
Our Interconnectedness

By Madis Senner

Mother Earth Press
Syracuse, New York
www.motherearthpress.net
motherearthprayers@gmail.com

Copyright © 2019 by Madis Senner
All rights reserved. No part of this book may be reproduced or transmitted without the written permission of the publisher.

Cover Design by Linda Donaldson of Imagine Design.
Illustrations are by Linda Donaldson of Imagine Design.

ISBN 978-0-9908744-2-3

The question is not whether a tree makes a sound if no one is around to hear it fall. It does because that is a given. The question is why did the tree fall and what are the ramifications?

That is because the Great Law of Karma connects everyone and everything that has ever been and that will ever be.

To my parents Linda and Helmar Senner.
Whatever good, compassion and love are within in me
is because of you.
Aitäh (Thank You.)

Table of Contents

Preface	ix
1. Everything Has Karma	1
2. The Illusion of Reality	15
3. Samskaras, The Root of Karma	23
4. Circles	35
5. The Pilgrimage of Reincarnation	53
6. The Web of Circles	67
7. Disconnect	77
8. You Shall Know Them By Their Fruit	97
9. You are a Keeper For All of Creation	127
10. Take A Break With a Mystical Experience	151
11. Working With Samskaras	167
12. Drink Living Water	193
13. Earth Magic	207
14. Blown Away	221
15. The Great Cleansing	231
16. You are Never Alone	251
Bibliography	257
Notes	263
Index	283

Preface

During the winter of 2017/18 as I was traveling around upstate New York talking about my book *Sacred Sites in North Star Country* and the transformative power of space, I began to notice people were interested in my thoughts on karma. Whenever I mentioned "everything has karma," everyone's ears perked up. People were intrigued and asked questions. It was clear that it resonated with many.

I thought back to last fall when I spoke at Gobind Sadan in Central Square, New York. Their now deceased leader, Baba Virsa Singh Ji, said it was one of the holiest places in the world. Indeed. I was there for a memorial service in remembrance of the burning of their temple in the aftermath of 9-11 and saw how they responded with love.

I was seated in the audience and was not slated to speak, but was asked to. What to talk about? I chose to discuss their leader Babaji's famous mantra, "Ek Onkar Satnam Siri WaheGuru," that has had a powerful affect on me on several occasions. The gathering was all too familiar with its transformative power. When I said that it was because of its karma, because "everything has karma," again, people were intrigued. They wanted to know where I received that knowledge from and I told them that I learned it as a student of Mother Earth. Years of meditating in the woods have made me sentient of Her and taught me that the land retains a memory of what has transpired on it.

Several people asked for my email address and requested more information. These were not New Age or alternative spirituality folks. They were devout Sikhs who were committed to meditation and had driven long distances to attend services at Gobind Sadan.

It is clear that people were interested in the concept that "everything has karma" and wanted to learn more. It is a new concept with an old body that has been with us since time began, meaning that it has always existed but people were not aware of it. Karma is a critical concept to understand if you are serious about your spiritual development.

My goal in writing this book is to present you the truth about karma and teach you how to work with it. That knowledge will help you understand the transformative power of space and Mother Earth, as well as mantras and much more. My hope is that you will be inspired to make a pilgrimage and visit sacred sites in North Star Country (greater New York State, America's Northeast); where I believe that Mother Earth's Soul resides. Such a sojourn will help elevate your consciousness and in turn help improve the world.

This book is meant to help you with your spiritual development. It does not provide a path, but instead will better help you navigate your path. You will learn how to hasten your spiritual transformation and raise your consciousness and that of the world. This is not about indulging in physical delights, or becoming rich, or anything similar, because I believe that prosperity and abundance are snares. I live in snowy and cold Syracuse, NY, for a reason. I am less interested in living in a warm environment and more interested in transforming my soul, helping others evolve, and creating a better world. Why Syracuse? Because I believe it is one of the holiest and most sacred places in the world.

I am a former money manager who felt called and committed to being God's servant in 1999, but not in the usual religious way. I endeavored to hear that inner voice of God to guide me, whether it be pursuing a rigorous regiment of meditation and spiritual exercises or coming to the aid of a Muslim doctor, Dr. Rafil Dhafir, at the height of Islamaphobia after 9-11 and just before the second Iraqi War.

In the summer of 2002 I was compelled to gather people to pray around Onondaga Lake, a lake sacred to the Haudenosaunee, also known as the Iroquois. That began my quest to learn about the wonder of Mother Earth and the role that the transformative power of North Star Country has had in raising our collective consciousness, and the movements and great souls born there.

Since then I have come to understand how critical Mother Earth is to our spiritual development. I also now realize that humankind, through our thoughts and actions, can enhance or retard that development. It became very clear to me that the Earth retains a memory (or karma) of what has transpired some place. Certain places have a special indefinable quality that facilitates mystical experiences, brings you to a higher state of consciousness, and/or blesses you with great insights. I have been fortunate to experience such sacred places in North Star Country that have been enhanced by the intentions, prayers, and ceremonies of spiritual pilgrims.

Karma, contrary to what many believe, can be powerfully healing and transformative. That is what I hope to teach you in this book: how to make Karma work for you. You will also learn how pervasive karma is, because everything has karma; and how to make better decisions of which karmas you take on in your life.

Following the call to get people to pray around Onondaga Lake in 2002 I realized that I had to learn how to dowse. Dowsing, which I do, uses dowsing rods made of brass or copper in the shape of an "L." You hold the shorter piece of the L-rod in your hand. Ask a question and rely upon your intuition to point the rods in a particular direction. As a geomancer, I use them regularly to find aspects of Mother Earth in the unseen world (invisible to the human eye). They are a vital tool in my Earth Healing work.

Several people have helped in this endeavor and I would like to thank them. Thanks to fellow lover of Mother Earth and healer Debra Schaffer for guidance and input with early drafts. You are a font of knowledge about Feng Shui and Energy Healing and I am glad that I could call upon that knowledge. Your editing help was most welcome.

Thanks to Suzanne Kotcher for taking the time to read the full manuscript and coming back with suggestions. Your encouragement was much appreciated.

Thanks to violinist Janice Carr for insight on how violins retain a memory. I would have been challenged to find the resources you provided. Special thanks to listening to me read those early drafts.

Thanks to Dr. Manfred Schleyer of the Institute of Flow Sciences (Institut für Strömungswissenschaften) for his correspondence and sharing his knowledge of water and distilled water.

Thanks to Steve Herbert, fellow lover of water and Mother Earth, for sharing your knowledge of living water and blind springs.

Thanks to Joscelyn Godwin a friend and font of knowledge of Esoterism and Hermeticism upon which I could call upon. Thanks for your encouragement after reading my manuscript.

Thanks to PMH Atwater for your kind comments and input. I am so glad that I have been blessed these last few years with your friendship.

To my friend and fellow spiritual traveler Ralph Singh, I give thanks to you for all your work and helping me to get 'Nam' right.

1. Everything Has Karma

In 1988 Claire Sylvia, a dancer, received one of the first heart-lung transplants in New England. Her donor was an eighteen-year-old man who had died in a motorcycle accident in Maine. Given the high profile of the surgery, two reporters interviewed her at Yale New Haven Hospital three days after her transplant.

One of the reporters asked Claire what she wanted to do more than anything else after this miraculous surgery. Her reply: "Actually… I'm dying for a beer right now."[1] She was mortified and surprised by her comment because she did not like beer, but her organ donor did.

Over the months ahead Claire would come to realize that certain aspects of the donor's personality were reflected in her.[2] Where previously she had loathed fast food, she developed an affinity for Snicker's bars, Reese's Peanut Butter Cups, green peppers, Kentucky Fried Chicken and MacDonald's Chicken McNuggets. These were all things her organ donor loved. She realized she had an increase in what she called "male energy." Claire also found that she had lost her desire to cook and her sense of fashion style.

It was clear that Claire Sylvia's heart lung transplant transformed her. Literally almost overnight she went from Claire the dancer, reserved, with refined tastes, to Claire the free spirit—impulsive, bursting with male energy and a desire for fast food.

Claire had received what some call the "cellular memories" of her donor. In other words, "who" her donor was—parts of his personality, preferences, and perspectives—had migrated to her along with his heart and lungs. We know about cellular memories thanks to the work of Dr. Paul Pearsall, a graduate of Wayne State University School of Medicine, who has researched transplant recipients extensively. His work on heart transplant recipients receiving the memories of their donors led to the formation of the Cleveland Clinic's Heart/Mind program.[3] Dr. Pearsall even met with Claire.

Dr. Pearsall believed that our cells retain a memory, particularly our heart,[4] implying that memories may also be stored outside of the brain. Dr. Pearsall notes that every heart transplant recipient he has interviewed, whether they were sensitive and in tune with their heart or not, were affected by the donor's heart; and it did not matter how many years had lapsed since their transplant. They all reported "some form of spiritual imprint of their donor."[5]

Karma

Claire Sylvia had taken on the karma of her donor when she received his organs. To understand this, you need to expand your view of karma.

Karma is about cause and effect, about the belief that our intentions and actions have consequences, about the fact that we will reap what we sow. Here's an example of cause and effect: if we show kindness in helping a stranger (cause), later at some point a stranger will help us (effect). Similarly, if we physically hurt someone, someone will hurt us. Our emotions and thoughts have karma to them as well. So if we are angry towards people, people we encounter will show anger towards us. It is important to know that our actions may not affect us until a later lifetime, meaning you will die and be reborn again (reincarnated) before the karma manifests.

Karma begins as an action (cause), that later will have a response (effect). So a record, or memory of the action (cause) must be kept. Without that record, or memory, there can be no response. So karma needs a memory to do its job.

Claire Sylvia took on the memories (karma) of her donor when she received his heart and lungs. The cause of her inherited karma was her donor's penchant for junk food that was a strong tendency in his character. It encouraged the consumption of more fast food (effect)—Chicken McNuggets, Kentucky Fried Chicken, Snicker's bars, Reese's Peanut Butter Cups, etc.

When we think of karma we automatically assume that it is the result of our own actions. Organ recipients such as Claire Sylvia demonstrate we can take on someone else's preferences, behaviors and thoughts—that we can assume someone else's karma through the transplant of their organs into our own body.

Transformed By Transplants

Taking on parts of an organ donor's personality and life preferences is a very real phenomenon. Often when I talk about Claire's experiences in public someone will tell the story of a friend, or loved one who underwent a transplant and they subsequently saw changes in them.

Dr. Paul Pearsall, in a paper for the Journal of Near-Death Studies,[6] along with Gary Schwartz, PhD, professor of Psychology, Medicine, Neurology, Psychiatry, and Surgery at the University of Arizona and Linda Russek, PhD, then assistant Clinical Professor of Medicine at the University of Arizona, reported on ten case studies of heart transplant recipients.

In one case, a forty-seven-year-old Caucasian man described by his wife as an "Archie Bunker" personality, received the heart of a seventeen-year-old African American male who was accidentally shot in a drive-by shooting on his way to violin class. He had been passionate about classical music and died clutching his violin.

The recipient's wife commented after the transplant that for the first time her husband was now inviting black co-workers to their home. He also began listening to classical music endlessly. His wife even noted that her husband whistled classical music songs that he never knew before.

In another case, a twenty-seven-year-old woman received the heart of a nineteen-year-old woman who died in an automobile accident. The mother of the donor said that her daughter had been a vegetarian who operated a health food restaurant. Her mother described her as being wild, with a new boyfriend every few months. In the final moments of her life she told her mom about the trauma of the accident.

The recipient reported dramatic changes in her life since the transplant. Almost every night for months after the operation, she felt the pain of the donor's accident, particularly in her chest. Admittedly once "McDonald's biggest customer," she now hates meat, and it makes her sick. What really bothered her (the recipient) was that she was now engaged to a man with whom sex was great. The only problem was that she used to be gay! She described herself as having a "gender transplant."

The recipient's brother describes the transformation even more radically, saying that his sister used to be militantly gay and would preach to his girlfriend about the "evils of sexist men." He called her the former "Queen of MacDonald's" who now hates meat.

In another case, a forty-seven-year-old man received the heart of a fourteen-year-old female who died in a gymnastics accident. The gymnast was so excited about life that she hopped around all the time. She was also anorexic and purged herself. Following the transplant, the recipient's brother described him as acting like a kid and jumping around all the time like a "fool." He stated his brother laughs like a young girl, is frequently nauseous, and throws up a lot.

Are there other ways to take on the karma of others besides through heart transplants? In fact, there are many ways to take on karma that is not our own. We are constantly influenced, pulled, changed, manipulated, and even altered by the karma of others. That is because everything and I mean absolutely everything—has karma. While not all karmic pulls are as dramatic as that of an organ recipient, they still affect us.

Inanimate Objects Retain a Memory

Sorcerers have long understood the power of objects to retain a memory and thus created talismans to achieve a certain effect. For example, they might create a healing stone by holding it and praying for or visualizing healing, or visualizing people holding the stone and being healed. They believed that the stone retained a memory of their words and intentions and thus would affect those who came in contact with it.

The belief that objects retain a memory is not confined to sorcerers and mystics. Many Christians view the robe that Jesus wore at his death as being sacred and having healing powers. They cite the bible story of how a woman who had been hemorrhaging for twelve years was cured by simply touching Jesus' robe. (Mark 5.25-30) A book entitled, *The Robe*, by Lloyd C. Douglas (and the subsequent movie), is the tale of how the robe of Jesus transformed a Roman solider. Over half a million people have traveled to Trier, Germany, to see what is believed to be the robe Jesus wore at his death, hoping for a miraculous cure similar to that of the hemorrhaging woman.[7]

Violinists will tell you that their violin is alive and retains the memories of its previous owners. Toby Faber describes this phenomenon in his book on Stradivari, the maker of the world's most revered violin (*Stradivari's Genius*). As an example, he tells how this happened to Ukrainian born master violinist Louis Krasner, who bought the Dancla Strad from the great virtuoso Nathan Milstein.

Krasner said that his predecessor's "playing and sonorities were, I would sense, still in the violin."[8] He noted, "A Strad violin, like a sensitive animal, knows its master and, like the living being that it is, has a memory and loyalty."

Yehudi Menuhin, who many consider the greatest violinist of the twentieth century, was even more passionate about the power of a violin to carry forward the memories of its previous owners. He stated in his autobiography that, "A great violin… is alive, …and its wood stores the history, or the soul, of its successive owners. I never play without feeling that I have released or, alas, violated spirits."[9]

Land Memories

Land has historically been held as being sacred by many cultures and faith traditions, particularly places where significant religious events happened. Christians and Jews see Jerusalem as being holy. Islam suggests that Muslims take a pilgrimage at least once in their life to Mecca. Similarly, Buddhists visit the Bodhi Tree in Bodh Gaya, Bihar, India where Buddha achieved enlightenment. Spiritual pilgrims from around the world, including the Dalai Lama, travel to experience the Bodhi Tree, as if the area around the tree retained the memory of Buddha's transformation.

It is clear that land memories influenced the unusual and sad phenomenon at Overtoun Bridge in Milton, Scotland. Since the 1950s, more than fifty dogs have jumped to their death from the bridge.[10] Others place the number of attempts at six-hundred.[11] No wonder it is called the "dog suicide bridge."[12]

Many theories attempt to explain the dogs' behavior, including that the dogs smell mink or that they sense the mood of the owners living in an economically depressed area. The smell of mink may have gotten the first dog or two to jump—but it was the land memory that got subsequent dogs to do so. Further, humans have also jumped from the bridge, and it's reported that a father threw his baby off the structure.

It is highly probable that land memories attached to Overtoun Bridge influenced the dogs to jump to their death. Just as Claire Sylvia gained an affinity for junk food from her organ donor's memories, the dogs picked up the memory of other dogs' desires to jump from the bridge. The more dogs that jumped, the stronger the imprint became, encouraging even more dogs to jump. Interestingly, all of the jumps occurred around the final two parapets on the right-hand side, lending credence to the 'memories theory.'

The notion that a particular memory, suicidal in this case, can spur us to act against our best interest is unfortunately all too common. T.C. Lethbridge (1901-1971) who served as the Keeper of Anglo-Saxon Antiquities at the Cambridge University Museum of Archaeology and Ethnology from 1923 to 1957 has written about this phenomenon. When he left the museum he studied dowsing and parapsychology, and subsequently wrote several books.

Lethbridge believed that our thoughts could attach to a particular location and cause subsequent visitors to act in a certain manner. He and his wife once traveled to Ladram Bay in England to collect seaweed. They both experienced a queasy and depressing feeling near the face of a cliff. When they investigated the cliff above, again both felt a thought enter their minds inviting them to jump off. Lethbridge commented, "We were surely picking up the thoughts of someone who had either jumped off the cliff, or wanted to."[13] He documented that at least five other people had experienced a variety of similar occurrences encouraging them to jump. Two years after their experience, a fellow who had parked his car some distance away, apparently looking for a place to commit suicide, ended up at the same place.

We are all Sin Eaters

One of the most haunting and riveting television programs I have ever seen, one that still clings to me, was a show called "The Sins of Our Fathers"[14] that aired on Rod Serling's the Night Gallery (2/23/1972). Serling was famous for his Twilight Zone television series that used science fiction, the curious, and weird to entertain and make social commentary.

The program was based upon an old Welsh custom of sin eating, where the poor and the pariah would have a ritual meal and eat away the sins of a recently deceased person. In doing so, they would take on the sins themselves, and it was believed that in doing so they would be damned for all of eternity. Basically, the sin eater was a karma eater who was supposedly negating (removing) the repercussions of bad karma created during a lifetime through violent and selfish acts.

The story begins at a time when plague and famine have been devastating the countryside. After days of searching for a sin eater, a servant arrives at the home of a sin eater named Dylan Evans. His wife tells the servant that her starved husband is dying, and instead she offers her son. She does not intend to have her son do the sin eating ritual; instead, he is to fake the ceremony and bring all the food back home.

When they arrive back at the deceased's the son persuades everyone to leave the room so he can be alone with the dead man. He begins the sin eating ceremony by shouting "God almighty ... let all the sins of this corpse flow into my body." As he speaks the words, he grabs the food around corpse and stashes it into his tunic. He howls and screams as he continues stuffing his tunic with food. With his tunic filled, the son bolts back home.

At home, he unloads all the food on the kitchen table. Before he can begin to eat it, his mother takes the food into the other room and places it next to her deceased husband.

The son realizes that his mother's intent was never to have them eat the food to end their hunger, but to serve as the feast for a sin eating ceremony for his father. The mother tempts her starving son by describing in detail the thick slabs of bacon and wedges of cake.

He tells his mother he cannot eat the sins of a sin eater. The mother responds that his father was no simple farmer: "He ate sin upon sin, year after year, hundreds of sins from hundreds of men. Someone has to take on the sins of the sin eater."

The son lunges towards the food, screaming, "Oh God almighty, give me this man's sins. Let me be damned forever," and begins devouring the food. We see his eyes gaze over as he howls and screams.

We are all sin eaters, consuming the sins, or karma, of others. More often than not we consume the cumulative karma of sin eaters, upon sin eaters over a long period of time. There is no formal ceremony with a feast to take on karma. Rather, we take on the "sins" or karma through what we eat, what we watch, where we go, what we think, through the groups we belong to, and more. Every interaction, thought, intention, and affiliation in our life has karma. We are affected by everything that we come into contact with.

This is not to say that all karma is bad and harmful to you. There is good karma; karma that can help you in many ways. For example, the memories attached to the violin of former masters improved the playing of subsequent violinists.

We Are One

I am hoping to expand your concept of karma beyond an egocentric perspective. Most of the teachings and books on karma speak to how you can free yourself of karma's influence. But the fact is that in a world where everything has karma, we are tethered and bound to a multitude of people past and present, the energies of locations, and to all sorts of things living and non-living. They influence us on a constant basis.

It is important to realize that not only are we affected by people's actions in the past, but we will also influence others in the future. The owner of a violin not only takes on the memories of its previous owners, but adds to them as well. So, in the future, the next owner of the violin will be experiencing the memories of all that have owned and played the violin before them.

Karma is not bound by time. It carries forward the memories of the past. It connects the present to the past and carries it forward into the future. It is the sum total of what has ever been and will be. It is timeless.

In this book, I am providing direction to help you navigate a world filled with karmic energies. It is a path not only to guide you, but also help you loosen the chains that bind others. You will learn that it is by freeing others, that we free ourselves. No doubt you need to help yourself, but ultimately you have to live your life with the understanding that we are all interconnected to each other, to Mother Earth and to all of creation; that everything is evolving and that there is greater reality to the world we live in.

Imagine if you undertook actions to make a better world, or improve a group you belong to, or turn a piece of land into a sacred space for all to enjoy. These actions would boomerang back to you. The world would look to improve you, your club or organization would lift you up, or members of other clubs would help you and Mother Earth would nourish you.

As we become aware of karma and its influence on our lives, we learn that "oneness" and "unity" are quite real. We truly ARE our sisters and brothers' keepers, as well as the keepers of all of creation and Mother Earth. We learn that karma is one of the ways we are bound together with all of creation and Mother Earth. More importantly, we learn that karma can be a powerful tool to advance our individual and collective spiritual evolution.

The Journey Ahead

The idea that everything has karma is a radical departure from the traditional view of karma. I write about karma as an extension, or expansion, of the traditional understanding of what karma is. I want to show you how pervasive karma is in your life.

This is a metaphysical book, and in it I write about ultimate reality, esoteric concepts, and other concepts which you may not have heard before. Although most of us have heard about, or are even familiar with, the concept of karma, few know the technical aspects of how it works. I will explain this in the next few chapters.

I will offer two ways for navigating a world where everything has karma: helping you better make choices about the karma that you take into your life, and teaching you how to make karma work for you.

The first few chapters will explain how karma works and how we take it on. You will learn why karma matters and how pervasive it is. As we go further into this book, I will teach you how to recognize the karma of certain organizations/ groups/religions and disciplines; and how you can lessen its impact. In a world where everything has karma, you will learn how you can lessen the affects of bad karma.

You will learn a variety of ways to reduce and possibly remove some of your karma. You will learn how to make better choices about the karma you take on, as well as ways that you can make karma work for you. Not only do I explain it, but I also provide clear examples and recommendations. Truly you can make karma work for you.

A book on karma would not be complete without a discussion of how it affects your spiritual development. That is because karma is ultimately about facilitating your spiritual transformation. As part of that I will be talking about the journey of the dark night of your soul; a painful and haunting experience you will encounter in this life, or in a next life in which you are going to lighten your load of karma.

I will be introducing several new concepts such as circles and spiritual nutrition. A few of them, such as the impact of others on your spiritual development, will be startling, arguably shocking, and may lead you to dismiss me as being a sensationalist, a fool, or worse.

Just because someone has had a difficult or troubled life does not necessarily mean it is the result of bad choices they made in a previous life. Someone may have decided to take on challenges in order to evolve, or they may have taken on someone else's karma.

What is happening on the Earth Plane may also be just the opposite of what is going on in the spiritual realm. When a rich young man asked Jesus how to get eternal life, he told him to give all his money to the poor and to follow him. Jesus told his disciples that it was easier for a camel to get through the eye of a needle than for a rich man to enter into the kingdom of heaven. (Mt. 19.24) Jesus concluded by saying, "…but many who are first will be last, and many who are last will be first.

(Mt. 19.30) Meaning that those successful and famous in the Earth Plane might not be so in heaven.

Basically: don't judge.

Chained to Our Past

The Bhagavad Gita, also known as the Gita, is a beautiful poem that comprises a dialogue between Prince Arjuna, and his charioteer, Lord Krishna. Through their conversation, Hinduism is revealed and explained.

Like all great scriptures, the Gita has many translations and interpretations. One of them was by Eknath Easwaran (1910-1999), an Indian—born scholar who came to America on a Fulbright Scholarship and never left. His spiritual transformation began shortly after the loss of two souls he admired, Mahatma Gandhi (1869-1948) and his grandmother who was his spiritual teacher. One day afterwards, he came home to find that a truck had killed his dog, and the loss was so inconsolable that he began to endlessly read and recite the Gita.

Easwaran in the preface to his translation of the Gita says, "Two forces pervade human life, the Gita says: the upward thrust of evolution and the downward pull of our evolutionary past."[15] The downward pull of our evolutionary past is our karma. Through our ignorance and egocentric view of karma, we have let it become a chain with an anchor attached to it that prevents our spiritual advance. Instead, we need to understand that everything has karma, and that karma can be like a hot air balloon that lifts us to higher states of consciousness and facilitates our spiritual transformation.

2. The Illusion of Reality

To understand why everything has karma and that we are all sin, or karma eaters, you need to know about the nature of reality, or what some call 'ultimate reality.' Karma forms in the unseen world and manifests in the physical world. By understanding the nature of ultimate reality, we can begin to see why everything has karma.

The world we live in is an illusion. It is not real, or perhaps it's more accurate to state that it is not as it appears to be. There is a greater existence behind what we call reality (the material world, the Earth Plane, the physical world). Hindus call this illusion "maya."

If you have seen the movie "The Matrix," you will have an idea of the concept of "maya." Neo, Trinity, and Morpheus lived in one world, but would enter another computer-simulated reality called the Matrix. It was a sophisticated and enormous virtual reality that most people accepted as reality. Yet it was not reality.

Instead, people lived in pods tethered to machines, which connected them to the Matrix. So while they thought they were living, walking around, and eating in one world, their reality was actually an illusion. Think back to how Morpheus freed Neo. We see Neo in a pod filled with a slimy, gel-like solution with numerous tentacles attached to him. He looks around and sees thousands upon thousands of other pods around him, all containing people. A machine, assuming Neo is defective, comes over and removes his tentacles and he is set free. Morpheus greets him by saying "welcome to the real world," implying that the computer-simulated Matrix he once called home was an illusion.

Right now, we are living in a Matrix-like reality. We believe it is real, but it is not. It is an illusion—a sophisticated simulation.

Our true being, our soul, resides in a spiritual existence. Though our physical body exists in the material world (physical reality, the Earth Plane), our material world is like the virtual reality called the Matrix. It is not real, but an illusion.

Our physical body is in the material world to help facilitate the spiritual evolution of our soul...to help us become more loving, giving, and compassionate...to make us selfless.

Another way to see our existence is as a sophisticated video game. Our true being, or soul, resides in the real world. When we play a video game, we become an avatar in the virtual reality within it, the material world. As we play the game, we become more absorbed within it. We may get so swept up in the video game that we lose track of what is going on around us and begin to think we are living in the virtual reality.

We Live in a Sea of Consciousness

The ultimate reality behind the Matrix-like world we live in is made up of "consciousness." Behind our true being and the world around us is pure consciousness. Everything is consciousness: our physical bodies, animals, mountains, and even our patterns of behavior and thinking.

Sri Aurobindo (1872-1950) one the great mystics and philosophers of the last few centuries teaches us that we live in a sea of consciousness. He was a prominent Indian political activist early in the twentieth century who advocated for India's independence from England. A shift in his focus from politics to spirituality began occurring around the time he and several other activists were implicated and arrested in a bomb plot.

A few months before Sri Aurobindo was arrested he broke from his activities and spent several days with a guru who taught him how to still his mind through meditation, and in doing so, he opened up the door to the divine. Later, he would tell a disciple that a voice within him had told him to hand himself "over to the Divine within me, enjoining an absolute surrender to its will…a seed force to which I kept unswervingly and increasingly till it led me through all the mazes of an incalculable Yogic development."[16]

In prison, his transformation continued, and he decided to dedicate himself entirely to a spiritual life. As his biographer A. B. Purani tells, his field of action was enlarged enormously, from the service of the country and its freedom to a worldwide work of intimately touching the future of humanity.[17]

Upon his acquittal, that voice within directed him to move to Pondicherry, India (French India) to spend the rest of his life in spiritual practices and teaching.[18]

Eventually, French-born Mirra Alfassa (who Sri Aurobindo dubbed the Mother) would join him. Interestingly, she began having dreams and visions of Sri Aurobindo ten years before they met. Shortly after meeting him she said that their joining together was not something to be pursued but was " a fact accomplished long ago"; and she was told "Do not revel in the ecstatic contemplation of this union, fulfill the mission I have confided to thee on earth."[19]

Sri Aurobindo viewed the Mother as an equal partner. She began to increasingly take over the daily duties of the household, which evolved into a spiritual ashram as the number of students increased. Sri Aurobindo would eventually focus solely on yoga, on which the Mother assisted him with.

Sri Aurobindo explained how pervasive consciousness is when he wrote, "Consciousness is a fundamental thing, the fundamental thing in existence—it is the energy, the motion, the movement of consciousness that creates the universe and all that is in it – not only the macrocosm but the microcosm is nothing but consciousness arranging itself."[20] He believed the evolution of humankind hinges upon the transformation of our consciousness.

Sri Aurobindo taught that everything is consciousness — energy, objects, liquids, gases, motion, organizations, and our individual, as well as, our group/collective thoughts. Everything is consciousness. The world as we know it, as Sri Aurobindo stated, "…is nothing but consciousness arranging itself."

So if we as people take on karma, whether individually or from others, as heart transplant recipients such as Claire Sylvia did, then organizations, objects, songs, places, religious groups, liquids, flora, and fauna can also take on karma. That is because everything is consciousness, and karma attaches to consciousness.

Karma makes no distinction between a heart, a violin, a cliff, or a bridge; it is all consciousness. It will attach to whatever the form of consciousness is. Because everything is consciousness, karma attaches to everything.

Whenever you consume something, go someplace, or join a group, you will be taking on its karma. So you need to be judicious about where you spend time, what you eat or wear, about the groups you belong to, etc. Everything in our lives carries karma because everything, at its core, is consciousness, and karma attaches to consciousness. Karma inexorably connects us to everyone and everything. Some of these interactions will have a powerful influence on you and others will have almost no influence at all.

Brahman, God

This sea of consciousness is all part of Brahman, or God, who is the source and end of all things. Brahman is the only thing that exists, the true reality. The great Hindu sage of the eighth century, Adi Shankara said, "All this universe known through speech and mind is nothing but Brahman; there is nothing besides Brahman."[21] Brahman is pure consciousness according to Shankara.[22]

Shankara was a spiritual prodigy who, as a child, went from town to town debating village and spiritual elders. He believed that true knowledge was gained through experience and not through reading books, chanting, or breathing exercises. We must meditate on the truth and get to know God.

Shankara taught that the divine spark of God, Atman, exists in all of us. He stated, "Atman is no other than Brahman... It is consciousness itself...It is unchangeable, eternal. It does not dissolve when the body dissolves."[23] Atman is the eternal soul. There is also the evolving soul, or the psychic being, as Sri Aurobindo taught. The evolving soul is looking to become pure consciousness (later in Chapter 4, Circles, I will discuss the psychic being in greater detail).

In Chapter 7 of the Gita Lord Krishna explains to Arjuna that all of existence takes place within and is the absolute:

The birth and dissolution of the cosmos itself take place in me. There is nothing that exists separate from me, Arjuna. The entire universe is suspended from me as a necklace of jewels.

Arjuna, I am the taste of pure water and the radiance of the sun and moon. I am the sacred word and the sound heard in the air, and the courage of human beings. I am the sweet fragrance in the earth and the radiance of the fire; I am the life in every creature and the striving of the spiritual aspirant." (7.6-9)

Spirit and Matter

Ultimate reality is pure consciousness and at its core is God. So how does the virtual reality we call the Earth Plane and material reality take place?

Consider it as the distinction between spirit and matter. Spirit, in this case, is pure consciousness, while matter is the material world. Consciousness (spirit) devolves to take on material form. Think of the stages of devolution being like floors in a tall skyscraper. As consciousness starts devolving with each step down, it becomes more like matter and less like spirit. It begins in the ethereal and ends on the ground floor of the physical world. Like steps in a staircase, each floor in its devolution consciousness becomes more like matter and less like spirit. When it finally reaches the ground floor consciousness is almost all matter.

Exhibit 2.1 Devolution of Consciousness shows how consciousness devolves to create the material world. With each step down the amount of spirit (consciousness) diminishes and the amount of matter increases until it reaches the point where there is very little spirit left. The gradients (ovals) in Exhibit 2.1 are not exact, but help to illustrate the devolution of consciousness.

There are many levels between pure consciousness and the physical world that is dominated by matter. Each of them has a distinct gradient, or blend, of spirit and matter. The closer to pure consciousness a gradient is, the higher the proportion of consciousness (spirit) relative to matter.

Some call these gradients Planes of Existence, or just Planes. Others see them as other dimensions, or alternative realities.

Ultimately, your goal is to reverse course and become more like spirit and less like matter.

The Devolution of Consciousness

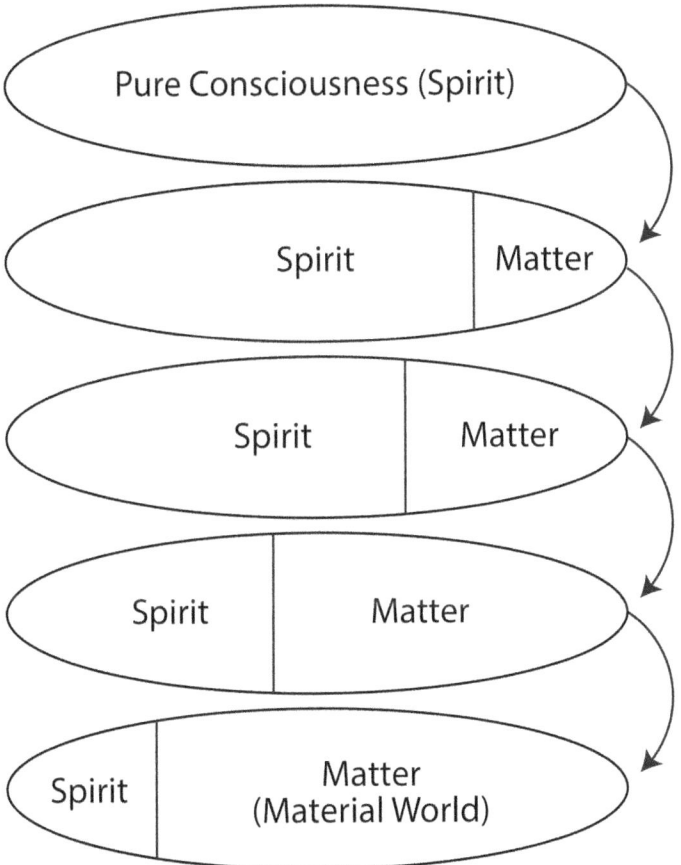

Exhibit 2.1 Devolution of Consciousness. The ovals represent steps down in the devolution of consciousness to create the material world (Matter). With each step down from pure consciousness (Spirit) the amount of Spirit diminishes and the amount of Matter increases for a respective gradient.

3. Samskaras, The Root of Karma

So karma attaches to consciousness, and because we live in a sea of consciousness, karma attaches to everything; because everything is consciousness. But, what attaches?

A memory or, a record of what transpired is what attaches.

At its core, karma is a memory. Everything else, from the boomerang affect of payback for our actions to reincarnation, is built upon a memory. Without a record (memory), karma cannot work. Memory, as you are about to learn, can be quite powerful and enduring.

Hindu Vedanta (the oneness of all of creation, the divinity of the soul, the universality of all) teaches that each thought or intention we have, or action we take, emotion we have, or sound we hear, creates an impression on our mind called a 'samskara.' These thought impressions/imprints (or samskaras) are like grooves on a vinyl album. We are covered with them and they reflect all that we have thought and done.

Samskaras are the root of karma and they exert a powerful influence upon us.

Vritti's — The Vortex Shape

To better understand the power and properties of samskaras we turn to their form. Samskaras are essentially thoughts. Hindus call our thoughts vrittis, literally translated as 'whirlpool.' So samskaras have a whirlpool, or circular-like pattern of movement. Basically, a samskara behaves like a vortex.

Think of a whirlpool in the water and how it pulls in everything around it into its eye. Tiny particles around the whirlpool are drawn to it and are eventually sucked into its whirlpool. The image of a vortex has been used to describe incredible power through descriptions such as 'hurricane force' and inescapability with phrases such as 'death spiral' and 'spiraling out of control.'

So it is no wonder how strong and dominating the samskaras attached to a heart are in influencing heart transplant recipients such as Claire Sylvia. They have been percolating for the donor's whole life. In essence, Claire's donor altered her food preferences towards junk food, had her lose her flair for dressing and cooking, and more. Again: think of the power and influence of a vortex.

Samskaras look to reassert themselves by causing us to keep thinking the same thought, or perform the same action repeatedly. If we think or do the same thing over and over again, the deeper that impression becomes, in the process increasing its influence upon us. Acting out or thinking about a particular thought is like fertilizer to a plant and makes it grow stronger.

Have you ever gotten a thought that you could not shake? Had an earworm, a song, play endlessly in your mind? Who has not fallen victim to a thought? The more you think about it the stronger it becomes. Samskaras if left unchecked, can create obsessive, compulsive and addictive behavior.

Over time, if samskaras get deeper, they begin to cloud our thinking and exert more and more influence over us. If allowed to grow they can begin to dominate and control our lives. They can become like weeds, that if unchecked, can take over a garden.

Meher Baba (1894-1969), in his book *Discourses*[24] that deals with the spiritual path, delves into samskaras, or what he calls "sanskaras," saying that they are deposits of previous experiences and are the most important determinates in our past and future experience. He feels that to understand the significance of human experience requires one to understand the formation and purpose of samskaras.[25]

Meher Baba was born (1894-1969) in India to parents of Persian decent who were Zoroastrians.[26] As a young man, he befriended an older woman, Hazrat Babajan, a Sufi mystic. One day (in 1915) she held his face in her hands and kissed him on the forehead and he was transformed and began his spiritual path with great intensity. Meher Baba practiced bhakti (devotion, praise to God) and was passionately devoted to, and worshipped, God, and achieved high states of God intoxication (what he called *"masti"*). He would actively seek other *"masts,"* those who were so intoxicated with God that they lost contact with the external world. Often they were indigent.[27]

In 1925, Meher Baba began a period of silence where he did not speak and communicated only through a rectangular board on which letters of the alphabet were painted. He maintained his vow of silence until his death in 1969.

Meher Baba believed that samskaras limit and control us, saying that "*sanskaras* or impressions form an enclosure around the possible field of consciousness. The circle of *sanskaras* constitutes that limited area in which alone the individual consciousness can be focused." He felt that, in the process, we become helpless captives of the illusions projected by our own false thinking.[28]

In other words, samskaras act like horse blinders and limit our perception of how we see and view the world. Meher Baba felt that samskaras help perpetuate the feeling that our body exists. This limiting affect of samskaras that Baba talks about is not confined to our perceptions of our body, but affects everything about us and around us. Basically: how we see things from reality, to judging people, our behavior, our likes, etc., are clouded by our samskaras.

Because samskaras attach to consciousness, and everything is consciousness, they (samskaras) attach to everything. Subsequently everything carries samskaras. So when Claire Sylvia got a heart lung transplant, she inherited the samskaras that had attached to her donor's heart and lungs. It was the donor's samskaras attached to his heart and lungs that got Claire into eating junk food, losing her flair for dressing and cooking, and brought a host of other changes. The influence of samskaras upon us is well beyond anything we have thought or done.

While Meher Baba said that samskaras overran our being and limited our perspective, he ultimately felt they played a vital role in our transformation. He said: "It is the evolutionary struggle that enables the soul to develop full consciousness…The process of reincarnation therefore is to enable the soul to eliminate the samskaras by passing through the furnace of pain and pleasure."[29]

Each impression or thought we have is like a seed that is capable of bearing fruit (producing more like-minded thoughts) and producing many more seeds. Swami Satyananda Saraswati speaks to this in his interpretation of Patanjali's *Yoga Sutras*. He references to a third century AD Indian philosopher, Nagarjuna, in telling how samskaras proliferate and bring about more future lives:

> It is said by Nagarjuna that a seed when not burned is capable of giving rise to many seeds and plants. In the same way when the chitta (individual consciousness, memory) is not freed from the samskaras, it is capable of producing many more samskaras, bodies and reincarnations.[30]

Many consider Patanjali to be the founder of yoga. It is believed he lived sometime between the second century BC and the fourth century AD. The *Yoga Sutras* contains 197 aphorisms on the theory and practice of yoga and provides a path to liberation with a heavy emphasis on meditation and achieving the meditative state of Samadhi.

When I began an intensive meditative practice to achieve the meditative state of Samadhi, I relied on the Yoga Sutras a lot, particularly on the Swami Satyananda Saraswati's version, *Four Chapters on Freedom—Commentary on the Yoga Sutras of Patanjali*,[31] because it was evident he knew first-hand about the nuances of the various meditative, or trance, states. He was the founder of the Bihar School of Yoga in India and a student of Sri Swami Sivananda, who founded the Divine Life Society.

The Yoga Sutras place heavy emphasis on achieving the meditative state of Samadhi. Samadhi has many definitions, or interpretations from ecstasy to union with God, to the loss of "I-ness" when meditating. Swami Satyananda Saraswati says the Samadhi begins when your consciousness has broken free from the physical sphere and the sense of individualism does not exist.[32]

Altered states of consciousness are an important concept that I will come back to later. By going into the trance state of Samadhi, our awareness is set free from the physical world and its trappings, and we lose our sense of individuality. In a gross oversimplification, we can say it is the ultimate vacation, hiatus, separation, or disconnect from the reality of the physical world. It is also the ultimate union with God.

It is said that the sage Sri Ramakrishna, who was credited with the revival of Hinduism in the mid-nineteenth century, would go into Samadhi for days, even weeks, on end. He would remain in Samadhi so long that he would have to be force-fed to stay alive.[33]

Patanjali advocates concentration as a meditative technique, picking an object, word, or image to focus on; the principle being that by feeding one thought, or samskara, it will become stronger and block out other thoughts (samskaras). Eventually your concentration becomes one-pointed to where all that you realize is your focus of concentration and awareness of everything else evaporates. This eventually leads to Samadhi. In other words, focusing and concentrating on one thing can elevate our consciousness and free us.

The Law of Attraction

Not only do our thought impressions, or samskaras, plant more seeds that bear fruit within us, but they also attract other like-minded thoughts, or bring similar actions upon us. They are like magnets, attracting similar thoughts/actions to us.

The Law of Attraction, that like-minded thoughts are attracted to each other, is the mechanism of action that facilitates the boomerang affect of karma. We reap what we sow. If we put out love, then it is love that we will attract. If we put out violence, then violence will be drawn to us. It is the Law of Attraction that makes this possible.

Madame Blavatsky is credited with first stating the Law of Attraction in the late nineteenth century when the New Thought Movement—we are what we think, the power of positive thinking, the mind cure—was at its height. Rhonda Byrne, with her wildly successful book and movie *The Secret*, is a popular manifestation of the New Thought Movement. Much of it is predicated on the Law of Attraction and how we can reap all sorts of material rewards by just thinking and visualizing prosperity and wealth.

Blavatsky noted that mystics and adepts have long known that like attracts like in the unseen world: "It is the universal law, which is understood by Plato and explained in Timaeus as the attraction of lesser bodies to larger ones, and of similar bodies to similar."[34]

Helena Blavatsky was a Russian-born immigrant who was one of the co-founders of Theosophy in 1875. Theosophy is a wisdom tradition that focuses on the occult and esoteric teachings to achieve Enlightenment. One of the sayings attributed to Theosophy is, "May you be blessed to be born in one religion and die in another."[35] When I first left Wall Street one of my early teachers was a Theosophist. I used to attend Theosophical meetings at the NYC lodge and considered myself a member. Interestingly, this was around the time that the movie The Matrix came out, and many Theosophists believed that the chain-smoking oracle was based upon the chain-smoking Blavatsky, with all her occult and mystical teachings.

New Thought leader William Walker Atkinson, who is credited with writing close to a hundred books under various pen names (Theron Q. Dumont, Yogi Ramacharaka), said that there was one great law in the universe: the Law of Attraction. He felt that we place so much emphasis on the Law of Gravitation but ignore The Law of Attraction, "the mighty Law that draws to us the things we desire or fear—that makes or mars our lives."[36]

Karma is based upon cause and effect. Put out love (cause) and love will come back to you (effect). The Law of Attraction is what makes the process of karma work.

Because the Law of Attraction makes karma work, it should be viewed as a component of karma, not as a stand-alone Law. It exists to make karma work—not to be a phenomena, or law, by itself, per se.

Samskaras Can Live Forever

Once formed, a samskara can last forever, especially if it is fed by repetition of action and/or thought; or if there was a strong emotion or trauma associated with its creation. It attaches to our being and remains there. If not cleared in this life, we carry it forward into a future life.

Because samskaras carry our karma forward into a future life, they facilitate the process of reincarnation. If it were not for samskaras reincarnation would be much different and most likely would not happen.

Samskaras influence our behavior, our tendencies, and even help shape our character, particularly those we feed through repeated behavior/thought. Swami Vivekananda (1863-1902), a student of Sri Ramakrishna, teaches that samskaras shape who we will be:

> Each work we do, each thought we think, produces an impression called in Sanskrit samskara, upon the mind; and the sum total of these impressions becomes the tremendous force which is called character...The sum total of the samskaras is the force which gives a man the next direction after death. A man dies, the body falls away and goes back to the elements; but the samskaras remain, adhering to the mind.[37]

Swami Vivekananda is credited with having introduced Hinduism, particularly Vedanta to the west when he gave his speech at the World Parliament of Religions in 1893 during the Chicago World's Fair. He believed that the divine spark is in all of us and that our goal was to spiritually evolve and become like the divine. While teaching in the Thousand Islands Park along the St. Lawrence River in northern New York State, he achieved the highest state of Samadhi, Nirvikalpa Samadhi. The Ramakrishna—Vivekananda Center New York purchased the property and erected a monument on the spot of this great achievement.

Patanjali calls the tendencies we create in our character 'vasanas.'[38] To understand this, remember that the Law of Attraction is one of the properties of karma: an action will encourage us to repeat or do more of the same action, or thought. So when we undertake an action, a samskara, or impression is created. It will encourage more of the same, and try to have us repeat the act. This will make the samskara stronger. It will also help fructify the karma we have taken on and encourage it to bear more fruit and manifest.[39]

By making the samskara stronger, it takes on a greater role in our life, creating a tendency and even shaping our character. Let's say we steal something. This may embolden us to steal again, or be dishonest in another way. It becomes a stronger influence in our life. So we have the beginnings of something more than an individual act—we have a pattern of behavior. If we do not clear up the samskaras that made this particular tendency, we will carry it forward into a future life. In this case, we will have a tendency to be dishonest.

The important thing to note about samskaras is how powerful they are. They determine our character and whom we are, and if not burned off, are carried forward into our future lives.

Our Thoughts Morph

There is another point to note about the behavior of our thoughts and samskaras. Over time, they will morph, become more powerful and will take on characteristics different than when they were first formed. The Bhagavad-Gita says, "When you keep thinking about sense objects attachment comes. Attachment breeds desire, the lust of possession burns to anger." (2.62)

Anger can turn into violence; violence can turn into murder. The point is that our thoughts can escalate and morph well beyond their original intent.

Think of a situation in your life when one simple action mushrooms. It could be something as simple as being on a diet, and you eat something you were not supposed to, and it cascades, and you blow your diet.

Seed Thoughts

It is the ability of our thoughts to morph and become so much more that makes our spiritual transformation possible. We can become spiritually transformed or, enlightened because our thoughts/actions have the ability to become something else; something different; something so much more than we could have ever imagined.

New Thought Movement concepts, such as the power of positive thinking and we become what we think, are based upon the concept that our thoughts morph. Basically, our thoughts will eventually change us dramatically.

Numerous books have been written about how we have the ability to radically transform ourselves through our intention. Spurring on this growth has been the development of neuroplasticity; the finding that we can radically re-alter our brain during our lifetime.

One of the authors in this new movement is Rick Hanson, who has written books with titles such as *Buddha's Brain, The Practical Neuroscience of Happiness, Love and Wisdom*; *Hardwiring Happiness, The New Brain Science of Contentment, Calm and Confidence*; *Resilient: How to Grow an Unshakable Core of Calm, Strength, and Happiness*.

Hanson is a neuropsychologist and meditation teacher. In his NY Times bestseller *Hardwiring Happiness*[40] he advocates what he calls 'self-directed neuroplasticity' by focusing and dwelling on positive experiences throughout the day. By taking in the good experiences and dwelling on them, we begin to rewire our brains (neuroplasticity) and start to develop the sense to see the positive in everything. There are several testimonials to the success of his method in reviews of his book online, at Amazon.

The morphing and transformative power of our focus and thinking speaks to the power of seed thoughts. Just as a tiny oak seed can grow to become an enormous tall oak tree, so can we become something so much more by planting that seed thought within us.

It is that first step, that seed thought, that will determine who you become.

When it Rains It Pours — The Levels of Karma

You have heard it said that when it rains, it pours; meaning that when things start to go bad they continue to get worse. The misery, or misfortune, or mishaps, become a trend that becomes almost irreversible at the time. So instead of a little hardship, the rain in your life becomes a downpour as misery keeps piling on.

To understand this you need to realize how the levels of karma may be behind this. Karma and its Law of Attraction work at every level of your being: your thoughts, actions, emotions, words and more.

Consider an accident where you break something. On one level, the physical or material level, it is the breaking of something. At another level, it may cause disappointment, or anger, or melancholy within you. Now you are putting out melancholy and disappointment. Karma and its Law of Attraction begin responding to your attitude and emotional response of disappointment and melancholy over your accident.

A cavalcade of experiences, images, events, or people that are guaranteed to elicit melancholy and disappointment within you begin appearing in your life, further fueling your sadness. You may break things or loose things—but it may not be physical tragedy you are bringing upon yourself. It is sadness and disappointment that you are beckoning towards yourself.

If you ever experience such a cascade of misery, put out love. Give and give. Help someone in need, spend some time at a soup kitchen, or donate your time someplace. The important thing is to find a way to give, and give, and give… Remember always try to maintain a positive attitude as best as you can, no matter what. This will help you prevent a boomerang of melancholy and disappointment. STAY POSITIVE.

Defining Who We Are

Samskaras exert a powerful influence upon us. They have the ability to influence our thinking and behavior. Longer term they shape our character over many lifetimes.

Not all samskaras bear bad karma. There are also positive samskaras: Ones founded on love and compassion that can elevate your consciousness and facilitate your spiritual transformation. In the pages that follow I will offer many other ways that you can make samskaras and their karma work for you.

The quest for immortality has been a pursuit of humankind since the earliest of times. The fact that samskaras can last forever shows that some things are eternal. One wonders if there something about samskaras that can help us transcend time? Indeed, there is.

4. Circles

So we retain a memory, a samskara, of all that we think and do and that becomes the root of our individual karma. What is the mechanism, or agent, by which we take on the karma of others? To understand how we take on the karma of others, of things, and of groups, you need to know about 'circles.'

A circle is essentially any union, whether it is you and a friend; you and a group of people; you and an organization; or you and an object; you and a place; you and a song; or you and a club, or team; or you and a trade. Circles like samskaras have a vortex form with a circular shape and exhibit the behavior of a vortex. You could say that they are samskaras, but that would be confusing. Just see them as being any union that you have with anyone else, an object, a concept, a discipline, a group, or a place.

A circle is also the mechanism through which you interact through in your relationships. For example, you can be a member of an organization, attending its meetings and acting in its interest. Because this organization is a separate and distinct entity with an existence of its own there has to be an independent, but related structure through which you can take on its karma. That structure is a circle that I call a 'connecting circle' because it connects you to another circle.

Again: any union forms a circle, however, your interaction with a particular circle requires the formation of a separate and distinct connecting circle through which you can take on the circle's karma. This newly formed circle is unique to you and a particular circle. While you can take on a circle's karma, it does not mean that the circle will subsume you and have you lose your identity.

Circles also give form to consciousness. In other words, they allow consciousness to manifest as a group, a theory, a song, an object, and more. A circle also provides a medium to which karma can attach. So a circle can and will carry karma.

Circles are an enormous concept that has a huge bearing upon you; one that you may have had inkling about, but have never heard about. I even drafted an outline for a book about them. I write about them now because in order to grasp how you take on the karma of others you need to know about circles.

Water Imitates Life

To better understand circles and see them at work, we look to water researcher Theodor Schwenk (1910-1986). Some might call him a hydrologist, and while he certainly employed a scientific approach to the study water, he also saw its spiritual nature. He felt that humankind had lost its reverence for water and no longer saw its divinity, having abandoned the water gods of old. He saw the wonder of water and its relationship with developing living forms.

Schwenk was an Anthroposophist. Anthroposophy is a philosophy developed by Rudolf Steiner (1861-1925), who believed that the spiritual world was accessible through intellectual rigor and observation. Steiner was a philosopher and esotericist briefly affiliated with Theosophy early in the twentieth century.

Schwenk's book *Sensitive Chaos, The Creation of Flowing Forms in Water and Air* is beloved many of us that see water as being magical and alive, what we call 'Living Water.' In it Schwenk discusses the many properties that water possesses and displays, such as, wherever water forms its takes on a spherical shape, whether it be a tiny drop of water or covering the whole spherical earth. Water is essentially a circulatory system, from the movement of rivers and streams to the cycle of precipitation, condensation, and evaporation. In particular, Schwenk focused on the movement of water.

In his observations Schwenk found that when two different liquid streams meet (whether it be at a confluence, after a bridge pier in the water, or a twig in a stream), a spiraling movement, or vortex forms. He called it the 'archetypal phenomenon of vortex formation', saying:

> Wherever any qualitative differences in flowing medium come together, these isolated formations can occur. Such differences may be: slow and fast; solid and liquid; liquid and gaseous. We could extend the list; warm and cold; denser and more tenuous; heavy and light (for instance, salt water and fresh); viscous and fluid; alkaline and acid…At the surfaces of contact there is always a tendency for one layer to roll in upon the other. In short, wherever the finest differentiations are present the water acts as a delicate 'sense organ', which as it were perceives the differentiations and then in a rhythmical process causes them to even out and merge.[41]

Schwenk notes that this archetypal phenomenon is an individual and separate form within the larger collective, saying, "[t]his important phenomenon—the curling in of folds or layer to create a separate organ with a life of its own within the whole organism of water—does actually occur in the forming of organic structures."[42]

It is important to note that Schwenk is saying that an independent structure forms whenever two different flowing elements come in contact with each other, creating a structure that looks to balance out their differences. In other words, there is an exchange between the two. This structure is what I call a 'connecting circle.' Furthermore, this structure has a vortex-like pattern of movement to it. Remember that our thoughts, vrittis and samskaras have a spiraling form. Basically, the movement of water mimics its underlying form, the vortex.

Exhibit 4.1, Connecting Circles, shows how a separate connecting circle forms between two different entities/circles when they come in contact with each other—in this case, you and another circle.

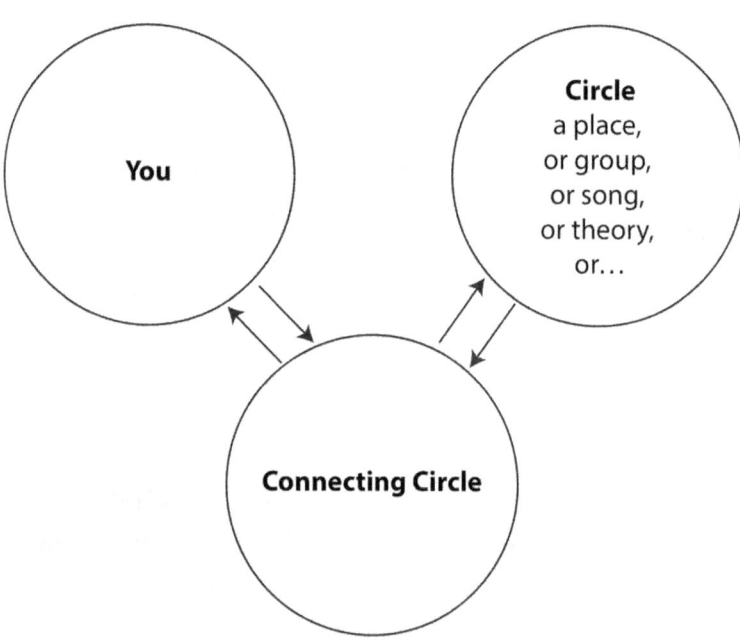

Figure 1 Exhibit 4.1 Connecting Circles. Whenever two circles come in contact with each other, a 'connecting circle' forms to merge, or act as an intermediary between them.

Circles

Circles are not confined to moving liquids, but are pervasive and found throughout all of existence, because they are a phenomenon of consciousness, and all of existence is made up of consciousness. You have an infinite amount of circles in your life—your relationships, the places you go, the objects you own, the groups you belong to, the activities you perform...

Think of a group, or circle of three friends—Tom, Bill and Terry. Each is part of the circle of friends. At the same time, each has a separate relationship with the other. Tom has a separate relationship with Bill and one with Terry, as well, and Terry and Bill have their own relationship separate from the circle. While the circle of the friendship can be strong and dominate their lives and thinking, each of the friends remains a separate and distinct individual.

As Above, So Below

The idea that the movement of water in the physical world is replicating its underlying movement in the unseen world may be difficult to fathom. One of the key concepts of esoteric and occult teaching is: "As above, so below; so below, as above," meaning that what is happening in the physical world is similarly occurring in the unseen world. It comes from the Hermetic text *The Emerald Tablet*.

"As above, so below" implies that the microcosm is like the macrocosm. We as individuals, in many respects, have makeups like Mother Earth and the world around us, in that we are similarly affected by things. I am fond of saying, "as it is one for one, so it is for many, because many are one and one are many."

Within as "above so below" there is the concept of replication that the form and function operating at a higher Plane of Existence manifests in a lower Plane. Just as we breathe air in the Physical Plane, our Energy Body absorbs energy from the Energy Plane for sustenance. Basically, what happens and how it happens in one dimension is mimicked in others. "As above, so below" implies that there is an oneness and connection to everything and everyone.

The Hermetic Tradition is credited to Hermes Trismegistus, who is believed to have lived in ancient Egypt. He is considered the father of occult wisdom, the founder of astrology, the discoverer of alchemy, and much more.[43] However, it is difficult to imagine that one person initiated all these disciplines, and it is more likely that several individuals, or groups thousands of years ago are behind Hermeticism.

Hermeticism has been a key concept in my work, particularly as it applies to what follows. I even developed a school of geomancy, The Eastern Hermetic School of Geomancy, much of it based on the Hermetic Tradition, in addition to Hindu Vedanta. Hermeticism and Vedanta helped me to understand the unseen world around us.

Taking on Karma

What Schwenk's archetypal phenomenon of vortex formation shows is that whenever two different elements come in contact with each other, a vortex forms. The vortex performs a blending process between the two different elements. Basically, a 'circle' (connecting circle) forms when two different elements come in contact with each other and looks to unite them and have an exchange between them. It is this exchange and blending that gives us a glimpse of what happens when we come in contact with another element, or consciousness.

It might sound like a simplistic question, but how do we come in contact with other circles or consciousness? We take on the karma of others through our contact with them; either through our close proximity to someone or something, or through our intention. Remember: we are talking about an interaction occurring in the unseen world, in the great sea of consciousness and thoughts.

As was noted in the first chapter, objects such as a violin take on the memories of their previous owners. By playing the violin owner creates memories (samskaras) that attach to it. This is because the violin was not only the focus of the owner's attention, but is because of its close proximity to the owner and the action of playing—constant playing, and practice for hours on end each day. So when the new owner plays the violin, they are picking up on these memories, to their benefit.

How close does an object to be to you for you to merge with it and pickup its karma? It depends upon the size of your aura. You will interact with everything within your aura. Your aura is your subtle body, the many sheaths or invisible bodies that surround your physical being, and can extend a few feet to hundreds of feet from your body. The size of your aura is a function of your spiritual development and your connection to Mother Earth. The further you have progressed on your spiritual transformation, the larger your aura. Similarly, the greater your connection to our Mother the larger your aura is.

Think of your aura as being your spiritual lungs. The larger it is, the more you can absorb of Mother Earth's emanations.

Similarly, a particular location will also influence you. When your aura comes in contact with the space, you will interact with it. The Overtoun Bridge in Scotland retained the memories of the many dogs that jumped from it. When a dog came in contact with the samskaras attached to the bridge, they similarly felt the pull to jump off. So proximity, or contact with other consciousness will bring about an exchange.

Joining, Thinking About, Participating, Using

We also come into contact with other's karma through our intention. When we join a group—an organization, religion, club, political party—read a particular website/ magazine/ book, we take on its group's karma; as well as add to it. Our intention is to become part of the group. Similarly, by using the name or products/services of a circle, we take on its karma. Even thinking about something will have us merging with it and possibly taking on its karma.

Again: we are talking about an interaction in the unseen world. Our focus and intention bring us in contact with a circle; whether it be a club, religion, or community group. Merely thinking about a circle will have us be in contact with it.

Madame Blavatsky speaks of group karma and how we can be swept up by the collective actions of others with whom we are united by community, religion, nation, and the world. She calls it "Distributive Karma" and it is based upon the "interdependence of humanity."[44] The implication is that karma is distributed within a group, or cohort. We are inexorably linked to others through the numerous circles in our lives.

To many, this may border on the ridiculous: that everything we do and come in contact with has karma, and we will be influenced by it and we will influence it. Others may think why walk out the door in the morning, because it seems so hopeless. It is not.

How much you will be influenced will vary from almost innocuous to severe. It will be determined by the strength of your bond with a circle, how much you are immersed in it and for how long, and the veracity/morality of the samskara, among other factors.

The Unity Principle of Circles

As Schwenk notes, the natural inclination of a flowing liquid when it is challenged and comes in contact with a fluid that is different is to attempt to balance out the differences. This is done by reverting to its underlying form, the consciousness behind it, a circle with a whirlpool-like movement.

Calling it "balancing" may be too mild if we consider that water is mimicking its underlying form. A circle, like a samskara, looks to exert its control and influence. Remember, they are like weeds looking to overrun a garden.

The process of balancing that Schwenk describes is going on all the time around us. Wherever we go, we all come in contact with samskaras. The results are not necessarily a dramatic balancing or evening out, but there is an exchange of consciousness. This implies a dynamic process.

Uniting disparate or different elements is a key feature of consciousness that is reinforced by its circular shape. The circle is a timeless symbol of oneness and unity. What Schwenk sees as the natural inclination of water to balance is a much more powerful force. Consciousness seeks to unite and merge with all the other consciousness it comes in contact with, or anything within its circle.

This is a very important concept because it means we are constantly being shaped by the consciousness that we come in contact with. By circle, I mean the many relationships in your life. Each one of them, at its core, is a samskara with all its features and form (circle). Just like any samskara their influence upon us will depend upon a variety of factors, such as its strength, our commitment to it, etc.

To better understand how consciousness merges (balances out) and affects us, think of how temperature works. Place an object outside in the cold, and it will freeze. Or think of the area of a dryer's hot air duct as it releases hot air into the cold air outside. The air around the duct will be warmer than the air outside but, not as warm as it was when it was first released by the dryer. As the hot air dispenses farther from the duct, its temperature keeps decreasing until it is the temperature of the cold air outside. The balancing out and merging out of consciousness is very similar to that of temperature, but not as dramatic as the previous examples demonstrated.

When consciousness unites, there is an exchange of the elements of each. We see the Unity Principle at work within a samskara when it tries to influence our thinking and behavior. The inclination to unite, as seen in the flow of water, is evident throughout all of existence, as all of existence is consciousness. The Unity Principle is a strong force.

So the merging of a circle will look to blend and exchange elements of each. One of which is karma. So when you come in contact with other consciousness, there may be an exchange of karma.

The Soup Theory of Space/Circles/Consciousness

When you interact with a circle, you will not necessarily be taking on all of its karma. In fact, it may have a minimal karmic affect upon you; or you can be influenced in ways that are not in keeping with what you may have thought. Or you could really be consumed by it. To understand how the karma of a particular circle you come in contact with will influence you, I turn to my 'soup theory of sacred space.'

While consciousness will try to merge with everything within its whirlpool, the consciousness it comes in contact with, not everything will be united. Tiny eddies and whirlpools will resist by not blending with the larger circle. In other words, some tiny individuality/differences are retained within the larger collective; there can be a modicum, or even a great amount, of individuality (differences) retained. This is particularly true for larger circles.

Over a number of years spent studying and experiencing sacred sites, I developed what I called the 'soup theory of (sacred) space,' because experiencing a sacred space, or any space for that matter, was like eating a soup.

A space (circle), like a soup, is made up of its ingredients, or in this case, samskaras. It is the blend of the ingredients that make the soup; similarly, it is the blend of the samskaras that make up a larger circle. These samskaras have karma and may be thought of as being karma.

At the same time: when you eat, let's say, a vegetable soup, you are eating the stock (the soup) and various vegetables. With every bite of soup you have, you may consume a vegetable or two. Each vegetable has the ability to stick out and dominate your eating experience. Similarly, the individual imprints at a sacred site have the ability to grab you. For example, I have had a variety of incredible mystical experiences at the Peacemaker's Sanctuary at Onondaga Lake (Syracuse, NY). Once my prayers were answered there; at other times, I have had revelations or gotten directional messages, and sometimes I just felt good being there. So if we compared it to eating a vegetable soup, most of the time I got the stock, but at times I bit into a mushroom, or a carrot, or a potato.

In other words: for larger circles, groups and organizations, there is the larger blend, or unity, that defines it, like a vegetable soup, or chicken soup; but within it are its component parts. When you come in contact with a larger circle you will experience its composite identity. Which component parts you experience will vary. Just like I had a variety of mystical experiences at Onondaga Lake's Peacemaker's Sanctuary, you will encounter different things at different times.

I believe that the soup theory of space describes how you take on karma for larger circles and organizations. In other words: an organization is made up of its constituent parts, with their own individual samskaras. When you join or partake in the organizations activities you are merging with its larger collective consciousness. Which of its individual component karmas you take on, if any, is difficult to determine.

However, a smaller or less diversified circle doesn't have a broad variety of karma, and there will not be that much divergence in the karma which you may take on.

Circles Connect to Our Very Being

Circles look to merge us, combine us, and unite us in ways that goes way beyond picking up karma to affect our spiritual development. To understand how profound and powerful this is, we have to understand the distinction between positive consciousness and negative consciousness.

Our thoughts have a morality to them, running along a continuum from the divine to the demonic (Bhagavad-Gita Chapter XVI). We may broadly classify them as either love/selflessness (divine) or violent/selfish (demonic). They may also be classified as positive (divine) or negative (demonic) thoughts.

Positive thoughts/actions (samskaras) adhere to the golden rule of "do unto others" and act out of love and the interest of others; this is at the core of every faith tradition. Call this the law of love.

Negative thoughts/actions are those that follow the law of self-interest, selfishness, and violence.

All thoughts (samskaras), circles, places and structures of any sorts, and all of creation, lie somewhere along this continuum, with varying shades of being either divine, or demonic.

Consciousness Quotient, Evolving Soul—It matters

We are constantly interacting with the consciousness we come in contact with, taking on its karma and being influenced by it.

The Unity Principle holds that when different circles (consciousness) come in contact with each other, they will merge to a varying degree, and look to balance out. This has important implications for us beyond taking on karma.

Consciousness, as was previously noted, has a morality to it, running from the divine to the demonic. Our goals in life, both individually and collectively, is to transform and evolve and become pure consciousness, or divine consciousness. Progress is measured by how close we are to becoming divine consciousness.

Hypothetically, if consciousness were measured on a scale of 0 to 100, demonic consciousness would be 0 and divine consciousness would be 100. Because consciousness runs the spectrum from divine to demonic, all consciousness would have a score somewhere along the continuum from demonic (0) to divine (100).

So a particular circle (consciousness) could have a score of 31, 81 or 44. I call this measure your "consciousness quotient." It is like a thermometer that measures your body temperature; only it's a measure of your evolving soul. You can gauge the consciousness quotient of any circle.

The progress of our spiritual transformation is reflected in our evolving soul. It is a measure of our compassion, love for others, and selflessness, among other things. So our evolving soul is constantly being influenced by the consciousness it comes in contact with.

Sri Aurobindo, and his associate, the Mother, call our evolving soul our psychic being. As the Mother teaches:

> The psychic being is formed progressively around the divine center, the soul, in the course of its innumerable lives in the terrestrial evolution, until the time comes when the psychic being, fully formed and wholly awakened, becomes the conscious sheath of the soul around which it is formed.

And thus identified with the Divine, it becomes His/Her perfect instrument in the world.[45]

The Mother teaches that the psychic being never dies because it is our eternal self, and carries that consciousness forward from life to life.[46]

So when we come in contact with a circle, not only may we take on some of its karma, but it also affects our soul development. This affect upon our soul can be very profound.

Years ago, when I began my intensive meditation regiment in hopes of achieving the meditative state of Samadhi, I employed a variety of meditative exercises, visualizations, yoga, readings of sacred texts... The core of my effort was the Hindu technique of concentrating on an object, which was a flower. I would meditate for hours on end. Initially this was challenging because I would get nauseous and would have to stop.

As my concentrative meditation on the flower progressed, I began to get revelations about it, such as insights about research done on it. I was beginning to merge with the consciousness of the flower. As Swami Satyananda Saraswati said in his interpretation of Patanjali's *Yoga Sutras* (I.41 Oneness of chitta [consciousness] with Object) as we progress in meditation, "there is a sudden flash of consciousness when the mind completely fuses with the object."[47] He goes on to say that there are stages in the fusing process, and ultimately the object disappears from our awareness.

I also began to get a very eerie sense about the flower. I eventually came to realize that my consciousness was merging with the consciousness of the flower (or should say, its karmic reading, or its consciousness quotient) and it was not good. I stopped meditating on the flower and began a mantra, a story mantra or word concentration meditation. It was because of this experience that I learned about circles and consciousness quotients.

It still may seem unimaginable that just by coming in contact with something, or joining a group, or walking through a particular place, your very being, your evolving soul will be influenced. Think about how drinking alcohol affects you, or how taking a prescription drug can save your life, or how you will be burned if you put your hand in a fire. These are all phenomena of the Earth Plane. As noted earlier the principle of "As Above, So Below" says that what transpires here in the material world is similarly occurring in the unseen world.

Another way to see it is to realize that alcohol, a prescription drug, and fire, at their core are all consciousness. So your interaction with each is just an interaction with some other consciousness. Similarly, taking on a circle's consciousness by just thinking about it, or walking through a particular place, or joining a group, is no different.

I am teaching you about your consciousness quotient not because I want you to be able to quantify it, but rather, to educate you about how your environment and relationships, or circles, affect your spiritual development. They are constantly shaping you. The Unity Principle is at work 24/7, having your circles influence your thinking as well as influencing your consciousness quotient and psychic being.

In other words: the consciousness quotient of the circles you come in contact with is one way that your psychic being can be nourished or, unfortunately, can also be depleted. To understand how your psychic being can be diminished, think of how working with, or being in contact with, negative people can deplete you and bring negativity into your life.

Whenever you travel, you come in contact with the samskaras and karma of space and objects, and they can either increase or decrease your consciousness quotient. Whether your consciousness is raised or lowered is a reflection of the relative difference between your consciousness quotient and the circle you are in contact with. How much your consciousness quotient is influenced will be a function of the samskaras strength, and how much time you spend in it, as well as your affinity to it, among other factors.

For example, a brisk walk in cold weather will have less influence upon your physical body than standing still in cold weather for a long time. Every time you walk out the door or drive to work, you are moving through a multitude of samskaras, each one with a different consciousness reading that may have an influence upon you. Unfortunately, most of the world is covered with negative samskaras with low consciousness quotients, and carry negative karma.

Similarly, the many circles in your life, from your family, friends, work and other associations, or a particular discipline or technique you might use in work or in your life, will have a consciousness to them that will influence you. Understand that, in many ways, you are a reflection of your circles.

Everything has a consciousness quotient, or a consciousness reading, because everything is consciousness and everything is evolving, or devolving.

The Unity Principal underscores how interconnected we are to each other, to places, and to all of creation. Your spiritual evolution is partly determined by the circles in your life. The consciousness quotients of those circles can either raise or lower yours. They will go a long way in determining whether your evolving soul, or psychic being, is progressing or digressing. That's why I wrote this book and it's critical for you to realize how interactions, affiliations and habitats shape you.

It is important to state that it is in your interest to raise the consciousness of everyone and everything in the world. That is because everyone and everything has a say in your spiritual evolution.

Earlier, I said everything has karma. Everything and everyone also has a consciousness quotient, and it might just be as important, or even more important, to you.

Circles

Circles are also dynamic and affect you in many ways. Here are two examples to better help you understand some of their nuances and properties. What follows are stories of two circles that came together briefly and then dissipated. They show how profoundly a circle can affect you.

Each year, I make an effort to visit Swami Vivekananda's Cottage on Wellesley Island in Thousand Islands on the St. Lawrence River near the Canadian Border when the Ramakrishna—Vivekananda Center of New York opens it up for a brief period. Swami Vivekananda's bedroom upstairs, now a sanctuary, has a large and powerful Energy Vortex in it. An Energy Vortex forms in response to positive human intention—love, compassion, giving, and altruism; or from intense meditation/prayer—and greatly enhances a space. One year, I walked into the room by myself and was instantly sent into a deep trance state so powerful that I left after a few minutes.

The following summer I organized a group of people to visit the cottage for a group meditation and satsang (singing and chanting). When we went upstairs to meditate in the shrine, Vivekananda's bedroom, it was so packed that there was no room to sit, so some people had to wait on the stairwell for someone to leave before they could enter.

Meditating in the room full of people, I felt nothing. Imagine, a year earlier I had only to walk into the room to be immediately blissed out and sent into higher states of consciousness. Now, a year later with a large group of neophyte meditators and people not strongly connected to our

Mother I felt nothing. That is the power of a circle. You fuse together for a moment of time and the group consciousness dictates your perception, being and much more.

Similarly, I spent a lot of the time, in the woods searching for sacred areas and surveying places that I found, or was told about. My ability to sense our Mother and Her essences, energies, and consciousness will be influenced by the number of people in the survey and their connection to our Mother. Too many people, particularly if they do not have a strong bond with our Mother, and my senses diminish. Conversely, if I am in the woods on a survey with others that are connected to our Mother, there is a synergy where all of our senses to our Mother improve—it is Amazing!

Again, both of these situations describe circles that formed spontaneously amongst a group of people and subsequently dissolved. There are many older more established circles like religions, institutions, and organizations that have a dramatic influence upon you as well, as you shall shortly learn.

Anyone that plays basketball knows that their game improves when they play with better players. I imagine it is the case for musicians and many other disciplines and activities.

Connecting Everyone and Everything

Circles are a complex subject. Just realize that whatever, or whoever, you are in contact with, whether it be consciously or unconsciously: you are part of circle with them. This will have an influence upon you.

Many of us embrace the concept of an interconnected world. Circles are one of the ways that we are connected to each other and to everything. They underscore how interconnected we are; in doing they show not only how linked we are, but how others affect us, and how we affect others.

We are ONE.

5. The Pilgrimage of Reincarnation

When James Leininger[48] was two years old he began regularly having horrible nightmares several times a week, where he kicked and screamed. He would blurt out, "Airplane crash! Plane on fire! Little man can't get out!" A few months later, his parents would learn that the little man that their son referred to was actually James himself.

Young James would draw vivid paintings of airplanes and boats in battle, signing his name 'James 3' at a time when children are supposedly unable to write. He told his parents he was the third James. James Leninger was probably one of the most detailed examples of reincarnation that provided a treasure trove of information about his past life and his death.

Through the diligent effort of his parents, Andrea and Bruce, Leninger James would come to learn that in his past life he was James Huston Jr., a Navy pilot who had died at Iwo Jima during WWII.

James Huston Jr.'s sister, Anne Barron,[49] was astounded by the minutiae that young James knew about her childhood and family—that her father was an alcoholic and that her mom (Daryl), a gifted artist, had painted pictures of her and her young brother that no one else but them knew about. She became convinced that young James Leninger was the reincarnation of her brother James Huston Jr.

Reincarnation is a very real part of our being.

A Doctor That Works With Reincarnation

Dr. Brian Weiss, a Miami based psychiatrist, has been studying reincarnation for over thirty years, has written numerous books on reincarnation, and regularly teaches workshops on what he calls past life therapy (also called regression therapy), a technique he has used to help thousands of his patients. During past life therapy, Dr. Weiss hypnotizes his patient and travels back with them to learn about their past lives. He has found that many of their phobias, issues, and problems can be traced back to experiences, or traumatic events in a previous lifetime, and that by facing and examining them, they are often healed. His patients have been cured of a variety of ailments—anxiety disorders, nightmares, fear, depression...

Dr. Weiss is no New Age believer or adherent of eastern traditions such as Hinduism that believe in reincarnation. He is a graduate of Columbia University and Yale Medical School, and Chairman Emeritus of Psychiatry at the Mount Sinai Medical Center in Miami.

It all began in 1980, when a lab technician at Dr. Weiss' hospital came to see him as a patient. Her name was Catherine.[50] She had grown up in a conservative family in a small town in Massachusetts, was very attractive and did modeling on the side. She suffered from fears (water, choking, airplanes, the dark, and was terrified of dying) and other phobias. She did not believe in reincarnation and knew little about it.

After eighteen months of psychotherapy Catherine's fears and phobias persisted, that all began changing after she went to a medical conference in Chicago in 1982. While visiting an Egyptian exhibit at one of the museums, she began to correct her guide about artifacts in public, in front of others in the group—and she was right.

When she got back home, she visited Dr. Weiss and told him about her Egyptian experience. It convinced her to move forward with hypnosis, something she had been unwilling to do for months.

During her second hypnosis session, she told Dr. Weiss that she saw a large white building with pillars and that her name was Aronda and the year was 1863 BC, and there was no water.

Dr. Weiss asked her to go back in time, and she began rattling off different people and different times. She talked about being Rachel, a twenty-five-year-old woman with a daughter named Claestra. In a subsequent regression she saw herself drowning, while clutching her infant daughter; and as Louisa, a prostitute in 1756 AD Spain.

All the time Dr. Weiss' brain was racing as he listened, wondering if it was schizophrenia that Catherine was suffering from. He ruled out hallucinogenic or other drugs because she did not drink. In his gut, Dr. Weiss wondered if he had come upon Catherine's past lives and reincarnations, something he knew very little about?

Surprisingly, when Catherine came for her next session she informed Dr. Weiss that her lifelong fear of drowning was gone, her fears of choking had diminished, and her nightmare of a collapsing bridge were gone.

Shortly thereafter Dr. Weiss became convinced that Catherine was telling the truth and reincarnation was for real after she relayed some very personal private information about Dr. Weiss to him. Catherine told Dr. Weiss that his father, whose name was Avron, was in the room with them, and that his daughter is named after him. So was his first son, Adam, who died as an infant baby after a few weeks. Catherine said both died from heart issues, and that his son had a backward heart like a chicken.

Dr. Weiss was shocked. Catherine knew nothing about his personal life. His young son Adam had died from a "total anomalous pulmonary venous drainage with an atrial septal defect..."[51] where pulmonary veins that are supposed to bring oxygenated blood back to the heart enter on the wrong side.

The loss of Adam was the greatest tragedy in Dr. Weiss' life. Upon hearing this information, any doubts he had about Catherine and reincarnation were gone.

What is also interesting is what Catherine said about Adam: "He made a great sacrifice for you out of his love. His soul is very advanced... His death satisfied his parents' debts."[52] Earlier, I had said not to judge others in this lifetime because they may be taking on other's karma. Adam's brief life is a testimony to this.

With the help of Dr. Weiss, Catherine would keep conquering her phobias. Ultimately, only a few minor traces remained, and she became a radiant and happy person.

The Pilgrimage of Reincarnation

Reincarnation is the pilgrimage of your soul from one lifetime to the next. The Gita compares it to the changing of clothes: "As a person puts on new garments, giving up old ones, the soul similarly accepts new material bodies."(2.20,22) Our physical body in each lifetime is like a new set of clothing; but it is much more than that.

It is the soul that reincarnates with a new body. Each new journey begins from the point of spiritual evolution where the soul last left off. We also carry forth our samskaras. Our tendencies, or vasanas will determine our personality and character from one lifetime to the next. So, in a sense, our vasanas connect us to our previous lives, as do our samskaras and their karma that we carry forward into our future lives.

Unless we clear up our samskaras in this life, we carry them forward into a future life. The purpose of karma and its samskaras is to make us more loving, self-sacrificing, and altruistic. It is also to have us grow closer to God, and to serve God. The Gita says it well:

Those who make me the supreme goal of all their work act without selfish attachment, who devote themselves to me completely are free from ill will for any creature, enter me. (11.55)

Implicit in the Gita's message is that we should be devoted to God and do things for God. The popular greeting "Namaste," literally interpreted means that "I bow to the God in you," implying that when you greet someone like this, you are greeting and bowing to God. So, in a sense, when we give, or help others, heal, we are directly helping God, because all of creation is part of God.

If we do not learn these lessons and remove our samskaras in this life, we will have to be reincarnated in a future life to do so.

The payback of karmic debt also negates, or removes samskaras. You hurt someone and someone hurts you, or you kill someone and someone kills you in a future life. However, it may well be that those samskaras have influenced your character and behavior, and karma's Law of Attraction will bring more into your life.

As for bad karma, you need to realize that, "you are not punished for your sins, but by them,"[53] so said American writer, philosopher, and businessman Elbert Hubbard (1856-1915). He went on to say that doing right brings good, and that doing bad brings misery; noting that these are eternal laws. Hubbard is best known for starting Roycroft Community of Artisans in East Aurora, New York, believing that work defines us and makes us who we are.

The purpose of yoga and sadhana (spiritual exercises such as pranayama and meditation) is the removal of samskaras and the liberation from them. Later I will provide several other ways that you can remove samskaras and their karma from your life.

The Lessons of Reincarnation

Psychic healer Edgar Cayce (1877-1945) was known as the sleeping prophet because he would lie down on his couch and go deep into trance to try and find a cure for what ailed someone. Often he would draw upon a person's past lives to find a remedy. Cayce was a devout Christian and Sunday School teacher who came to believe in reincarnation.

When first told about reincarnation and his own past lives, Cayce was skeptical. He was similarly challenged to believe that his inclinations in his current life were the result of his actions in past lives. Or that he was once a monk and had attained considerable soul development, but had squandered it with a series of lives with a downward trajectory.[54]

Cayce developed his psychic gift during a past life when he had been left for dead in battle. Unable to move and in serious pain, he began to focus on his mind. Just before he died, he was able to separate his mind from his body.[55] His challenge in this life was to use his gift for good, and in doing so, he could return to the pinnacle of his soul development. But if he used his psychic gift for materialistic and selfish purposes, he would move to the lower levels of humanity.

Cayce tells us that people (souls) are challenged by the same issue lifetime after lifetime, refusing to change, and often with the same people. As author Noel Langley writing on Cayce's view of reincarnation says: "Throughout the Readings, one comes across cases of individuals whose karmic sin was their determination to clutch onto their obsolete guilt and shame, rather than make a positive effort to balance it by the "forgiveness of others."[56]

One reading was for Stella Kirby,[57] divorced and with a child, who Cayce described as quiet. She became a nurse and took a private position at twice the going rate only find that her patient was a fifty-seven-year-old man who did not have his

The Pilgrimage of Reincarnation

wits about him. He lived in a cage that surrounded his bed and would rip and tear apart everything he came in contact with. When Stella touched the man she was overcome with nausea and had to leave the room.

Cayce told Stella that she and the caged man's paths had crossed twice before. The first time was in Egypt, when he was her son. The second time was later in the Middle East, when he was a wealthy philanthropist. At that time, he maintained a harem, of sorts, and women were required to perform weird sexual acts. It was that memory of degradation and disgust that triggered her nauseous feeling when she encountered the man again; only now he was living in a cage. Cayce remarked about the irony of the situation, on how the man was now surrounded by enormous material wealth, but was locked in a cage, too feeble to use it.

Cayce told Stella that she must give him love and nurture him, something she found very difficult. She fed him and slowly he began to respond. All the while, she struggled to stay the course with the man's care. He died within two years. She was released from his torment and Stella moved forward with a rewarding life.

Cayce concluded that Stella must not have been kind to her son when they lived in Egypt. The Middle East experience was another chance for her to make amends and help the man overcome his depravity, which she did not do. Now they came in contact with each other again for the third time, and she was able to provide the love he needed, and they both put their karmic debts to rest.[58]

Stella had a karmic debt to pay for her treatment of her son in ancient Egypt. Retribution was not the goal of repaying the debt, but rather for Stella to learn love and caring so that her soul could evolve. It was a lesson she had to learn, and she had to repeat the class over and over again before she got it.

The Pride Before the Fall

You don't have to die and be born again to see how karma is looking to teach you. We are continually challenged to learn, evolve our soul, and get closer to God. If we have a particular lesson to learn, behavior to change, or character feature to develop, the Law of Attraction will ensure that we will be continually be confronted by that same issue over and over again.

Consider the pride before the fall. "Pride goes before destruction, and a haughty spirit before a fall." (Prov. 16.18) Being overconfident or arrogant is a character flaw.

Have ever felt yourself overconfident only to find yourself quickly knocked off of your pedestal? I have, many times, especially when I was managing money. Jokingly, I thought I could have set my watch to it, as success led to exuberance and overconfidence, then the crash or failure. Eventually it got to the point where I would get nervous whenever I found myself getting overconfident; knowing that shortly I would have a setback. It is a lesson I hope that I have learned.

Soul Groups

Stella Kirby and her son point out how we are intimately connected to the same person, or groups of people, over several lifetimes through time. Stella first met him in Egypt as her son; next as part of his harem in the Middle East; and finally in America, as a nurse to the now feeble and insane man locked in a cage.

Edgar Cayce notes that, depending upon how we deal with karma, we may tether ourselves to others for several life times:

> He is taught that if an innocent man, having suffered injustice at the hands of a powerful enemy grimly takes a "just" revenge, he will gratuitously handcuff himself to that same enemy, and both of them will be compelled to return

together and reenact the whole dreary negative conflict until they develop enough common sense to bury their hatchets and call it quits.[59]

Dr. Brian Weiss talks about soul mates—not the loves of our lives, but souls we reincarnate with over and over. He believes that we have many soul mates that are part of a larger soul group. Sometimes these are people that we felt we have met before, but generally they are people that we get close to. We grow through the interaction with our soul mates in our soul group as we ascend the ladder of lifetimes. All the while, our soul group gets larger.[60]

Instant Karma

"Instant Karma gonna get you" are the beginning words to John Lennon's song, Instant Karma. It took him about an hour to write it one morning.[61] All told it took less than ten days to write, record, produce, and release it. The song grew out of conversation that John, his wife Yoko Ono and her former husband and his wife had about how fate affects us in this lifetime and how its not necessary to die and be reincarnated to experience karma.

While critics say this song is noteworthy because it was the first hit for a single Beatle on their own, it also highlighted the eastern concept of karma in the western psyche.

Why does some karma affect us immediately, some at a later time, while still others in a future lifetime?

Swami Satyananda Saraswati, in his interpretation of Patanjali's *Yoga Sutras* says that it depends upon the possibility, the conditions, and the ripening of the karma, noting that sometimes people do bad things and have no karmic repercussions in this lifetime, while others lead good and virtuous lives and suffer.

He compares the fructifying of karma to growing vegetables, saying some ripen soon, while others take a long time. Plant spinach today and you will be harvesting in two or three months, while a guava tree will bear fruit in three years and a mango tree takes five to ten years to bear fruit.[62]

Part of the reason that some karma needs a lifetime or several lifetimes is because of its severity; or we take on so much bad karma that we cannot obliterate it one lifetime.

It could also be a function of your soul group, meaning that the actions of your soul group does not allow someone karmic payback in this life.

There is also the fact that bad karma can and will begin to influence our character, and may develop a strong vasana that is not easily eradicated. It takes time to learn, develop, and transform your soul.

Synchronicity

Synchronicity also helps explain when and how we pay back our karmic debt. Psychiatrist and psychoanalyst Carl Jung (1875-1961), a student of Sigmund Freud, developed his concept of synchronicity to explain the simultaneous occurrence of unrelated events that were beyond coincidence. Describing it as "the concept of a meaningful coincidence of two or more events, where something other than the probability of chance is involved."[63]

Jung was an eclectic thinker who explored eastern religions, mythology, alchemy, and astrology in his work. His development of the concept of the collective unconsciousness (that humankind shares an unconscious collective memory) is arguably his defining work.

As examples of synchronicity Jung talks about the duplication of cases found in hospitals, or when someone notices the number from their streetcar ticket and comes home and receives a telephone call and the same number is mentioned. It was just such an unusual occurrence that first got Jung thinking about synchronicity. He tells of a young woman he was treating, who at a critical moment in a dream, was given a golden scarab:

> While she was telling me this dream I sat with my back to the closed window. Suddenly I heard a noise behind me, like a gentle tapping. I turned round and saw a flying insect knocking against the windowpane from outside. I opened the window and caught the creature in the air as it flew in. It was the nearest analogy to a golden scarab that one finds in our latitudes, a scarabaeid beetle, the common rose-chafer (Cetonia aurata), which contrary to its usual habits had evidently felt an urge to get into a dark room at this particular moment. I must admit nothing like it ever happened since.[64]

In letter dated 1953 Jung notes how it was Einstein who, in the 1920's, provided the impetus for developing his concept of synchronicity by getting him "thinking about the possible relativity of time as well as space, and their psychic conditionality."[65] It also initiated Jung's friendship with theoretical physicist Wolfgang Pauli, who would help him formalize his theory of synchronicity.[66]

Jung called synchronicity an acausal connecting principle,[67] meaning that it was responsible unto itself for making events take place that had no other cause. It was not bound by time or space. It was a phenomenon unto itself. It was a very radical idea that went against traditional western thinking.

Jung stated that "I have picked on the term 'synchronicity' to designate a hypothetical factor equal in rank to causality as a principal of explanation…I considered synchronicity as psychically conditioned relativity of space and time."[68] He went on to say that in the psyche time and space are "elastic," noting that concepts such as time and space only became fixed with humankind's mental development and with the development of measuring devices.

Synchronicity is a big concept, no doubt influenced by the time period and the work of Einstein. Psychotherapist and Jungian scholar Ira Progoff said that it took Jung decades to formulate synchronicity, and Jung felt that it,

> Was principle equal to, and commensurate with the theory of relativity developed by his friend Einstein. His theory had added merit of including the dimension of the psyche in a comprehensive view of the universe.[69]

Progoff says that Jung was frustrated that he could not adequately communicate his vision of synchronicity, but that he did lay the groundwork for others.

To me, synchronicity is much more than Jung described. One could argue that the attraction of a golden-like scarab was a function of the Law of Attraction. When Jung heard and thought about the golden scarab in his patient's dream he put the thought out there, and a similarly colored beetle came back in response. The synchronicity I am talking about is far more complex. It is about balancing multiple karmic debts that have to be repaid by multiple parties that are part of a soul group and related soul groups through the prism of time.

Think about it. You have your karmic debt to repay, as do others in your soul group. You may also have a need to connect with someone for a specific karma debt to pay, as Stella Kirby did with her son. This all needs to take place in the larger context of groups and nations. The number of interconnections is mind-boggling.

See the Wonder of Synchronicity

There is a wonder and beauty within the enormity of the concept of synchronicity. To ponder how a myriad of apparently unrelated elements can coalesce together to become the one key that opens a special door, and that a multitude of special doors are simultaneously being opened all around us in many places, and at many levels simultaneously. It is simply breathtaking to imagine.

How does this happen? That remains a mystery, as does the rationale behind why our thoughts morph and become transformative. Both speak to the amazing possibilities that exist in our reality.

What is known is that you can be spiritually transformed by seeing the process of synchronicity blossoming around you. Believe it. See it. Seek it. In doing so you begin to grow and tap into the divine consciousness behind it.

Grace

As much as there are karmic consequences for our actions there is also 'grace.' Grace is a forgiveness given to us by God for something we have done. It is more than that; it is a gift—a divine gift from God.

On the surface it may seem that Grace is the equivalent of a 'get out of jail card' to circumvent our karma. Such an argument fails to consider our purpose for being on the Earth Plane. We are here to spiritually grow; to be transformed and become more loving, compassionate, giving, altruistic, selfless… and to grow closer to God. Does it matter if we do not fully pay off our karmic debt if we have learned our lesson? Do we need to keep falling down over again until we have fully exacted and paid off our karmic debt?

Grace is the love of God. It could be something as simple as the timing of when we pay our karmic debt. Making a loan payment when you are working is not a big a challenge, but having to do so when you are unemployed and flirting with bankruptcy can be devastating. Several times in my life I have felt spared from having to pay back karmic debt, only to do so later when I was better able to handle it.

Grace can also be a gift from God to prod you along and encourage you to turn more to the light. It could also be a gift when you are challenged and desperate, to save you from mishap.

Grace is a blessing from God.

Paul Brunton (1898-1981), a mystic who educated the west about mysticism and Hinduism in the first half of the twentieth century, wrote a wonderful book about Grace. I know about him because of a lovely spiritual community on the southeastern shore of Seneca Lake, in the Finger Lakes region of New York, Wisdom's Golden Rod. John Damiani, who was a student of Brunton's, started it.

Brunton felt that we could attract Grace by cleansing our hearts, saying that Grace was critical: "You cannot conquer your desire nor subdue your animal nature by your own strength. In the final outcome, it is divine Grace which releases you from bondage."[70]

"This is the paradox that when you take the first step on this Quest, it is grace which impels you to do so. Yet you think and act as if you have never been granted the divine gift."[71]

Grace is a gift from God. May you be blessed with it.

Carrying the Past into the Future

We are here to learn and evolve. Karma is our teacher. If we do not learn our lesson in this life, we will have to learn it in a future life.

Reincarnation helps karma transcend time. It connects us to our past lives and carries us forward into the future. Who we were was different than who we are today, and will be even more different in the future.

Learn your lessons well.

6. The Web of Circles

Circles pervade all of creation. They give structure to the physical world and are repositories to which samskaras can attach. They are also a vehicle by which we can take on the karma of others. Circles link and connect all of life. They perform a variety of functions besides taking on karma. By looking at circles in a different context besides karma, we begin to see how they operate.

Morphic Resonance

Have you ever wondered why a spider knows how to spin a web at birth without learning from other spiders? Or why some birds fly south for the winter, and why others have particular courtship patterns, or behaviors?

Dr. Rupert Sheldrake will tell you it is because of a shared collective memory that they can call upon. He believes that all of Nature has a memory. Specifically, all organisms inherit a collective memory of their species from previous organisms by a process he calls 'morphic resonance.' Basically this is a term to describe the mechanism of how self-organizing systems inherit a memory from previous members of the same system.

Sheldrake also believes that individual organisms are subject to the same morphic resonance from themselves in the past; and that this self-resonance provides them the basis for their individual memories and habits.[72]

Sheldrake's perspective that a species, individual organisms and all of Nature retain a memory is very similar to the concept of samskaras/memory that are the building blocks of karma. The idea that this inherited memory provides individual organisms with their habits sounds like the Hindu concept of vasanas. Remember that vasanas form over several lifetimes from our samskaras, and are our traits, or character.

Morphic resonance is the process, or what makes possible the influence of an organism's ancestors upon it. Structurally, morphic resonance occurs in a field; what Sheldrake calls a 'morphic field.' It is similar to what many developmental biologists call biological fields, or developmental fields, or positional fields, or morphogenetic fields: basically, organizing fields for an organism. Think of a field being like a cloud surrounding an organism that consists of a memory and its organizational system. Again the parallel to karma is striking. Samskaras attach to consciousness and have a whirlpool-like form and movement; aka this is like a field.

Sheldrake has impeccable scientific credentials. He studied natural sciences at Cambridge University, where he was a Scholar of Clare College, earning his Ph.D. in biochemistry (1967). However, while there he became increasingly disillusioned with what he was being taught—or at least its perspective. He was interested in the living and not the mechanistic approach that he was being taught, that views life as a machine. As Rupert notes in his autobiography: "The first thing they did in the Biochemistry Department was to kill the organisms we were studying and then grind them up to extract the DNA, the enzymes, and so on."[73]

Returning from a trip to British Malaya where he had studied rainforests, he stopped in Sri Lanka and India. It was an eye-opener that changed him. Upon returning to England Rupert began to explore the holistic tradition in biology. Soon his concept of morphic resonance, or what he calls the memory of Nature, followed.

Rupert wanted to be in India. So he left Cambridge and took an agricultural research position in Hyderabad, India, which allowed him to study agriculture firsthand year-round. While he had been brought up a Christian, he was persuaded to become an atheist around age fourteen by a biology teacher. However, while in India he began to visit various ashrams and gurus, and even studied with Sufis. It was a Benedictine monk, Bede Griffiths, who had an ashram that bridged Christianity and Hinduism, which drew him. He found new meaning in the Christianity that he had rejected as a teenager and ended up spending a year and a half there before returning to England.

It was while living at Bede Griffiths' ashram that he wrote his first book, *The New Science of Life*. It put forward his theory of morphegenic fields, the belief that Nature retains a memory. It posits that past organisms shape the form and behavior of a particular species: in essence, a species is defined by the behavior of its ancestors.

The scientific heretic was born.

John Maddox, the then editor of *Nature* called *The New Science of Life* "heresy," saying it was "the best candidate for burning there has been for many years."[74] Probably what so inflamed the scientific community was that Sheldrake was one of their own. He had a doctorate from Cambridge and was the winner of its botany prize, a researcher at the Royal Society, a fellow of Clare College, and a Harvard scholar.

Sheldrake would go on to write many books dealing with topics taboo to science such as telepathy and precognition, with titles such as *The Presence of the Past: Morphic Resonance and the Memory of Nature* (1988), *Seven Experiments That Could Change the World* (1994), *Dogs That Know When Their Owners Are Coming Home* (1999), *The Sense of Being Stared At* (2003,. *Science Set Free* (2013) *The Physics of Angels: Exploring the Realm Where Science and Spirit Meet Science* (With Matthew Fox 2014) and *Spiritual Practices: Transformative experiences and their effects on our bodies, brains and health* (2017).

Over time attitudes regarding Sheldrake's work have begun changing. In a 2012 review of Sheldrake's *The Science of Delusion* Christopher Potter of the Sunday Times said that he "would not be surprised if in years to come Sheldrake will be seen as a prophet rather than an eccentric."[75]

While Sheldrake's work does not specifically deal with karma, it posits that living systems retain a memory of their ancestors. It shows that learned behavioral patterns transcend time and connect members of a particular species or living systems through eternity, or as long as a species remains in existence.

The concept of Morphic resonance is not confined to living systems. Sheldrake believes that there are insulin fields, beech fields, swallow fields… that morphic resonance shapes everything; atoms, molecules, crystals, societies, customs, habits of mind, stars and galaxies.[76] Even societies, cultural and social groups, religious paths and artistic schools are organized by morphic fields. There are fields within fields. Sheldrake sees schools of thought, such as scientific paradigms as morphic fields; and within them are the fields of physics, biology, geophysics, metallurgy…[77] Basically, everything has a memory that shapes its form and behavior.

What Sheldrake calls morphic fields, is very similar to what I call circles, or even samskaras. Whereas morphic fields unite similar organisms, such as members of the same species, or planets in a solar system, a circle can be a much larger organizational field. It unites anything that has a relationship with something else, whether it is members of the same species or different species, or inanimate objects. It based on intention/focus and affiliation. So when you talk to a stranger, or pet your neighbor's dog, read about a particular theory, or work on your computer, you create a circle with them. This circle can be ephemeral, or long lasting. How much influence it has upon you will depend your commitment to it and how much time you focus on it.

Space and location also create a circle. Wherever you are, and whenever you are, there you are, merging with the space.

Inheriting Karma

According to morphic resonance a species learns behavior over time and the more that its members repeat a particular behavior, the more readily successive generations learn and exhibit the behavior. In his first book, *A New Science of Life*, Sheldrake makes his case for morphic resonance and provides a research study that used white Wistar rats.[78]

The study was to determine if learned behavior improves over time with successive members of a species. It was a test of Lamarckian Inheritance, also known as the Theory of Inheritance of Acquired Characteristics, which hypothesizes that the changes an organism learns during its lifetime in order to adapt to its environment are passed onto its offspring. In other words, the learned behavior is transferred to the progeny of an organism.

The task was to have rats learn to escape from a specially constructed water tank by swimming to one of two gangways, only one of which led out of the water. One gangway was illuminated; the other not. The illuminated gangway was the wrong one and provided an electric shock; the dark gangway provided an escape route. They would alternatively switch which gangway was illuminated, but always retained that it was the one that gave a shock. It took some rats as many as three-hundred-thirty immersions before they learned to choose the dark gangway.

The initial study (McDougall) looked at thirty-two generations over fifteen years and found that the number of immersions required before learning occurred declined from an average of about two-hundred and twenty to under forty.

A subsequent study (Crew) that included untrained rats did not validate the original study. But the inbreeding of the rats, only brother and sisters, led to huge abnormalities within the population.

A final study (Agar) over a period of twenty years used trained and untrained rats for fifty successive generations. The results of this test were even more remarkable because it found that the rate of learning improved for both the trained and untrained lines.[79]

One of the best examples of spontaneous learning of species according to Sheldrake[80] was found with birds opening milk bottles in England. Beginning in the 1920s blue tits (Parus caeruleus) and related species began stealing the cream from recently delivered milk to homes by learning to remove the caps of the milk bottle. Once the cap was removed, they could consume the cream.

Because the birds do not travel more than a few miles from their home and the behavior was found throughout England, it was assumed that it was passed along within the species. Once the behavior began in one area it spread fast.

The habit of opening milk bottles also appeared in Sweden, Denmark, and Holland. Interestingly the home delivery of milk bottles virtually stopped during WWII. However, beginning in 1947/48, the opening of caps in Holland vigorously picked up. None of the birds would have had the longevity to survive WWII.

Sheldrake also points out how the introduction of barbed wire late in the nineteenth century led to numerous deaths and injures to horses as they ran into wired fences. By the middle of the twentieth century it was no longer a problem as horses as a species learned to avoid barbed wire.

You Can Change the Future

Sheldrake's work with Morphic Resonance shows that the members of a circle influence it over time, implying a dynamic process. Basically, a circle evolves based upon the thinking and behavior of its members. So what the circle was a few hundred years ago can be quite different today.

Furthermore, because the behavior of members changes over time, the circle changes, and subsequently, so do its new members. So while you might think it ridiculous that somehow birds learning to open milk bottles has something to do with you, it similarly shows that the circles you belong to are dynamic; and that they will begin to shape your behavior in ways you might not be aware of, or even like.

It also means that we can alter the behavior of others in our circle through our thoughts and actions. If enough people begin to act or think a certain way, it may have an impact upon others in the circle.

Bottom line: your circles will influence you over time; and at the same time, you can influence the circles you belong to.

Collective Unconscious

Sheldrake's concept of morphic resonance assumes that humankind similarly has morphic fields. The closest comparison to be drawn is with Carl Jung's collective unconscious, our shared collective memory. Sheldrake even acknowledges this:

> The approach I am putting forward is very similar to Jung's idea of the collective unconscious. The main difference is that Jung's idea was applied primarily to human experience and human collective memory. What I am suggesting is that a very similar principle operates throughout the entire universe, not just in human beings.[81]

Jung believed that in addition to our immediate consciousness, "there exists a second psychic system of a collective, universal, and impersonal nature which is identical in all individuals...does not develop individually but is inherited...It consists of pre-existent forms, the archetypes..."[82] He said that "[t]he unconscious is the unwritten history of mankind from time unrecorded."[83] So, in essence, we inherit the collective memory of our ancestors.

He goes on to say that these preexistent forms, or Archetypes, which we inherit, can only become conscious secondarily (through us), and "give definite form to certain psychic content."[84] Basically, there are universal patterns of behavior, and they affect our thinking and behavior.

The concept of archetypes includes character types of behavior, such as the Mother figure (birthing, nurturing, inner strength, feminine... earth mother, life giving...), and the trickster (joker, prankster, magician...). as well as all universal forms of human nature. For example, there are archetypes of transformation that typify situations, places, ways, and means, that bring about change.[85]

Harold Coward a professor who wrote about the Hindu religion said: "[T]hroughout his life Jung admitted his strong attraction to Indian karma and reincarnation theory, but its lack of empirical evidence was the obstacle to its full acceptance."[86] Jung even credits karma theory with helping him fulfill his notion of archetypes,[87] something Coward points out that many of his biographers refuse to acknowledge.

Jung recognized samskaras and said that they were the equivalent of archetypes.[88] You see this vividly in Jung's description of how archetypes like samskaras form from continuous repetition over the ages. As Jung tells:

> There are as many archetypes as there are typical situations in life. Endless repetition has engraved these experiences

into our psychic constitution, not in the form of images filled with content, but first as forms without content, representing merely the possibility of certain type of perceptions and actions. When a situation similar to the archetype occurs the archetype is activated and compulsiveness appears.[89]

The memory of our ancestors transcends time and controls us in many ways. We are powerless against our collective unconscious and its archetypes and are at their mercy. They exert an incredible influence upon us. Jung said that: "[M]ankind always stands on the brink of actions it performs itself but does not control. The whole world wants peace but prepares for war, to take but one example. Mankind is powerless against mankind.[90]

Jung's description of the evolution of our psyche is very similar to the evolution of a species' habits in Sheldrake's morphic resonance. In 'Mind and Earth'[91] Jung compares it to the development of a multistory building. Its upper story was constructed in the nineteenth century, its ground floor in the sixteenth century, and its masonry reveals that it was reconstructed in the eleventh century. In the cellar we find Roman foundations, and under the cellar is a cave with Neolithic tools in the upper layer and remnants of fauna from the same period in the lower level. Jung felt we live in the upper story and are only aware of the lower story. We remain totally unaware of what lies below the earth's surface.

The process of the evolution of our psyche as described by Jung similarly tells us how samskaras and circles are sculpted over time. What is today, was shaped by its past. Samskaras, like Jung's proverbial house are continually being remodeled, but their roots are buried deep down in their past.

The development of our psyches from a root cellar with animal bones to a modern building shows that our thoughts, both individual and collective, can morph and be so much more.

Interestingly, Jung felt that our collective unconscious was buried in the earth, saying that, "our contact with the unconscious chains us to the earth and makes it hard for us to move."[92]

Sheldrake's morphic resonance and Jung's collective unconscious and archetypes show how we are shaped and influenced by exogenous factors over which we have little, or no control. These are factors, or behaviors, or perceptions, or ways of thinking and more that have been shaped over time by our ancestors; as well as for species by their ancestors over time, according to Sheldrake's morphic resonance.

We are defined by our past, and help define the future for others. The past lives in us, and we will live in the future.

7. Disconnect

The great Tibetan Buddhist Milarepa (eleventh century) who achieved Enlightenment lived many years in isolation in caves in the Himalaya Mountains, away from society. He would meditate for hours on end, eating little if anything at times; always in solitude. It was the breaking away from society and spending time in Nature by himself that facilitated Milarepa's spiritual transformation. All of us should consider Milarepa's example and find time for solitude, particularly in Nature.

The story of Milarepa and his metamorphosis is as tragic as it is remarkable. Born to a prosperous family when his father died his aunt and uncle fleeced the family of their wealth. Bitter, his mother asked her son to study sorcery and exact revenge. Milarepa learned well, and among other things rained down violent hailstorms and killed many, including thirty-five at one time in a wedding party.[93]

Eventually, remorse set in and Milarepa searched out a new teacher to guide his transformation, Marpa the Translator. To expiate the bad karma for Milarepa's evil deeds, Marpa had him construct stone and clay buildings by hand. When Milarepa was halfway through constructing a building, Marpa would have him take it apart and return the components to where he had gotten them.

After some time, and several buildings built and torn down, Milarepa was initiated as a priest. He was led to a rock cave given some provisions, and told to meditate in solitude. After eleven months in seclusion, his guru Marpa and his wife visited and they had a religious feast.

Many more stints of solitude in rock caves would follow, one of which was a three-year period of seclusion to achieve Siddhis (spiritual gifts). Known for writing songs Milarepa would sing about how to attain such gifts:[94]

Within the close confinement of a solitude,
By noise of men and dogs untroubled,
There is a boon of quickly gaining *Siddhi*.[95]

Milarepa developed the ability, to levitate and fly, well up bliss and compassion in others, and produce flames of fire and springs of water in his body. He was able to transform his body into any object at will, and became a miraculous healer and more.

Milarepa would become a teacher. Once, he was headed with five students to meditate on a snowy mountain. When one of his disciples fell ill, they were forced to live in a desolate mountain in Upper Lowo. Locals realizing that Milarepa was there, came and offered their respects and asked him to teach them. Milarepa sang to them:

Lowo is the devil's dark country.
Towns are the devil's prisons.
Respect and status are the devil's ropes.
Distraction is the devil's obstruction.

Here, in desolate mountains empty of men,
Yogic awareness blossoms.
Here focused concentration grows strong.

Rest you well, you gathered here—
I supplicate for your fortune and spiritual welfare.[96]

Milarepa knowingly allowed himself to be poisoned by the girlfriend of a guru jealous of his notoriety. He forgave her and told her that he would try and remove the karma of unhappiness and suffering that would be the consequences of her actions. As the poison worked slowly, he spent the remainder of his days with his pupils.

One of Milarepa's caves contains an impression in the rocks of where he sat meditating, as well as an imprint of his hand that was left after he thrust it into the cave's wall.[97]

Desert Hermits

Living as a recluse for long periods of time away from society is a universal practice of the mystics of all faith traditions. Jesus spent forty days in the wilderness before he began his ministry. John the Baptist and other prophets lived in the wilderness away from society. Eventually this became a larger exodus whose members would be called the Desert Hermits, or Desert Fathers.

As Thomas Merton (1915-1968) tells us:

In the fourth century A. D. the deserts of Egypt, Palestine, Arabia and Persia were peopled by a race of men who have left behind them a strange reputation. They were the first Christian hermits, who abandoned the cities of the pagan world to live in solitude.[98]

Merton notes the irony of the timing of the formation of the Desert Hermits at a time when the Emperor was now a Christian and the Cross was a sign of strength. Feeling that these developments only strengthened the resolve of the Desert Fathers, he said: "These were men who believed that to let oneself drift along, passively accepting the tenets and values of what they knew of society, was purely and simply a disaster."[99]

Merton was a Trappist monk who spoke from experience about the Desert Hermits' life of solitude. He was a noted mystic, theologian, social activist, and author who wrote dozens of books. His *Seven Storey Mountain* is the moving tale of his own quest to become a monk. It inspired many to enter monasticism.

Noted activist and priest Daniel Berrigan (of the Berrigan Brothers) called Merton the 'conscience of the peace movement' in the 1960s. Merton was an active supporter of the nonviolent Civil Rights movement saying it was "certainly the greatest example of Christian faith in action in the social history of the United States."[100]

Merton was fascinated by eastern religions, most notably Buddhism, and in promoting an East—West Dialogue. Unfortunately, he was accidentally electrocuted and died in 1968 in Bangkok, Thailand while attending a monastic conference.

One of the more recognized Desert Honks was Anthony the Great, also called Abbott Anthony and known as 'The Father of Monks.' In central Egypt at the age of thirty-four (285) he began his life as a recluse. He attracted followers and became their spiritual father. His compassion and belief in the power of solitude is seen in the following where he compares a monk away from his isolated cell to a fish out of water: "Just as fish die if they stay too long out of water, so the monks who loiter outside their cells or pass their time with men of the world loose the intensity of inner peace."[101]

The Empowerment of Solitude

Mystics, adepts, pilgrims, monks, yogis and seekers from a variety of faith traditions have found solitude to be a magic elixir that hastened their spiritual evolution and transformation. By breaking the shackles of society, they broke their connection to the many circles in their lives. No longer encumbered by the karma and group consciousness from a host of circles, they were able to break free and have a growth spurt in their spiritual transformation.

To understand why breaking free from your circles can be so transformative remember that a circle at one level is a samskara; and samskaras, as discussed earlier, will try to control your thinking and actions to suit them. In other words, they will try to hog your attention and have you serve them, think in a certain way, or see the world through their eyes. They also (as noted earlier with Meher Baba) will limit your perspective. Basically, they blind you to a degree. You will also be merging with the circle's consciousness quotient, and that is generally not good.

The cure of solitude provides you with the freedom that can help you change yourself. It can bring a host of benefits:

Reflection. Solitude allows for reflection. Not encumbered by life's challenges and the demands of your many circles, you can reflect upon your life.

Freedom. Solitude brings freedom to think and do whatever you want, whenever you want. While a vacation can be a period of solitude, solitude is ultimately a vacation from your 9 to 5 self, or who you have become in the material world. You can just "be," if you want.

Learning. Solitude provides the opportunity to learn about yourself. At some point you will ask yourself, "who am I?", or "what do I want?", or "where I am going?" Free from society and the many circles in your life you see yourself in a new light.

Distance. Solitude gives you the chance to see yourself from a distance. Not being enmeshed in life's daily challenges, you look at things with a clearer perspective. Like a historian who looks back at a period of time after the dust has settled, you see things clearer because you are not bogged down, or overwhelmed by the moment.

Cathartic and Healing. Solitude can bring about a catharsis as you distance yourself from what ails or challenges you; and in the process, heal you.

The Ultimate Vacation. Solitude is the ultimate vacation because you are breaking from the life you have known, no matter for how long.

My Canoe Trip Ritual

Just about every summer in the 1980s and 1990s I would travel to Algonquin Provincial Park in southern Ontario, Canada for a solo canoe trip for a few days. The longest trip I took lasted ten days. Toronto's population was much smaller then and the Lake District close to Algonquin was just beginning its exponential growth. So there was a greater sense of isolation back then.

To reduce my chances of seeing people, I would try to go in early May. It even snowed lightly one year, on May 2nd. I would also chose routes with long or strenuous portages uphill where I would have to carry my canoe and gear. I felt this would discourage some. I think that the longest I ever went without seeing someone was two and a half days. If I met someone, well, I could not shut up.

Those were grueling, but joyful days. While I would feverishly paddle during the day, it seemed I would frequently stop for a spectacular view, or watch a moose feeding or one blocking a stream ahead of me on my path. I enjoyed the physical regiment, but I had little choice, as I would stay up late watching the campfire. In the morning I would read and reflect, so it would be some time before I began my daily paddle. My favorite read was a collection of short stories by Jack London about the Yukon and the great outdoors, which I brought with me one year. Sometimes if I had a big lake to cross, I might have to wait a few hours for the wind to die down along with the waves it had whipped up.

While there, I was untethered from my life in Manhattan and my Wall Street career. My biggest concern were the weather and my journey. Often, it was just the joy of being there. My canoe trips were always a cathartic and enlightening experience. No matter what challenges I faced, they melted away the more I paddled. Over the years my trip became a Ritual. I knew I was going to go to Algonquin to be purified and healed. The cleansing and healing got better each time.

The last time I went to Algonquin was in October of 2002. I wanted to experience the southern part of the park where I had never been, and felt the fall would have less people traveling this usually busy area. I had left Wall Street and begun meditating a few years earlier. I spent the bulk of my trip on a rock peninsula in a hidden area on a small lake and heard people paddle by, but saw no one while I was there. I did my yoga in the morning and meditated several times during the day. I read a host of books and scripture. In the early evening the loons would wail and the coyotes howled. Most of my time was spent reflecting and thinking about whatever came to my mind.

Looking back at those decades of solo canoe trips with the knowledge I have learned since, it is clear that I had made them a potent ritual. Over time, through continual repetition, I carved my experiences into myself. I had turned my pilgrimage into a samskara; one that could heal me and bring me great joy, as what I experienced each year only got stronger with each successive year. It is with great gratitude and happiness that I look back at my experiences at Algonquin Park.

Take A Vacation From Your Circles

You need to find time for solitude in your life. This does not necessarily mean a monastic life. It does mean finding time for breaks, like I had with my solo canoe trips. You need to have periods of solitude if you want to spiritually grow and not be at the mercy of others' karma. You have to take a vacation from your circles.

Solitude can be challenging and bring loneliness. So start slow. Do it for only a few hours the first time. Disconnect from all electronics, don't talk or visit with others, don't watch TV or play video games. Just be with yourself or, read a book that helps you reflect, or gain perspective. You need to work the ability to be alone as if it were a muscle. Over time, small steps will become large steps as you are able to spend more and more time in solitude.

Solitude is a vacation from your life; or from whom you have let your circles turn you into. Solitude allows you detach and explore who you really are. You may be surprised by whom you meet after an extended period of solitude.

In speaking on solitude, psychiatrist and former Oxford professor Anthony Storr notes, in his book *Solitude, A Return To The Self*:

> Removing oneself voluntarily from one's habitual environment promotes self-understanding and contact with those inner depths of being which elude one in the hurly-burly of day-to-day life... [T]he most profound and healing psychological experiences which individuals encounter take place internally, and are only distantly related, if at all, to interaction with other human beings.[102]

Take inspiration from Henry David Thoreau, who spent two years of relative solitude at Walden Pond in Concord, Massachusetts. He went into the woods because he wanted "to live deliberately, to front only the essential facts of life and see if [he] could learn what it had to teach, and not, when [he] came to die, discover that [he] had not lived."[103] Speaking of solitude, Thoreau writes that he "never found a companion that was so companionable as solitude."[104]

As a Naturalist, Thoreau writes in *Walden* about the flora and the fauna, the changing of the seasons, his neighbors, and surrounding ponds. It is through this simplicity and observation that we see Thoreau grow. He asks why travel to Africa, visit the Nile, go to the Northwest Passage, or the Mississippi if we have ourselves to discover, writing:

Direct your eye right (eyesight) inward, and you'll find

A thousand regions in your mind

Yet undiscovered. Travel them, and be

Expert in home-cosmography.[105]

Thoreau concludes *Walden* with an inspiring story that gives hope to all of us, that we too can break free and become who we were meant to be. He begins by saying that there was a story that been going around New England at the time, of how a beautiful bug emerged out of the leaf of a table made of apple wood that had stood in a farmer's kitchen for sixty years; first in Connecticut, then in Massachusetts.

So an egg planted long ago in a living apple tree that was cut down and became what Thoreau called its "well-seasoned tomb" had finally hatched and broken free. Thoreau asks,

"[w]ho knows what beautiful and winged life, whose egg has been buried for ages under many concentric layers of woodenness in the dead dry life of society?... may unexpectedly come forth from amidst society's most trivial and handselled furniture, to enjoy its perfect summer life at last!"[106]

Find time for solitude and become who you can be.

Disconnect From Some of Your Circles

Solitude is a powerful transformational act. However, everyone is not interested, or capable of, pursuing a life of solitude and contemplation. Or you may not be interested in taking periodic retreats of solitude in your life. You can certainly gain greatly by reducing the number of circles in your life, as well as reducing the time, energy, and devotion you apply to others.

When I left Wall Street and accepted God's call a few years later in February of 1999, I knew I had to break my connection to Wall Street and money management. I did not know why: just that I had to.

Wall Street is a very large circle with lots of bad karma. It is guided by Adam Smith's Law of Self-Interest (act selfishly in your own interest and you will be rewarded)[107] and not by the 'law of love' and 'do unto others, as you wish others to do unto you' that is at the core of every faith tradition. In other words, Wall Street is diametrically opposed to the foundation upon which every faith tradition rests.

It is a difficult circle to break free from. Our capitalist society is based upon Adam Smith's law of self-interest. We are fed business news and stock reports on a regular basis. Over half of Americans own stocks, many are business owners, and many of those that are not, aspire to become rich.

Then there is money, the unavoidable medium of exchange that represents power and prestige in our materialistic society. You need to follow the advice that Jesus gave to the rich man who wanted eternal life in heaven: "sell what you own, and give the money to the poor, and you will have treasure in heaven; then come, follow me." (Mark 10.21) That was a difficult thing for the rich man to do, as Jesus notes, as it is for all of us.

You should strive to have the minimal amount of money and its material accouterments in your life as possible. As Paul's apostle Timothy said, [f]or the love of money is a root of all kinds of evil. (1 Timothy 6.10) He goes on to say that it brings on all sorts of pain; aka, bringing on other's karma and negative consciousness.

Avoid the false teachers that preach abundance, the gospel of prosperity, using the Law of Attraction to bring money into to your life and the like. Such endeavors will only increase the number of reincarnations and future lives you will take on. As Edgar Cayce noted with his own life, his challenge was not to use his gifts for materialistic purposes.

You may say that you do not prey on the poor like Pay Day lenders who charge usurious percentage from people in need. You can say that you that you do not exploit and pollute the land with drilling and mining operations. You can claim that you do not operate sweatshops in foreign countries where workers are paid meager wages. You can say to yourself that you are not some paper pusher that makes millions, bundling, trading, or selling financial instruments. Or that…

You are guilty of this to a degree, and much more, by participating in Wall Street directly through your investments, your pension, by supporting corporations, by watching financial news, by… There are so many ways that we join in the circle of Wall Street. There are so many ways that we take on its bad karma; bad karma that has been accumulating for millennia.

What is so dark about Wall Street is that there is little or any good to counter-balance its cruelty, negativity, violence and selfishness. So when you gauge its consciousness quotient it is very negative, which means it will be a negative draw on your psychic being and spiritual evolution.

While you may not be actively involved with Wall Street and Big Business, you are actively involved with many other circles, all which carry karma and have a poor consciousness quotient reading. Less is better. You need to reduce the number of circles in your life.

This does not mean removing yourself from all the circles in your life. It means making an assessment of which circles you want to maintain participation in, and by how much.

While you cannot eliminate all the circles in your life you need to do an assessment of your relationships, memberships, associations and more. The chapter that follows, 'You Shall Know Them By Their Fruit' will better help you make your assessment. Reflect on what you belong to and why? Then determine how much to continue participating, or whether you should at all.

Break Free from Social Media

You need to reduce and hopefully eliminate the use of social media in your life. It is an impediment in your development as a person, and to your spiritual evolution.

Jaron Lanier is a computer scientist and philosopher and one of the founders of virtual reality who has written about the dangers of technology. He calls social media "The Cage that Goes Everywhere With You."[108]

In *Ten Arguments For Deleting Your Social Media Account Right Now*, Lanier lists a litany of things of how social media is hurting you, from losing your free will, turning you into a bad person, destroying your capacity for empathy, making you unhappy, and more. Probably Lanier's biggest truth about social media is that it "hates your soul" and does not allow you to experience, saying that experience is the deepest of mysteries.[109]

Lanier recommends quitting social media because it is the most finely targeted way to resist the insanity of our times.[110]

SOCIAL MEDIA BLOCKS YOU FROM YOURSELF.

Having lots of friends and followers may mean you are popular; but it could also be that you are good at networking and spend lots of time on social media. Do all the hoops you jump through, such as posting pictures and telling stories to attract more friends and followers, define who you really are, or do they tell who you have let yourself become? Do you know, yourself?

Before there was the Internet and social media people communicated in person, or through letters. Consider the wisdom of Thoreau. In reading the following, change 'letters' to 'social media:'

> In proportion as our inward life fails, we go more constantly and desperately to the post-office. You may depend on it, that the poor fellow who walks away with the greatest number of letters, proud of his extensive correspondence, has not heard from himself this long while.[111]

You need to break free from the circle of social media and find time for yourself.

Make Your Own Path

Jiddu Krishnamurti (1895-1986) had a profound insight when it came to one's spiritual path saying it was a "pathless path." Meaning that there were no religions, religious texts, gurus, or spiritual advisors, that provided a clear path to freedom—rather, you had to make your own path. Essentially your guide was within yourself. That is certainly very true for your spiritual path and is sound wisdom and guidance for navigating your own life and its many circles.

In 1909, Theosophist Charles Leadbeater, a noted clairvoyant, discovered fourteen-year-old Krishnamurti on the grounds of the Theosophical headquarters in Adyar, India. What captured Leadbeater's eye was Krishnamurti's luminous and beautiful aura. As mentioned earlier, your aura is your spiritual lungs, it is also a reflection of your spiritual acumen. What Leadbeater saw indicated that Krishnamurti was an old soul with occult powers, something of great interest to the Theosophical Society.

What made the finding of an individual with such a magnificent aura even more appealing to the Theosophical Society was that its leadership was looking for a World Teacher, a messiah, to lead the Theosophical Society and the rest of the world in its spiritual advancement. Krishnamurti became the chosen one and would be groomed for that role. The Order of the Star in the East (OSE) was established for this purpose in 1911.

In a way, it was odd for the revolutionary and independent non-religious Theosophical Society to follow the path of traditional religions with a messiah-type figure. Clear divisions broke over this as well as other issues within the organization. There were departures, as with Rudolf Steiner in Switzerland.

Even though Krishnamurti was a slow learner, he was tutored for his role in the years that followed. By the mid 1920s his inner circle felt that he had in fact learned his lessons well and was the authority he was destined to be. Indeed. Biographer Roland Vernon notes that in 1928, when Krishnamurti was asked whether he was the Christ, he replied that, "[T]he great spiritual teachers of the past had not come to found religions, but to free people from them."[112] One must wonder whether he was rebelling against his last fifteen years of tutelage under the thumb of the Theosophical Society, or whether that is what he had come to understand.

On August 3, 1929, on the first day of the Order of the Star gathering in Ommen, Holland in front of three-thousand in attendance, Krishnamurti dissolved the organization and freed himself, saying,

> I maintain that Truth is a pathless land, and you cannot approach it by any path whatsoever, by any religion, by any sect... Truth, being limitless, unconditioned, unapproachable by any path whatsoever, cannot be organized; nor should any organization be formed to lead or

to coerce people along any particular path. If you first understand that, then you will see how impossible it is to organize a belief. A belief is purely an individual matter, and you cannot and must not organize it. If you do, it becomes dead, crystallized; it becomes a creed, a sect, a religion, to be imposed on others.[113]

There is a truth to what Krishnamurti speaks of—to not follow the path set by religions, but to find your own path. There is a price to pay when you have an institution, or organization, act as an intermediary and control, or limit your experience. You want to experience God first hand by yourself.

However, there is a benefit to be gained from the knowledge and experience of a religion (or any institution, for that matter). They can teach you. I would say to spend some time and learn, but do not fully commit to anyone group or organization for the long term. View organizations as stepping-stones on your path.

When I began my spiritual quest I took a very ecumenical path. I studied and went to religious services of many faith traditions. In New York City I went to Buddhist meditation classes and attended Theosophical meetings and classes. I went to traditional Christian services and became a member of St. Mary's Episcopal Church in West Harlem. I even attended a B'hai service. When I moved back to Syracuse, I attended Muslim prayer service, Hindu pranayama (breathing) classes, Sikh group meditations, and was a member of Grace Episcopal Church for a short while. I would also periodically attend the services of various Christian ministers I had become friends with through social justice actions we participated in together.

I learned much. Some services I attended only briefly; others, such as the Wood Hath Community, I was actively involved with, and attended their bible classes regularly, on and off again, for well over a decade.

Basically, I cobbled together my own path. I learned and shared with many others. It seemed as though as my path progressed I would gain a particular knowledge or perspective from each respective group. Rather than seeing a specific and worn path, I created a mosaic. I would gather little bits of knowledge, love, and experience unique to each group. They were all helping mold who I was becoming, to varying degrees.

I must also add that I spent enormous amounts of time meditating, often in the woods. Those were wonderful and joyous experiences that nourished my soul in unbelievable ways. I developed a very strong and loving bond with Mother Earth. A bond that provided me with insights and what I believe was ancient, arguably advanced, knowledge of our dynamic relationship with Mother Earth and the critical role She plays in our spiritual evolution.

By creating my own path I was not encumbered by the karma and consciousness quotients of mainline religions. In other words, the backpack of my soul was not weighed down as I climbed.

You can take that same principle and apply it to other circles in your life. Join a group, learn from a group, help a group, but at some time, move on. Most of all consider, creating your own group and helping others. By starting a group you are starting a new birth and will be keeping the intent and spirit of an organization alive, but not necessarily carrying forward its karmic baggage.

Bear Witness to Your Mind

You need to make an effort to not take on negative samskaras through your thinking. You do this by bearing witness to your thoughts. Become aware of your thinking during the day. Observe your thoughts. Try to move from the person living the novel to the author writing the novel. Begin to see how your mind works.

Do your best to keep your thoughts positive and loving. When you have a negative, selfish, or violent thought, label it mentally as such, as you would during meditation. Then counter this with a positive, loving and giving one. If you think ill of someone counter it by sending them a blessing. You want to neutralize the negative in your life.

After some time spent trying to be positive and loving in my focus, I began to get sensations in my parts of my body when I had strong loving or altruistic thoughts. These sensations were similar to the chills, or a rush of energy, or arguably what some may call kundalini. They were meant to help me become selfless. This went on for years and years and still does so periodically.

Conversely, if I had a selfish or violent thought, or an emotion such as anger, I would have some minor mishap: slip slightly when I was hiking, or stub my toe, or feel a slight pain. They were nothing major, only slight, trivial errors. Often I would have to reflect back on what I was thinking at the time of the mishap to determine what I was to learn. Why did that happen? What's the message? This still periodically happens.

Learning to bear witness to your mind is invaluable and can be of great aid to you if you are ever experiencing trauma or hardship.

As beneficial as learning to bear witness to your mind can be, you need to periodically get out of your own head and stop focusing on yourself. Pray for others during the day, repeat a mantra, do a contemplative walk, or give thanks to our Mother. Mix it up. Just as a good athlete does a variety of exercises and plays different sports, you need to keep changing how you exercise your heart and mind. Most of all, you have to make sure it is not always about you.

In our narcissistic and self-absorbed world you have to make sure that you are not too much in your own head. So, pray for others, visualize peace in the world, and think loving thoughts of others; just don't bear witness to your own mind all the time.

Path of Karma Yoga

Another way to reduce the impact of a circle is to practice karma yoga. Karma yoga is the path of selfless service where you don't reap the fruits or benefits of your actions, but just do them. It is as if you entered a contest and won a prize and did not show to pick it up. You are either performing your acts for the sake of performing them, or for God or the greater good. So karma yoga calls for you to act selflessly and not in your own selfish interest.

As the Bhagavad Girts teaches:

[W]ithout being attached to the fruits of activities, one should act as a matter of duty, for by working without attachment one attains the Supreme. (3.19)

I envy no one, nor am I partial to anyone. I am equal to all. But whoever renders service unto Me in devotion is a friend, is in Me, and I am also a friend to him. (9.29)

By not attaching to the fruits of your actions, you are less tethered to them and the circle to which they belong. The more you are disconnected from a circle, the less sway it and its karma have upon you. Not partaking in the fruits of actions reduces the amount of karma that you take on, if any. So karma yoga can be one way to reduce the karma that you take on.

However, I strongly disagree with the idea of blindly following your duty. In essence the story of the Gita is of Krishna telling Arjuna to follow his duty, go against his wishes, and go into battle and kill his fellow man. No matter how noble your actions may be, if you follow a path that involves violence, you will be strengthening the already powerful grip it has upon the world. No doubt the solider is the hero in a violent world. But do we really want a violent world? Remember: Jesus was a pacifist.

In his book on karma yoga Sri Swami Sivananda advocates Seva, or selfless service:

> By doing service you purify you heart. Egotism, hatred, jealousy, the idea of superiority and all the kindred negative qualities will vanish. Humility, pure love, sympathy, tolerance and mercy will be developed. The sense of separateness will be annihilated. Selfishness will be eradicated…Be kind to all. Love all. Serve all. Be tolerant and generous to all. Serve the Lord in all.[114]

Sri Swami Sivananda also known as Sivananda Saraswati founded the Divine Life Society on the banks of Ganges River in India 1936, recognized for its free distribution of spiritual literature. Many of his disciples went on to educate and serve others, and founded other organizations, such as Swami Satyananda Saraswati who founded the Bihar School of Yoga, as previously noted.

Disconnect From Some of Your Circles

Eknath Easwaran, in his biography of Mahatma Gandhi, tells of a reporter who had been following him for years and had great admiration for work. One day the reporter asked Gandhi to tell him the secret of his life, to which Gandhi replied, "renounce and enjoy."

Easwaran said that:

> It was a reference to the Gita (Chap V Renounce and Rejoice). Meaning to enjoy life we cannot be selfishly attached to anything—objects, family, friends, power, prestige…Because once we attach to something we become its prisoner.[115]

In a way, we are all prisoners under the control of a multitude of samskaras and circles. You need to make choices about which ones you belong to.

DISCONNECT AND REDUCE THE CIRCLES IN YOUR LIFE AND LIMIT YOUR EXPOSURE TO THOSE THAT YOU RETAIN.

8. You Shall Know Them By Their Fruit

We are constantly interacting with a myriad of circles that we come in contact with; whether by choice or unknowingly, they are shaping us and we are shaping them. You have to disconnect from some of them, and reduce your participation in others, but how do you choose? Certainly personal preferences play a part: why you are part of a group, what do you get out of being a member, what do you contribute, and the involvement of your friends are only a few of the variables you need to consider. Or you may feel it your mission to turn around and improve a particular circle.

Before you can make a proper decision about the circles in your life you need to know if a circle is bad, and carries bad karma. Does it have negative consciousness, or a negative consciousness quotient that will diminish your soul? Will you be possibly taking on karma that may be harmful? A circle may actually bear good karma.

These are not easy questions to answer. Groups generally put forth their best face and don't advertise that they are violent, have a checkered past, or that horrific things were done in their name.

Then there is the added challenge that a group, organization, or action can be dedicated to a great cause such as helping others, but can have a very negative consciousness and contain lots of karmic baggage.

It is a challenging task to determine the merit of a circle and what your participation should, or should not, be.

You Shall Know Them By their Fruit

One of the ways to ascertain the consciousness of a circle, group, or even an individual is to look at their actions. Is their behavior in sync with their principles and words? Are they saying one thing and doing another? We regularly see the conflict between actions and words in religion, where we are told that such and such religion is a religion of peace, even reciting scripture and versus; yet we see its members mercilessly and cruelly hurt and kill in its name.

Jesus introduced the concept that actions speak louder than words when he taught that you shall know them by their fruit (actions). Watch out for false teachers who say one thing but do another:

> Beware of false prophets, who come to you in sheep's clothing but inwardly are ravenous wolves. You will know them by their fruits. Are grapes gathered from thorns, or figs from thistles? In the same way, every good tree bears good fruit, but the bad tree bears bad fruit. A good tree cannot bear bad fruit, nor can a bad tree bear good fruit. Every tree that does not bear good fruit is cut down and thrown into the fire. Thus you will know them by their fruits. (Mt 7.15-20)

Jesus' wisdom that behavior is a better barometer of character and integrity than words came at the end of his Sermon on the Mount, one of his most profound and famous teachings. It contains the Beatitudes (Blessed are the meek, Blessed are the Peacemakers…), the "love your enemy" teaching, the Lord's Prayer, and more.

You shall know them by their fruits was an exclamation point at the end of the Sermon on the Mount. It was meant to educate about false teachers/prophets, as well as to advocate for following Jesus.

Our culture is full of teachings similar to "you shall know them by their fruit." A few of them are, 'practice what you preach,' 'actions speak louder than words,' 'the fruit does not fall far from the tree,, 'do as I say—not as I do' (irony)... Hypocrisy is when you say one thing and do another.

So, one of the things you should consider to determine the karma that a circle carries, or its consciousness quotient, is to look at its fruit. The actions and words of members in the past are a good barometer. What has happened recently is an even better gauge. Who are its members, and why are they members? These are some of the fruits that you should look at.

Are the actions and words of the circle in keeping with the spirit or love, do unto others, caring, or giving? Are they in sync with the intentions and principles that the circle espouses? Do we hear people talking about love but hurting people to achieve it?

This is far from being a black and white decision. You may find circles' members often perform loving acts within its embrace, while others may be abusing the circle or performing violent or selfish acts. You need to balance the good with the bad.

We Learn by Observing Behavior

Not only do actions speak louder than words in reflecting our character, but they also help develop, or influence, the character of others. Alfred Adler, like Carl Jung, was a protégé of Freud. He was the first understudy to break from Freud and go on this own.

In his autobiography *Memories, Dreams, Reflections*, Carl Jung notes how his colleague Adler was shaped by the behavior of his parents, saying, "[L]ike many sons, Adler had learned from his "father" not what his father said, but what he did."[116]

Nobel Peace Prize winner, physician, and theologian Albert Schweitzer (1875-1965) said, [e]xample is not the main thing in influencing others. It is the only thing."[117] Schweitzer, a devout Christian set a brilliant example by becoming a physician at the age of thirty to serve those in need in Africa. He established a hospital in Lambarene, Gabon (then a province of French Equatorial Africa) and attended patients there until his death.

Repeated behaviors or actions become powerful samskaras. As noted earlier, Jung said that it was repetitive behavior that created an archetype.

The idea that the behavior of others shapes us shows how important the actions of a circle are in molding us. You may say, "Well I did not see, or the circle did not see, this behavior." The fact is that a memory of the behavior of its members in its name has attached to the circle.

Remember, there is a reason that they say that the "fruit does not fall far from the tree," meaning that children are often a reflection of their parents. For our purposes, a member is a reflection of its circle. The only question is the degree to which they are.

The Dynamics of a Circle

When you are talking about taking on the karma of a circle, you are talking about older and more established circles. In discussing circles earlier, I had mentioned how, when I went to the meditation room upstairs at Swami Vivekananda's Cottage in the Thousand Islands by myself, I was immediately struck and felt blissed out. However, when I went back the next year and meditated with a group of people, I felt nothing.

The people in the room had formed a new circle, which was balancing the meditative skills and connection to Mother Earth based on the participants that were there. The circle had no history to call upon. It was a reflection of the moment.

Similarly, when I am out the woods looking for sacred sites, or special aspects of Mother Earth, it is the group dynamic that can either enhance or reduce my abilities. If the participants in the group are not connected to our Mother, my skill level drops. Conversely, if other members are connected to Her, a synergy develops within the group, and everyone's skills are enhanced.

This effect of members influencing each other in a newly created circle is not confined to me. I have been out with others who have seen depreciable drops in their ability. A friend who is connected to Mother Earth and sentient of Her energies and essences noticed how she felt nothing in a powerful place when several people in our party (circle) were in the space. Later, I took her back to teach her about this phenomenon and had her experience the space again. She was blown away and immediately felt the power of the place.

During its formation, it is the focus and actions of the members while together that shapes the circle. You should not pick up the karma of individual members.

When a circle is in the process of forming, its early members play a dominant role in shaping it. More importantly they plant a seed and create a samskara. The members and their focus and intentions will determine the initial consciousness quotient of a circle; as well as define its focus and direction. So the initial planting of a seed, creating a samskara, plays an important role in defining a circle and its consciousness. Although that nascent, or newly formed samskara is not very strong—its original intention is extremely important.

That initial seed thought, intention, or purpose is critical and will shape the circle throughout its life. It is like a stream running down a mountain: if it starts going towards the east, it will be difficult or next to impossible to get it to end up on the western side of the mountain.

Remember: as it is for one, so it is for many. The same process that you undergo takes place in a circle. Circles are dynamic, changing, and evolving—and it is the karma of its actions that determine its character.

A Circle's Karma

Once a circle has formed and taken on a life of its own, it is the actions of its members acting out for it, or actions performed while in the circle, that will define it and make it what it becomes. These are actions done within its embrace through the member's intention, guidance of members, or in its name or those working for it. During this process, the actions and thoughts of its members while in the circle will help form what the circle becomes. This is how a circle takes on karma.

The circle has begun a life of its own, which may or may not adhere to its founding intention. You are all familiar with how institutions and organizations can stray from their original intent. The Catholic Church is the classic example of how an institution becomes as important (if not more important) than the principles, or spirit, upon which it was founded—that of Jesus Christ. This was very evident when senior officials were more concerned about covering up the pedophile scandal rather than following and exemplifying the teachings of Jesus. Unfortunately, the circle, the Roman Catholic Church, has in essence become a separate and distinct entity unto itself. You also see this clearly with large corporations and institutions that have been given personhood status by the courts.

Earlier, I mentioned that I initially chose a flower as the object of focus for my intensive concentrative meditation practice, but changed it to a mantra, or tale/story; a story mantra. I would repeat my story mantra endlessly for hours on end, day after day. Over time, I created a very powerful samskara that could put me deep into trance as soon as I began to recite the words mentally.

Something interesting happened when I led group meditations with my story mantra. The collective focus of the group would add to the mantra. There were times where I would shake because of all the energy that was coming into the mantra's samskara, or circle. Then, when I would next repeat my story mantra in a contemplative mind, it was much more potent.

My mantra had absorbed and retained the memory of the intentions of the participants in the group meditation. That collective experience of all us meditating on that same mantra was now contained within it. It was if the collective intentions of the meditators had been captured and bottled, with my story mantra being the bottle—a bottle I could open up any time. All I had to do was focus my intention on the mantra; in fact, I did not have to meditate on it to tap into it, although meditating made it much more potent.

It is the same with the karma of actions. Change the intentions of the meditators to the actions of meditators. Had the meditators performed various actions during the group meditation, the mantra's samskara would have similarly retained them, as well. The circle of my mantra meditation was taking on the karma—focus and intention—of those that had heard and-or repeated it.

While my meditation had a very clear story (uniting the consciousness and teachings of the greatest spiritual teachers that had ever lived), it was also affected by how it was used. It was at about this time that I began to have sleep issues. To help me combat my insomnia when I awoke in the middle of the night and could not fall back asleep, I would occasionally repeat the mantra.

By reciting my story mantra to help me sleep by putting me into trance, I had begun to alter the intention of my meditation. I was adding an element of yogic sleep.

Over time, I began noticing that periodically someone repeating or hearing the mantra meditation would go deep into yogic sleep; sometimes almost instantaneously, as if they had been hypnotized. They had picked up the kernel of sleep that I had added when I began to use the mantra meditation to help me fall back asleep. This shows how a circle can change over time.

Why did some pick up the sleep bit and not the regular meditation?

Earlier, I talked about my Soup Theory of Sacred Space and how sacred space and circles are like a vegetable soup. There is the stock that defines the soup overall, but within it are also the individual components: the potatoes, the carrots, the mushrooms, the onions, the celery, the green beans, and... With each spoonful, you are taking in the stock, but you may also take in a particular vegetable. You may bite into a mushroom or a carrot—two very different vegetables, each with a distinctive taste.

My story mantra had become like a 'vegetable soup.' The mantra was the stock and the features I added, like sleep, or a strong emotional experience, or a focus on love, or… they were its vegetables. So whenever anyone participated in the mantra, they could have a slightly different experience than others because they equivalently bit into a different and distinctive vegetable; yet they were still participating in and experiencing the same mantra.

We see a similar concept of 'vegetable soup' in Jung's collective unconscious that is populated by archetypes which remain hidden, but are always looking to enter consciousness. In speaking of 'archetypal personalities,' Jung notes how they are always lurking below the surface: "[T]hey always remain strangers in the world of consciousness, unwelcome intruders saturating the atmosphere."[118]

It is the same with all circles. How a particular circle affects you, or the karma that you take on, can vary. Ultimately, a vegetable soup is a vegetable soup.

The Vortex Test

For many years I have been searching for sacred sites and often working to resuscitate them. During this journey I learned about the wonder of our relationship with Mother Earth and how the land retains the memories of what transpired some place. I was blessed and gifted with the knowledge about the Earth Magic in that relationship and how we can co-create a new birth with our Mother.

One of those births is what Earth Healers and geomancers call an Energy Vortex. I call them Natural Vortex(es) (Vortices)[119] because they form in places in response to where positive human intention—healing, giving, selfless acts, praying, ceremony, meditation—have occurred over a long period of time. They are a whirlwind of energy in the form of a vortex and are very therapeutic and can nourish your soul. Like the funnel of a hurricane or tornado, the vortex pulls in extra nutrition.

While a hurricane or a tornado is incredibly destructive, a Natural Vortex is therapeutic, healing, and possibly consciousness-raising. Think of a vortex pulling in energy from around you and funneling it into you.

I often find them in hidden places in the wilderness that clearly were, at one time, a sacred site. I came to realize they were barometers: an indicator that a location was truly a sacred site, and that good deeds and prayer had occurred there in the past.

I almost never found Natural Vortices in the places of worship for mainline religions. The only mainline places of worship that had Natural Vortices were those that had been located over old Native American sacred places.

It was only years later that I realized that the group karma of the religious institutions were casting a pall upon the grounds of their place of worship and preventing a Natural Vortex from forming. It was my first inkling about group karma and the realization that everything has karma.

The fact that religious organizations can prevent the formation of a Natural Vortex has staggering implications. Before I can explain that, you need to understand the mechanics of how our soul evolves.

Nourishing Your Soul

Have you ever wondered about the mechanics of how your soul evolves? Think 'As Above, So Below.' It is very similar to the way that your body grows, or builds muscle. To build muscle, you need to exercise and consume protein. You can exercise all that you want, but if you don't consume enough protein. you will not build muscle. No Protein = No Muscle.

Similarly, you need to spiritually work your soul. You do this through your actions and intentions such as loving, giving, forgiving, healing, practicing nonviolence towards all of creation, helping others, praying, and meditating. Just like your muscles need proper nutrition to grow, so does your soul need nourishment to evolve. Instead of consuming the proper nutrition yourself, God though Mother Earth blesses you with that nourishment. When you love, help, meditate, or help others you get an extra dose of spiritual nutrition that helps your psychic being, or evolving soul to evolve.

Again, think "As Above, So Below." The processes occurring in the physical world are similar to the processes in the unseen world. Just as your muscles need nutrition to grow, so does your soul need spiritual nutrition to evolve.

To better understand this, consider the practice of energy healing and how it nourishes your Energy Body. When an energy healer lays their hands upon you they tap into the Life Force (also known as chi, qi, prana, orgone). In doing so, they pull in extra amounts of the Life Force. This nourishes your Energy Body and can help physically heal you. See Exhibit 8.1 Energy Healing, and how the healer's hands pulls extra Life Force into someone during a healing.

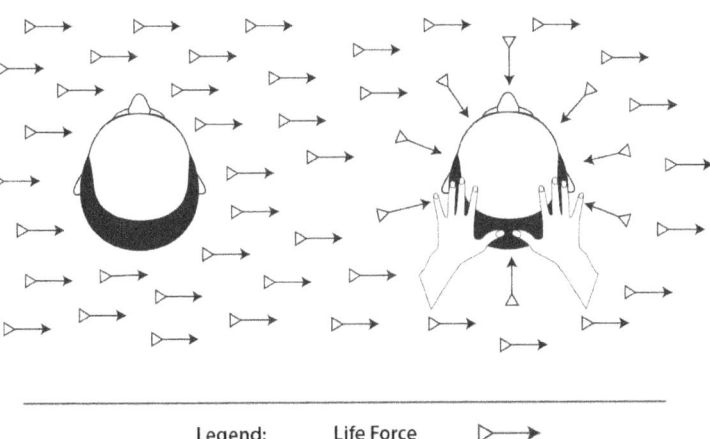

Energy Healing

Legend: Life Force ▷→

Exhibit 8.1 Energy Healing. Arrows represent the Life Force moving across the landscape. The Life Force (arrows) is pulled towards the healer on the right and into the person being healed, forming a circle of inward pull around their head.

A similar sort of process to energy healing takes place to nourish your soul. Instead of an energy healer guiding the Life Force into you, it is God, through Mother Earth, that nourishes your psychic being, or evolving soul. When you do a good act, help someone, or meditate, you pull in an extra dose of Cosmic Prana. This nourishes your soul and helps it evolve, and in the process, you become a better person. Think of it like being protein that helps your muscles grow, but instead, it feeds your soul and helps it evolve.

Cosmic Prana is of a higher order than the Life Force. Where the Life Force gives life to and nourishes your Energy Body, Cosmic Prana nourishes your soul and in the process helps develop your spiritual being. Just as foods have various nutritional components—protein, carbohydrates, fat—so does energy.[120] Think back to Exhibit 2.1, the Devolution of Consciousness, and the various levels, or gradients of Spirit and Matter. Cosmic Prana is a higher gradient that has more spirit than matter compared to the Life Force. Exhibit 8.2 Soul Nourishment, shows how meditating attracts Cosmic Prana.

Soul Nourishment
Meditating, giving, and the like nourishes your soul by drawing Cosmic Prana

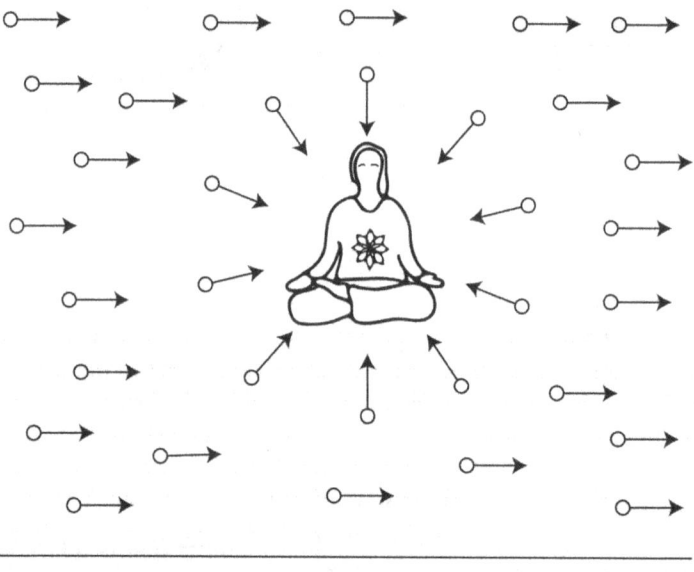

Legend: Cosmic Prana ○⟶

Exhibit 8.2 Soul Nourishment. Notice how the meditator is pulling in Cosmic Prana (soul nourishment) towards themselves.

The more you love, give, heal, and act selflessly, the more our Mother nourishes your soul. In the process, your aura gets larger, and as it does, it begins to pull in more of Mother Earth's nourishment. In other words: the capacity of your aura to absorb and assimilate nutrition, whether it is for your spiritual being or for your Energy Body, increases. It is a self-rewarding loop—you act selflessly and Mother Earth nourishes you, and in the process your aura gets bigger, which means that next time, you absorb even more because your aura is larger. You can further enhance the size of your aura by developing a strong bond with our Mother.

Blocking the Flow of Spiritual Nutrition

Preventing the formation of Natural Vortices (Energy Vortices) by mainline religious institutions has staggering and alarming consequences that go far beyond not allowing the formation of a Natural Vortex.

Basically, the circle and karma of mainline religions prevents the formation of a Natural Vortex by blocking the flow of spiritual nutrition—in this case, Cosmic Prana. By not allowing Cosmic Prana to be pulled to a location, an Energy Vortex cannot form. Cosmic Prana, as was just noted is what we attract when we meditate, perform loving and selfless acts, pray, give, and do unto others. It nourishes our soul and in the process makes us a more loving and compassionate person.

This blockage of spiritual nutrition (Cosmic Prana) by mainline religions is not confined to their grounds. Whenever you are in the embrace (membership, participating in its activities, accepting its theology that is unique, thinking about it, etc.) of a mainline religion through your physical being or your intention, you will similarly have the flow of spiritual nutrition to you blocked, to a degree. Some spiritual nutrition will get through, but less than if you were not in the embrace of a mainline religion.

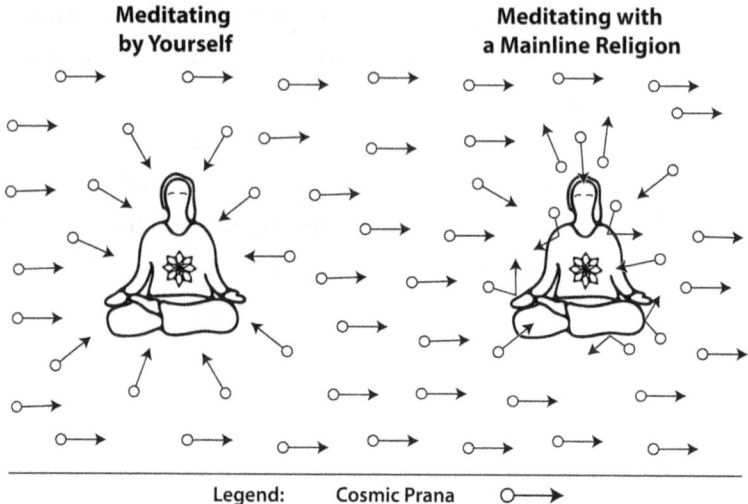

Exhibit 8.3 Meditating with a Mainline Religion shows how a Mainline Religion impedes the flow of Spiritual Nutrition. The meditator on the left is absorbing all the spiritual nutrition (Cosmic Prana) that she is attracting, while the meditator on the right is having some of it blocked, as seen with some of the arrows (Cosmic Prana) bouncing off.

Exhibit 8.3, Meditating with a Mainline Religion, shows what happens to your intake of spiritual nutrition when you are in the embrace of a mainline religion. The meditator on the left is pulling in spiritual nutrition (Cosmic Prana); while the meditator on the right is practicing a meditation unique to a particular religion. Not all of the spiritual nutrition is being blocked because of the circle with the mainline religion. Some is getting through.

Let me explain what I mean by 'being in the embrace' of a mainline religion. You are within the circle of a particular mainline religion when you become a member or attend its services.

You also merge with the circle of a mainline religion when you interact with its manifestations. Earlier, in speaking about archetypes, I quoted Jung on how we can trigger them by mimicking them, '[w]hen a situation similar to the archetype occurs the archetype is activated and compulsiveness appears.'[121] It is the same with all circles, whether they are mainline religions, corporations, clubs, theories, or otherwise. Whenever we mimic, recite, act out or behave in a manner unique to a particular circle, we merge with it. For a mainline religion, this could be things like reading its sacred texts, holding a particular belief unique to the religion, acting in its interest, talking or thinking about it, and the like.

This Cannot Be? How is this Possible?

To understand how and why this process, works think back to Theodor's Schwenk's 'archetypal phenomenon of vortex formation' and how a vortex forms whenever two different liquids, or elements, come in contact with each other. The vortex forms to merge the two and balance out the differences. This is the basic process of a circle. It looks to merge with other circles it comes in contact with and exchanges karma and consciousness.

The property of a mainline religion is part of its circle. So any property owned by a mainline religion bears its karma and its consciousness quotient. Sadly, their consciousness quotients are generally not positive.

So when you are performing acts, thinking about, or spending time with a mainline religion, a connecting circle forms between the two of you; the mainline religion and you. In the process, the new circle is blending both of your consciousness quotients. This new circle's consciousness quotient will disproportionately be influenced by the negative consciousness quotient of the mainline religion. This means that if you are meditating or doing good works within the new circle, your spiritual nutrition will be curtailed, to a degree, by it's negativity—a negative consciousness quotient.

While religions are committed to helping people, are spiritual in nature, and generally help the poor and needy, they have a checkered past. Consider Christianity. When Christianity merged with Rome it took on all the karma of the Roman Empire. It also fostered the inquisition, killing of pagans, the Crusades, the burning of witches, the selling of papal indulges, the pedophilia scandal, and much more.

A larger challenge is faced when the founder (seed thought) of a religion like Islam's Mohamed commits violence, as with the slaughter of Jews in Medina and his critics, and the raiding of caravans. The behavior of members during the formative period of a circle has a huge bearing in defining what a circle will become. Upon Mohamed's death, the violent Sunni Shia divide appeared, and still rages. Its fruits of violent jihadists are regularly on parade.

The other challenge presented by mainline religions, or much of organized religion, for that matter, is that they often act as intermediaries, or gatekeepers, to God. This, to a degree is the equivalent of a fence. Then there is the proselytizing of a religion, with the intention of control and manipulation. Does the act (fruit) of selling make for a better religion? No, just the opposite.

However, the negatives of mainline religions must be balanced out by the good works and intentions that religions provide; from helping the poor, to consoling the sick, praying, mediating, and much more.

When you pray on the property of mainline religion, your circle is merging with theirs. During prayer, you draw Cosmic Prana towards you. When you do so in the embrace of a mainline religion, a shroud forms around your connecting circle (the merger of your circle with that of the religion's circle). This shroud blocks and seriously impedes and reduces the amount of Cosmic Prana you pull in. It does not totally block it, but severely curtails the amount that you and the location draw towards you.

How much will be blocked?

I cannot say what percentage, or how much will be blocked. It will not all be blocked, but enough will be blocked to reduce the affects of your actions. In other words: your soul, which should be nourished, will be deprived to a degree.

When I say mainline religions, I am referring to organized religions; religions that have been around for centuries and have had time to accumulate karma. It does not matter whether they have are western, eastern, or have an earth-based focus.

There are other circles, such as technology, that are much more hideous and damaging to you, as I shall shortly discuss.

Outrageous?

I imagine that, to many my claim that mainline religions and other circles block the flow of spiritual nutrition may seem outrageous. Unfathomable. That I am making such a wild claim to draw attention, or…

While I have known about the inability of vortices to form on the grounds of mainline religions for some time, it is only recently, while working on this book, that I realized what this was indicating: that the flow of Cosmic Prana is blocked to varying degrees by circles whose consciousness quotient was less than stellar. In other words, many circles block the flow of spiritual nutrition and reduce the amount that comes to you.

The implications are staggering; such as, that instead of spiritually transforming humanity is stuck on a treadmill going nowhere. That no matter how loving, selfless and nonviolent that your life is, being part of the wrong circles will retard your spiritual evolution—significantly, to the point that it requires more reincarnations and future lives.

I still have trouble accepting this, and wrestled with it for a long time.

I thought back to a story I heard on NPR and wrote about in my book, *Vortices and Spirals*. It was a story about how location/geography played a pivotal role in helping heroin addicts kick their habit; and because the results were so dramatic, no one believed them.

Working for the Nixon administration, psychiatric researcher Lee Robinson[122] found that twenty percent of soldiers in Vietnam were addicted to heroin. By staying in Vietnam to be cured ninety-five percent of them remained heroin-free after returning home to the USA. Compare this to a ninety percent relapse rate for those treated in the USA. Speaking to NPR Duke University psychologist David Neal said that, "[P]eople, when they perform a behavior a lot — especially in the same environment, same sort of physical setting — outsource the control of the behavior to the environment."[123]

The results were so startling that Robins spent years trying to defend that she was not lying, or politically motivated.

Your Meditation is Impacted

This is not to say that meditating does not bring benefits if you are in the embrace of negative circle. You are still going to get spiritual nutrition, but the amount will be reduced.

To better understand the impact of circles on your meditation we need to examine it through two influences: 1) External and 2) Internal.

External. External influences will be impacted when you meditate in the embrace of a negative circle. The amount of Cosmic Prana and other spiritual nutrients you draw to you will be diminished. However, your prayers and positive intentions will help those that you pray for.

Internal. Internally, you will develop, fine tune your mind, reduce the challenging aspects of your life, improve your concentration, become mindful, get control of your thoughts, and reduce negative aspects of your life. Meditation will still help you spiritually evolve because you will be reducing negativity in your life and detaching from bad influences, or thoughts. In other words, by focusing on the positive you will not feeding the bad samskaras and they will dwindle. You will still become a better person, but just like trying to build muscle and consuming scant amounts of protein, it will take longer and many more lives. That is, assuming that the negative circles in your life do not drag you down.

Technology Kills

Technology kills. In the sea of consciousness that we live in, it is particularly pernicious. While certain circles will inhibit or partially block the inflow of spiritual nutrients, technology turns the spigot off.

Exhibit 8.4 Meditating With Technology Blocks Spiritual Nutrition (next page) shows how, when you use technology (in this case, listening to music on a cell phone while meditating), you are blocking the flow of spiritual nutrition to you.

The larger problem that technology creates is that most people use it for much of their waking hours. As a consequence, vast amounts of people are being blocked from getting spiritual nutrition.

We are meant to be immersed in, and bathed by Cosmic Prana (spiritual nutrition) 24/7. When we perform loving acts we get an extra dose. Technology totally turns off the spigot to our Mother's love.

Meditating With Technology Blocks Spiritual Nutrition

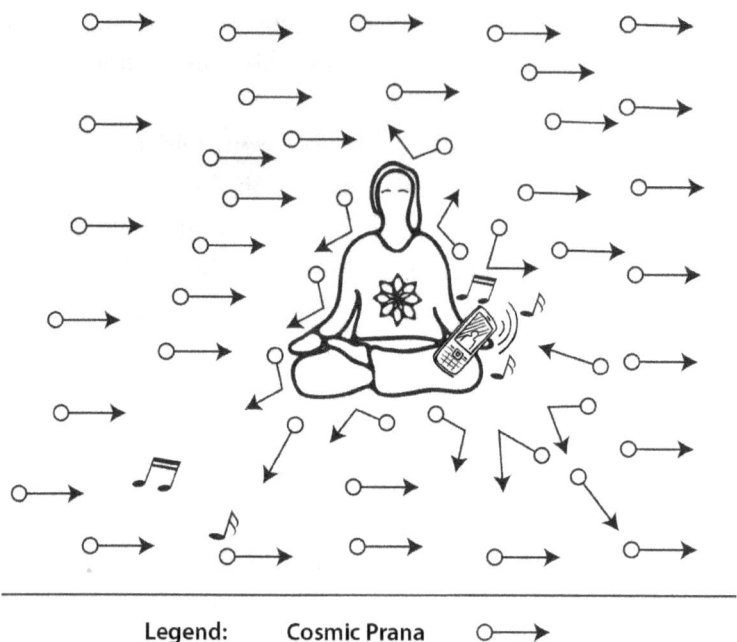

Figure 2 Exhibit 8.4 Meditating With Technology Blocks Spiritual Nutrition. The person holding cell phone and listening to music while meditating is having the flow of Cosmic Prana to them totally being blocked.

Technology has the focus and intention of control, destruction, and the conquering of Mother Earth; Our Mother who is our source of nutrition and our partner in our spiritual evolution. Arguably, technology's intent is the destruction and killing of all of creation. This has a karma, and it is horrific.

Author Nicholas Carr in writing about the dangers of the Internet, sums it up well in describing the intention of technology: "Every technology is an expression of human will. Through our tools, we seek to expand our power and control over our circumstances—over Nature, over time and distance, over one another."[124] This intention has karma, and we are all victims of it: think control; think destruction.

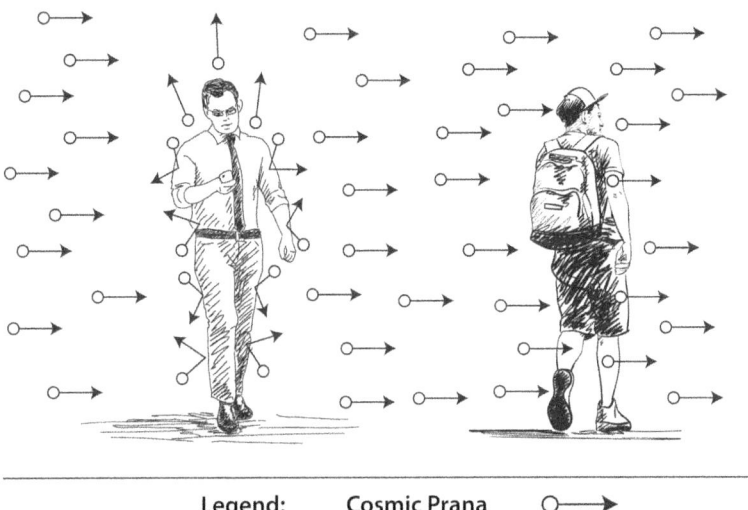

Exhibit 8.5 Cell Phones Block Out Spiritual Nutrition. We are bathed in Cosmic Prana (Spiritual Nutrition) 24/7. The man on the left is using a cell phone that is blocking the inflow of Cosmic Prana; consequently, he is being deprived of spiritual nutrition. The man on the right is not being deprived because he is not using a cell phone—as it is meant to be.

We believe that technology puts us in control and helps us navigate in the world—instead, we are the ones that are being manipulated. We are reaping what we have sown. KARMA.

In *The Axemaker's Gift—A Double Edged History of Human Culture*,[125] James Burke and Robert Ornstein tell how, throughout history, technological innovation created a double-edged sword where the costs outweighed the benefits. For example, the Gutenberg press reduced the power of the church and altered the map of Europe. Monarchs and their governments were now empowered to begin enforcing the local tongue with laws, taxes, armies, and the state bureaucracies that went with them.

Burke and Ornstein call these technological innovators "axemakers." With each new innovation, their power to force changes upon society increased and brought with it more alienation, as well as increasing social and economic inequality:

> Throughout history, mysterious axemaker knowledge always strengthened social conformist as at the same time it increasingly distanced the change-makers and their institutional masters from the general public whose lives they controlled. The sheer scale and number of new control systems generated by late-eighteenth century technologists and entrepreneurs widened this gulf and imposed rigid conformity as never before. Such was the rate of industrial innovation that it would force sudden and fundamental change on a society politically and administratively unready to deal with them. The changes would in turn bring into being new ways to manipulate the proletariat, because thanks to the factories there was a proletariat to manipulate. The new gifts would be an ideological tool for control… The new industrial towns cut off the new village immigrants from Nature and from any regard for it."[126]

No doubt, technology brings us benefits. At what cost? We think we are benefiting, but ultimately we are loosing out.

The karma of control and destruction that we are spawning with technology continues growing. Renowned theoretical physicist Stephen Hawking said that technology (artificial intelligence in particular) "could spell the end of the human race."[127]

The fruits of technology are control, manipulation, death, and destruction. It is a dark and evil circle that has a very negative consciousness quotient.

The Lost Generation

In an article for the Atlantic psychologist and researcher of generational changes, Jean Twenge asks, 'Have Smartphones Destroyed a Generation?'[128]

It is all too reminiscent of the 'Lost Generation' popularized by author Ernest Hemingway and 'coined by his mentor and colleague Gertrude Stein to describe a generation who came of age during the first Great War (WWI). Beleaguered by a war of epic portions, Stein felt they were lost because they cared about nothing and drank themselves to death.[129]

WWI was fought on a grand scale never seen before. It was also fueled by technological advancements that allowed for carnage on a massive scale—air warfare, submarines, tanks, machine guns, grenades, flame throwers, and chemicals weapons such as tear gas and mustard gas.

We, too, have lost a generation to rapid advances in technology—cell phones, digital technology, the Internet, and social media. While the specter of modern technological warfare disillusioned the Lost Generation and had them abandon tradition and, in some way, hope, the new generation Twenge speaks of has had their humanity and souls snatched by the grim reaper of technology.

The research is proof positive that digital technology, cell phones, and social media diminish your humanity. Their FRUITS are becoming ever more apparent.

A University of Michigan study found that students are forty percent less empathetic today than they were thirty years ago, and that the biggest drop occurred after 2000.[130] This is not surprising because it coincides with the advent of the Internet, social media, cell phones, and then smartphones. Less empathy and compassion is what you would expect to see if you were being deprived of Cosmic Prana, which makes you more loving.

Psychology professor Jean M. Twenge coined the term 'iGen', those born 1995 to 2012, to describe the generation brought up in the age of the Internet, social media, and cell phones. 2012 is only an arbitrary cutoff point; however, Twenge notes that 2011-12 was when the majority of Americans began owning smartphones. Twenge says that 'i' in iGen is meant to define the generation, but is open-ended about specifics, saying that it could stand for the Internet, the iMac, the iphone, or even the first personal singular (I).[131]

As a generational researcher, Twenge looks to see how different generations behave at the same age to determine changes between them. For example, what were Baby Boomers like at fifteen-years-old compared to Millennials when they were fifteen-years-old, compared to iGener's at fifteen-years-old.

What Twenge has found is that iGener's are growing up slower, today eighteen-year-olds act like fifteen-year-olds did a generation ago. She has found that iGener's have higher rates of mental issues and are more anxious and depressed, to the point of being more suicidal. They are less religious and spiritual. They are, however, more accepting of others.[132]

If you take nothing else away from this book get rid of your cell phone, don't partake in social media, and reduce technology in your life. These simple steps will go a long way in preventing the devolution of your humanity and consciousness and will help reduce the chances of increasing the number of your future lives.

The Best Intentions Can Go Awry

It can be very difficult to accept that a religion, mainline or not, can hurt you in some ways. They are supposed to help you spiritually evolve. They are also about control: for the longest time the Roman Catholic Church did services in Latin and kept people in the dark. To get to God, you had to go through them.

Often circles, organizations, movements, and efforts begin with the best of intentions and incredible dedication and focus, but as the organization evolves, things begin to change.

Growth brings power and struggles may ensue within the ranks. Jealously and petty fights over control, direction, membership and other matters within the circle form samskaras that attach to it, in the process encouraging more of the same from others

Growth attracts people who care less about the intent of the circle, but instead what it can provide them in their career or help with their ambitions. To others, the circle is a social networking opportunity, a resume builder, or... These intentions attach to circle blending and altering it ever so slightly, which causes its consciousness quotient to begin diminishing.

Others come with their biases or focuses on things such as money. Money is a very big thing in our capitalistic materialistic world. Because of this, many initiatives end up being business enterprises rather than their original altruistic focus. Money also links the circle with the circle of money, to a degree. These intentions attach to the circle.

Others in the circle may commit horrific violent acts within the sphere of the circle. Again: these acts attach to the circle.

Consider Mindfulness, the practice of being present and aware of what is going on presently with you and your surroundings. Robert Meikyo Rosenbaum and Barry Magid are two practitioners of Zen Buddhism. As editors of *What's Wrong with Mindfulness (And What Isn't): Zen Perspectives*,[133] they had others discuss what Zen Buddhism is and how mindfulness has been appropriated by the "Western Marketplace." They said that mindfulness has:

… expanded beyond it traditional training venues, religious practices, and cultural contexts. Mindfulness has become a generic term whose meaning becomes less clear in direct proportion to the hype it generates. It can be found everywhere: corporate retreats, medical centers, sports facilities and even the military have adopted it as a way to decrease stress and improve performance."[134]

Fortunately, this negativity is balanced with the good in many circles such as religions, spirituality, social work, health oriented, justice, and other circles dedicated to helping. People commit themselves to the circle, and others help or volunteer. Religious or spiritual circles will have people praying or meditating. All of these positive intentions and actions are balanced against the negative.

Heal the Body, Starve the Soul

We can see circles with the most beautiful of intentions go awry with practices such as Energy Healing, a favorite in the New Age community. Reiki, a particular form of Energy Healing, has gone mainstream, beyond holistic fairs and practices among friends to being offered at posh spas, hospitals, universities, and other commercial venues.

Reiki has successfully institutionalized itself with certification, training levels and more; all for a price. It like every other Energy Healing discipline, and so much else in the 'New Age Community' has mutated into a financial enterprise. What Rosenbaum and Magid said about mindfulness applies to Reiki and so much else in our world today:

> As mindfulness gets absorbed into a society that runs on the engines of consumerism, competition, and glorification of the individual self, its runs the danger of turning into one more brand trademarked for purely personal gratification.[135]

In the process, Reiki has picked up that karma, and in doing so has diminished its consciousness quotient. That is not to say that Reiki or other Energy Healing modalities are bad. They do help and most certainly provide sustenance for your Energy Body and ultimately aid in physical well-being.

At the same time, it starves your soul and diminishes your consciousness quotient because when you are having a Reiki session, you are merging with not only your health practitioner, but with Reiki itself. Unfortunately, this is no longer positive consciousness, so when you have a Reiki healing, you will be diminishing your consciousness quotient. By how much is difficult to say.

I had my suspicions about Reiki, but it really rang home with what happened at a sacred site. Some very good and dedicated people began talking about (intention) and practicing Reiki there and within some charged areas, with Natural Vortices. Unfortunately the vibe diminished discernibly and the Energy Vortices disappeared. Think back to the Vortex Test and how Natural Vortices do not form on the grounds of mainline religions. When you merge with a circle that carries bad karma and has a negative consciousness quotient, you are merging with that circle, and it attaches to where it is taking place.

It was no use telling these practitioners about how to treat the sacred space, and the potential harm they would be doing by practicing Reiki on the grounds. They were doing good, and I was nuts. What was even worse was that these people did not know where the vortices or specials places were located. I had showed them. When I told them how the space was to be properly used, they sadly ignored me and in the process trashed the wonder of the space.

Make Your Own Path

Energy Healing is a wonderful therapeutic process. When you practice a particular modality you may be taking on some bad karma. Take a page from Krishnamurti and create your own path, or healing modality/technique.

Attend classes, learn from others, and spend lots of time researching what the ideal modality should be. Then put it all together and make it your own distinctive and unique Energy Healing technique.

Then practice, practice, practice... Make every effort not to have negative karma attach to it. If you need to get paid ask for a donation rather than charging.

Energy Healing is a very intimate act. You merge with both the practice and the practitioner. If you are having it done you want to have someone with good intentions and moral integrity practicing on you. Ask about your healer's background. Are they, or were they a teacher or a social worker? Do they volunteer? What groups do they belong to? You will be spending thirty to sixty minutes merging with your healer, so you need to know about them.

Young/Newer is Better

Earlier, I had stated that you should be cautious about joining older, established religions or circles, and consider starting your own. That is because newer circles are often better. The longer a circle exists, the more the chances increase that it will be taking on bad karma and will begin diminishing its consciousness quotient. In a more perfect world, older circles would be better because they would develop powerful samskaras with a positive vibe over time; ones that could lift you up and help leapfrog your spiritual evolution.

Interestingly, I have found Natural Vortices on the grounds of newer spiritual groups. For example, I have found them on the grounds of a new spiritual leader, particularly if she/he is genuine and loving and people seriously meditate on the grounds.

I believe this is because they are not carrying forward and bearing all the karma that has attached to an older circle.

Corporations

Corporations have little if any redemptive value, and often have very negative conscious quotient readings. There is no counterbalance to their self-serving, manipulative, and controlling behavior, as there is with mainline religions whose members pray and do good works.

Corporations are focused on profit. They are artificial constructs that serve no good except to make money for their shareholders. They brand us with their corporate logos and look to manipulate us into buying their products and services.

Through their activities they may pollute and harm Mother Earth. Many corporations donate to politicians to influence their voting, to the detriment of society. They are looking to sell, sell, sell...

You need to distance yourself as much as possible from corporations. Don't brandish their logos. Don't buy into their silly arguments or actions to do good. Avoid them.

Objects have Karma

All objects have a karma and consciousness to them, which generally is not good. Often there are no fruits to judge objects by. However, you can look to their intention and purpose, and what were they meant to do. For example, guns are meant to kill, have a very negative consciousness quotient, and should be avoided.

Material objects are constituted of:
- Intention, or purpose, or function.

- Component parts. What are they made of?
- How was it constructed?
- Is it natural or organic?

A specific object also picks up the karma from what it was used for and who used it.

Everything Has Karma

Land will also carry samskaras, from how it was treated and what transpired on it. This will have an influence upon you like everything else.

Just remember everything has karma and a consciousness quotient to it. So the circles in your life will have a large say in your life and spiritual development. Choose your circles wisely.

9. You are a Keeper For All of Creation

In an interconnected world where we are all affected by each other and everything, you have a greater responsibility beyond yourself.

You are your Sister's Keeper, your Brother's Keeper, and you are the Keeper for all of creation, for Mother Earth and for all of the creations, structures and organizations humankind has constructed. Not only is it the right thing to do, but also because all of it affects you, since you are inexorably linked to everyone and everything.

The idea that you are, yourself, an independent and separate being and an entity unto itself—is simply false. You have been deceived, led astray by false beliefs and illusion; from the deception of material reality to the belief that your physical body is who your are to selfish doctrines such as Adam Smith's 'law of self-interest.'

You need to break from the chains of the physical world and see your connection to all of creation. This will help with your and other's spiritual transformation. The material world binds you to ego, separateness and sense pleasures. You need to rise above it and help others do the same.

How well you are progressing on your spiritual path depends upon everyone and everything. It is not just about you, but also about all of creation.

Gandhi summed it up well in saying how we are inexorably tied to each other in our spiritual evolution:

> I believe that if one man gains spiritually the whole world gains with him and, if one man falls, the whole world falls to

that extent. I do not help opponents without at the same time helping myself and my co-workers.[136]

Your Sisters and Brother's Keeper

The prophets, sages, and teachers tell us that we are to be kind and friendly to all. In the Golden Rule Jesus educates that not only should we treat others as we wish to be treated, but that it is the law: "In everything do to others as you would have them do to you; for this is the law and the prophets."(Mt 7.12)

Similarly, Buddhism teaches: "The disciple should treat all beings with kindness and compassion."[137]

Jesus taught that in addition to do unto others, we should also love our enemy:

> You have heard that it was said, 'You shall love your neighbor and hate your enemy.' But I say to you, Love your enemies and pray for those who persecute you, so that you may be children of your Father in heaven; for he makes his sun rise on the evil and on the good, and sends rain on the righteous and on the unrighteous. For if you love those who love you, what reward do you have? (Mt.43-46)

The point is not to distinguish between friends and foes when you help or give compassion.

The Gita says similar: "That one I love who is incapable of ill will, who is friendly and compassionate....who looks upon friend and foe with equal regard." (12.13,18) As well as mentioning a connection to others beyond empathy to compassion when you experience the happiness, or sadness of others: "When a person responds to the joys and sorrows of others as if they were his own, he has attained the highest state of spiritual union." (6.32)

Love is the Guiding Principle of the Universe

As much as loving your neighbor and your enemy is the moral and right thing to do as taught by the prophets and sages, it is one of the guiding principles upon which the universe rests. Love does make the world go round and brings a host of benefits in infinite ways; from our physical well-being to our spiritual development and more.

When we love, gather in community, help, heal, and act altruistically we are nourished.

This is a mystical truth; one which our individual and collective spiritual transformation is predicated on.

Earlier, I talked about the Earth Magic in our relationship with Mother Earth and how we can co-create a new birth with Her, an Energy Vortex (what I call a Natural Vortex, or Vortices). They form in response to positive human intention—healing, giving, selfless acts, praying, helping, ceremony, meditation and more—that has occurred over a long period of time. They are a whirlwind of energy in the form of a vortex and are very therapeutic and can nourish your soul, providing you with many more times the amount of nourishment we are usually blessed with, for our good acts and intentions.

Natural vortices are a testament to what is possible when we follow the law of love, live life altruistically, and help all of creation. We have it within ourselves to create a wonderful world that builds upon its altruism producing a wonderful synergy—a Heaven on Earth, where the lion lies down with lamb

Guided by Selfishness, Violence, Scientific Materialism

Unfortunately, instead of following the law of love as prescribed by the prophets and teachers, we have built a world based upon selfishness and competition. Our guiding principal is Adam Smith's law of 'self-interest.' Instead of cooperation and working together we revel in competition; believing it makes us work harder and breeds success. But, does it?

Are the Golden Rule, do unto others, and love your enemy merely slogans for religious services and spiritual adherents? I think not.

The law of love is the guiding principle of the universe. Go against it at your own peril.

Take science and disease. Instead of employing the law of love the scientific approach looks to conquer and defeat. Beat back and destroy that nasty disease; or learn how to control the weather; or how to better extract minerals, rather than developing a holistic alternative based upon cooperation and love. Because of this 'kill the enemy approach' we have created numerous Frankenstein's that are coming back to haunt us.

As German philosopher Friedrich Nietzsche famously said, "Whatever does not kill me, makes me stronger."[138] Science has made some very wicked things very, very strong.

The CDC (Centers for Disease Control and Prevention) calls them "superbugs": "nightmare bacteria" that have developed unusually resistant genes that do not respond to antibiotics, killing tens of thousands each year in the USA and posing an enormous risk to the health of Americans.[139]

Richard D. Smith and Joanna Coast note that medicine thought it had conquered infectious diseases with antibiotics, but all it has done "is made diseases stronger and more resistant. A new class of superbugs from ear infections and strep throat to malaria and tuberculosis formed in response. And the resistance is growing."[140]

We created superbugs with resistant genes because of the resistance training we put them through. We tried to wipe them out, defeat them, kill them, and exterminate them; and because of this, they developed resistance to our assaults.

You all know about and probably have even practiced resistance training. When you go to the gym and lift weights, you are practicing resistance training. By lifting weights, you are putting extra pressure on your muscles, and in response, they get stronger. This is a basic law of the universe.

Understandably, helping people get well is a good thing. Unfortunately, we have chosen a violent approach of killing and defeating a particular disease, and in the process have created new mutations that are even more dangerous. We need to consider alternative approaches not based on violence—and we have to be creative here—but some other alternative, or approach or doing something unrelated, that helps. Secondly, we need to understand that it may take time, a very long time, to develop alternatives. It took centuries, arguably millennia, to get to our current state of curing individuals.

Our approach to disease is a microcosm of our approach to the world around us. It matters to you, because you are linked to its karma. You don't need to be a scientist creating new drugs, or a researcher testing those drugs on animals, or even a consumer of them; although your degree of linkage will be how duplicitous you have been in the process.

The question is: what are you going to do about it?

Take Care of the Needy

Not only are we to love, we are called to help those who are in need and suffering.

Consider the beauty and wisdom of Jesus words as he tells who will get to heaven and why, on Judgment Day, saying it will be the ones that helped those in need and that were suffering:

> [F]or I was hungry and you gave me food, I was thirsty and you gave me something to drink, I was a stranger and you welcomed me, I was naked and you gave me clothing, I was

sick and you took care of me, I was in prison and you visited me. (Mt 25.35, 36)

Implicit in this is the concept that it was God with, or even in, the stranger, the prisoner…Those that failed to help the needy reply to Jesus that they did not see God. To which, Jesus answers: "Truly I tell you, just as you did not do it to one of the least of these, you did not do it to me." (Mt 25.45) Again, he was reaffirming that we are called to help those in need, and in doing so we help God.

Research has consistently shown that compassion and altruism improve our health and well-being. People that give to and help others are happier, healthier, and live longer. One study found that children are happier giving treats, rather than receiving them from other children.[141] A study done over five years "found that when dealing with stressful situations, those who had helped others during the previous year were less likely to die than those who had not helped others."[142]

In other words, giving of yourself and helping those in need is good for you because the karma of your actions boomerangs back to you.

God/Brahman is in all of Creation

You need to see God in all of creation. When we adhere to a materialistic view of reality, we bind ourselves to our lowest common denominator and deny our spiritual being. Similarly, if we prescribe to a dualistic vision of reality that heaven is in some far off place, as espoused by many western faith traditions, we become vulnerable to egotism and the illusion of self. When we begin to see God in everyone and everything, the notion of 'the other begins to diminish.' God is in all, God is everything.

Seeing God in all makes compassion towards others easier because of our link to them. This extends not only to all of humankind, but to all of creation, as well.

The Gita teaches that when we see God in all, we begin to walk the path of nonviolence:

> He alone sees truly who sees the Lord the same in every creature, who sees the Deathless in the hearts of all that die. Seeing the same Lord everywhere, he does not harm himself or others. Thus he attains the supreme goal (13:27-28)

Furthermore the Gita notes that by seeing God in all of creation, we get closer to God: "I am ever present to those who have realized me in every creature. Seeing all life as my manifestation, they are never separated from me." (6.30)

Both of these quotes from the Gita underscore the karma of seeing God in all of creation. The love we give in seeing God in all of creation has the love of God boomeranging back to us as we grow closer to God.

Jainism is one of most ardent supporters of ahimsa, the practice of non-violence, non-injury, and the non-killing of all of creation. It is so dedicated to non-violence that the first of its five vows is the commitment to ahimsa:

> I renounce all kill of living beings, whether subtle or gross, whether movable or immovable. Neither shall I myself kill living beings, nor cause other to do it, nor consent to it.[143]

To aid the Jain devotee in fulfilling their vow they should meditate on five things—carefulness of speech, carefulness of mind, care in walking, care in lifting and laying things down, and ensuring that their food and drink in no way brings harm to a living creature.[144] One is supposed to have universal love for all of creation.

This means a strict vegetarian (preferably a vegan) diet. I am a vegetarian, and would encourage everyone to pursue such a diet; it is both a moral act, as well as one that is good for your health. Many Jains also cover their nose and mouth to avoid accidentally inhaling an insect.

When ahimsa is applied both physically and mentally, a wonder of sorts can transcend upon an individual's life. It is said that Patanjali practiced ahimsa and did not harbor an evil or violent thought towards anyone or anything. Because of this, no animal ever harmed him and he could be among tigers with no consequences.

To begin to see how nonviolence and universal love for all of creation can allow one to not be harmed anywhere, even among wild animals, think of the Law of Karma and its Law of Attraction. Love does not sow violence, but only brings back love.

In his biography of Gandhi, Eknath Easwaran tells something similar about Patanjali's nonviolence, saying that when someone harbors no hostility, no one can be hostile to him or her. He then goes on to tell a story of Gandhi's love towards all:

> Towards dusk one evening at the ashram in Sevagram hundreds were gathered for prayer. Gandhi was seated on a platform in the front wearing only a shirt and loincloth. A ripple of terror swept across the floor as a cobra snake slithered across the room. There was a danger that a panic would cause a stampede and many would suffer.
>
> The snake approached Gandhi and crawled over his bare legs. All the while Gandhi was silently chanting his mantra, "Rama, Rama, Rama...."[145]

Easwaran noted that the snake must have lost all sense of fear, saying "in its own way it must have sensed it was in the presence of someone who would never cause it suffering." Slowly the snake crawled away without harming anyone.

The boomerang of karma can certainly work wonders.

Biodiversity and the Importance of All of Creation

Biodiversity (short for biological diversity) underscores how linked to and dependent we are to all of creation. It also shows how important that the littlest, or least, of creation is.

Biodiversity is a measure of how diverse a species or location is. It is viewed as consisting of three levels.[146] At the top are ecosystems such as rainforests, coral reefs, and lakes. Below that are species that constitute an ecosystem, such as bacteria, birds, animals, and people. At the bottom is the diversity of the individual species what scientists call genes; how biologically diverse a species is.

The premise of biodiversity is that the more diversity there is, the better and healthier an ecosystem, or the world, is. Implicit in biodiversity is the linkage and interconnection of all of creation.

The concept of biodiversity was not recognized until Edward O. Wilson (E. O. Wilson) introduced it in 1985 with a research paper titled 'The Diversity Crisis.'[147] In it, he declared that [b]iological Diversity…is in a state of crisis. Quite simply declining." He stated, that species are going extinct at an unprecedented rate, yet we have no measure of how many species there are, or how biologically diverse life is.

Wilson is an entomologist who gained notoriety for his research and writing on ants and their sociological behavior. Throughout his lifetime, he has continued to be passionate about biodiversity, particularly the protection of ecosystems. Later in his life, Wilson said that humankind's impact on biodiversity "is an attack on ourselves."[148] He has even advocated that half of the earth be dedicated to Nature.[149]

Biodiversity Matters

At every level of life, diversity increases the chances of survival for a species and those that are linked to it and helps maintain the continued functioning of an ecosystem. It is the biodiversity of different kinds of plants such as grasses, herbs, and fruits with their varying food values, that supports a broad assortment of animals. Similarly, a greater variety of plants and trees allows for more diverse types of habitats and shelters, increasing the variety of animals and species. The diversity of biochemical composition of various kinds of plants has kept them from being eliminated by predators. It is the diversity of bacteria and microorganisms and plants that allows for the proper functioning and viability of the soil.

In an anthology on biodiversity, Ruth Patrick sums it up well: "High diversity ensures the continuation of the functioning of our ecosystems."[150]

Biodiversity shows the importance of our linkage, connection, and dependence to all of creation in the physical world. We are truly responsible for the littlest of these. In that spirit, E. O. Wilson educates us that oceanic phytoplankton, composed of microscopic photosynthesizing bacteria, archaeans, and algae are major players in the control of the world's climate.[151]

There is more to biodiversity than insuring the continued existence of creation. Plants and animals have many benefits. Just as there are health and well-being benefits to being compassionate, caring, and altruistic towards others, there are similar benefits to interaction and companionship with animals. For example, pet owners have better physical and mental health.[152]

All of Your Circles

You are bound to, affected by, and responsible for a multitude of circles; from governments (national, state, local), clubs and organizations that you belong to, teams you are a member of, and who you work for, and much more.

You are also responsible for other circles you have no involvement with; because if some group is doing bad things—hurting others, destroying the environment—you need to do something about it. Yes, you cannot monitor every organization or individual, but you can be vigilant and try to help where you can.

Step out of yourself and see the unity of all—as it is for one, so it is for many. In our interconnected world, what others do and have done affects us, and we affect them. Focus on the unity of creation and see what has to be done.

For example, you may be a loving person that does selfless acts. What do you do for the larger communities you belong to? After all, you are taking on their karma. Do you speak out when injustices occur, or do you come to the aid of the pariah when they are persecuted? Do you criticize the group? Do you try to help the group?

In a world where everything has karma, you are tethered to everything. How much you are affected will vary, based upon your involvement. Just understand that you cannot sit by. You are duplicitous, to a degree. There is no escaping it: you are affected by group karma of all your circles, and to others to a degree.

Group Karma

Group karma, where all members of a circle suffer because of the behavior of some of its members is all too real. You cannot sit back and watch, even if you are born into a circle and did not voluntarily join. The fact is that you need to speak up and do your best to stand up to transgressions.

Swami Sivananda says that that the collective karma of a nation is like that that of any individual. The same principles underlying the karmic laws apply to national and collective karma: "Nations rise and fall, empires flourish and are dismembered on the same ground."[153]

We need only look to the Old Testament to see how Israel was punished for its transgressions.

Amos, the shepherd turned prophet, spoke on social responsibility and how Israel would suffer because of inequities and the selling of the poor into slavery for very little:

> Thus says the Lord: For three transgressions of Israel, and for four, I will not revoke the punishment; because they sell the righteous for silver, and the needy for a pair of sandals. (Amos 2.6)

There is no escaping group karma. In Isaiah 24, God says all will suffer for the acts of Israel:

> Now the Lord is about to lay waste the earth and make it desolate, and he will twist its surface and scatter its inhabitants. And it shall be, as with the people, so with the priest; as with the slave, so with his master; as with the maid, so with her mistress; as with the buyer, so with the seller; as with the lender, so with the borrower; as with the creditor, so with the debtor. (Isaiah 24. 1-2)

Group karma speaks to the consequences for the actions of a group, for the good and for the bad.

As it applies to one, so it does for the many, because the many are one and the one are the many. It is difficult to cast blame on all the woes of a circle, whether it be a country, a religion, or an organization of any sort, based on past actions; but that is their group karma.

Edgar Cayce said that everyone involved with the Conquistador invasions of Mexico and South America paid proportionately for their plunder and slaughter of the Aztecs. Biographer Noel Langley noted that Cayce felt that they "returned en masse to Spain during the period of the Spanish Civil War... There, brother and mother and father and sister turned against one another until their civilization was a shambles."[154]

However, Cayce believed that collective karma was never "entirely preordained. A given Country, for example, has the power to alter and reshape its destiny in exact accord with the altering behavior pattern of that people of the country."[155] Cayce felt that a stronger and more determined German public might have been able to stop Hitler.

Madame Blavatsky tells that we influence and are influenced by groups we belong to:

> [T]hat no man can rise superior to his individual failings, without lifting, be it ever so little, the whole body of which he is an integral part. In the same way, no one can sin, nor suffer the effects of sin, alone. In reality, there is no such thing as "Separateness"; and the nearest approach to that selfish state, which the laws of life permit, is in the intent or motive.[156]

As noted earlier, she calls group karma Distributive Karma because the karma is distributed amongst the members of a group, nation, or any other amalgam.

You are so much more than yourself.

Jesus was a Snitch

We live in a world in which many think that helping authorities by reporting a crime, or testifying against someone, is wrong; that some how by testifying you are violating a secret code. This is a ruse perpetrated by criminals. It is a sad reflection of the decay of our modern world.

A community, a society, or an organization like a building needs upkeep and maintenance to survive and thrive. We do this by helping and participating even when it is not our assigned role. Would you sit by and watch a baby drown because your job title was not 'baby rescuer?' It is the same with civil society, organizations and clubs you belong to, your friends, and any other circle in your life: you need to be involved and proactive.

Jesus specifically stated that you are to point out to someone if they have hurt you, and escalate it from there if they don't listen:

> If another member of the church sins against you, go and point out the fault when the two of you are alone. If the member listens to you, you have regained that one. But if you are not listened to, take one or two others along with you, so that every word may be confirmed by the evidence of two or three witnesses. If the member refuses to listen to them, tell it to the church; and if the offender refuses to listen even to the church, let such a one be to you as a Gentile and a tax collector. (Mt 18.15-17)

Someone I was very close to took it upon herself to teach and help someone, as if they were their own child. Unfortunately, this person decided, unbeknownst to my friend to use her credit card for their personal expenses. She fired this person, but did not report the crime to the police. I told her it was her duty to report the crime because the person would keep stealing and others would subsequently be ripped off, and the thief needed to be confronted. She told me that karma would take care of the thief. Wrong.

When we refuse to report a crime, or help authorities, we become complicit, and take on some of the karma of the action ourselves.

You need to be an active participant in all the circles you belong to. This means you have to report crimes, testify, volunteer, vote, teach others...

Bear Witness

How are we to deal with the faults, wrongs, and transgressions of a circle we belong to; or other circles that we don't belong to, that are doing wrong?

We do this by bearing witness—testifying to the truth and pointing out the wrong. The truth and the story need to be told. Bearing witness is a powerful tool that can bring about change and healing. It is one you need to make part of your life.

Think of the process of meditation, where you label your errant thoughts. While meditating, when you get a thought outside of the focus of your mediation you label it as such and get back to meditating. Over time, this trains your mind to concentrate, and you become a better meditator.

Bearing witness works the same way. Remember as it is for one, so it for many; the macrocosm is like the microcosm. When we bear witness, we are de facto labeling the wrongs of a particular circle. In doing so you are trying to get them back on track.

We reaffirm God through the action of bearing witness and helping others. This is because we are reinforcing one or more of the eternal truths: that we are to do unto others; that we are to love our enemy; that we are called to respect all of creation and treat it as being sacred and practice ahimsa; and that we are to honor and treat Mother Earth as the divine being She is. All of creation is sacred, because all of creation is God.

How do you label others? It could be a conversation, a letter, or it could something more overt, where people gather and carry placards highlighting the wrong. It can be an action where people refuse to participate in what they see as the transgression. The key is that you want to point out and educate about the wrong.

Speak Truth to Power

Governments and large organizations need to be publicly challenged.

Walter Wink (1935-2012) said that many of us are blinded to the reality of the world around us because the powers have created a 'delusional system' that serves them. Because of this, Wink believed that it was our responsibility to 'unmask the domination system' and show the reality of who the powers are: "The struggle for a precise "naming" of the Powers that assail us is itself an essential part of social struggle."[157] He felt that the Powers are buoyed by concealment and deception, and that by bearing witness, we pull away their masks and expose them for what they are.

Walter Wink was a pastor, theologian, and activist. In his obituary, the National Catholic Reporter called him "our best teacher of Christian nonviolence."[158] Although he is remembered for his workshops on nonviolence, he also practiced what he preached in places like South Africa during Apartheid.

Wink had a very radical view of Jesus message of nonviolent resistance. It was neither fight, nor flight, but rather what Wink called Jesus' 'Third Way', of direct action. It was sort of a jiu-jitsu move where we turn the violence of the transgressor back on them.

For example, in his Sermon on the Mount, Jesus offers the following advice about retaliation:

> You have heard that it was said, 'An eye for an eye and a tooth for a tooth.' But I say to you, Do not resist an evildoer. But if anyone strikes you on the right cheek, turn the other also; and if anyone wants to sue you and take your coat, give your cloak as well; and if anyone forces you to go one mile, go also the second mile. Give to everyone who

begs from you, and do not refuse anyone who wants to borrow from you. (Mt 5.38-42)

Wink felt that in each case—turn the cheek, give your coat, walk the second mile—Jesus was telling us not to respond in kind to violence, but rather with an action that does not allow the oppressor to humiliate us, and possibly jeopardizes them. For example, by giving your cloak along with your coat, you would have no clothes on. At the time of Jesus, it was thought more embarrassing and sinful to see a nude person rather than be the nude person themselves.

I met Wink at a Fellowship of Reconciliation conference at their old Nyack (NY) headquarters and served as actor for a skit on the Third Way, playing the guy who gave his coat and cloak when asked. Instead of giving my coat, I pretended to get angry with my partner and stripped down to my gym shorts underneath my pants. The audience was laughing as I left the room, feigning anger.

You must speak truth to power and challenge those in authority to stand true to the principles of a circle, whether it be a country, community, or club. Stand up for the pariah, the abused, the defenseless and the meek.

Saul Alinsky (1909-1972) was a noted organizer whom many consider the founder of modern community organizing, who dedicated his life to standing up for the have-nots. His theories and tactics were widely used in the counter movements and demonstrations of the 1960s. Time Magazine called him the 'Prophet of Power,' saying, "It is not too much to argue that American democracy is being altered by Alinsky's ideas."[159]

Alinsky's *Rules for Radicals*, published a year before his death, is a classic and is considered the bible of tactics and strategies to bring about change. His fourth rule is, "Make the enemy live up to their own book of rules,"[160] noting that they can no more do that than the Christian church can live up to Christianity.

A circle behaves like a samskara. It is about control, focus, and blocking out competing thoughts and actions. It is like a song that wants to become an earworm.

A circle also looks to merge its membership. When you bring in an alternative view, it must be registered and recognized; especially if it is a strong public statement.

By speaking truth to power and exposing the hypocrisy, the injustice, and the hurt, you begin to get the circle back inline. In doing so, you reaffirm its principals. The reaffirmation gives strength to the principles.

Voices Need to Be Heard

Bearing Witness is also about testifying to the truth and letting people tell their story. This could be a public witness, or one between two people. The important thing is that people wronged or hurt in some matter should be allowed to speak.

Elie Wiesel (1928-2016) was a political activist and writer who wrote about his life in a Nazi concentration camp. In his nomination for the Nobel Peace Prize in 1986, the committee called Wiesel,

> ... one of the most important spiritual leaders and guides in an age when violence, repression, and racism continue to characterize the world. Wiesel is a messenger to mankind. The message is in the form of a testimony, repeated and deepened through the works of a great author.[161]

In his acceptance speech, Wiesel noted how important it was to be a strident voice for the oppressed. Telling a young boy (which one assumes was himself) how the horror of the holocaust could have ever happened. He said:

> And then I explained to him how naive we were, that the world did know and remain silent. And that is why I swore never to be silent whenever and wherever human beings endure suffering and humiliation. We must always take

sides. Neutrality helps the oppressor, never the victim. Silence encourages the tormentor, never the tormented.[162]

Author, blogger, and founder of an Integrative Health Center (The Ommani Center for Integrative Medicine) that holistically approaches healing, Rose Kumar M.D. has found the power of bearing witness to be transformative, saying:

> As a physician, I feel that bearing witness is the most sacred part of what I do each day. Holding space and bearing witness to sometimes unbearable suffering deepens my heart and fortifies my soul. It makes my patients feel that they matter, that their pain and suffering matters. To be asked to bear witness for another is a profound honor. Life presents us with so many ways to bear witness to each other every day. We must embrace these opportunities for loving.[163]

Bearing Witness can similarly be transformative when we do it for a circle. For ourselves knowing that we have spoken truth to power and have not idly sat by. For those damaged, so that their story may be told. For others, so that they may know the truth and see the circle in another light and encourage them to help bring about change. For the circle itself, which will hopefully change and become the better for it.

Bearing witness will also help alter the karma that a circle carries both in this lifetime and for lifetimes to come. In doing so, people will be embracing a more loving world. Sheldrake's work with morphic resonance shows that the behavior of a species can change over time. We can similarly alter the behavior, attitude, and consciousness of a circle.

Put Forth the Positive

Bearing Witness is about reaffirming the truth.

When you bear witness, you need to put forth a positive alternative; what are you for, at the same time. If all you do is criticize and complain, you can become a Donnie, or Debbie Downer, spewing negativity. Remember the Law of Attraction.

You need to put forth the truth, a positive alternative: Love your neighbor/enemy, Mother Earth is our Mother, Mother Earth needs to be protected, or something else close to your heart.

To deny is to affirm. When we don't say what we are for, we give strength to what we are against. When we say we are not for war, the mind hears 'war.' So when we say we are against war, we are de facto affirming it.

You may also wish to have a motto or placard, based on scripture, or some sort of philosophical phrase. For example, "You shall love your neighbor as yourself." (Mark 12.31) "Blessed are the Peacemakers." (Mt. 5.19) "Love is the only force capable of transforming an enemy into friend." (Martin Luther King Jr.)

When we put forth the positive we give strength to it. Dwell on it. Think about it during your day. Ask yourself what it means and how you can embody it.

Bearing Witness is a Spiritual Experience

To better embody the spirit of the positive you wish to put forth, especially in public actions, you should contemplate and meditate on your advocacy.

Praying, meditating, and contemplating can work wonders. They will better help you understand what you are trying to say and why. They will empower you and give you clarity and strength. They will also bring you closer to God and help you better put forth God's message of love.

More importantly, they will help you counter the negative, the dark, and the evil. When you speak truth, you will be challenging a powerful circle that can have negative elements. You will be in direct contact with this.

Or you may challenge an authority, and its minions may come after you. There is always a chance you will be confronted by those who see things differently and are not too pleased with you.

Think about the circle you are now forming with those elements. Some of the people you may be dealing with might not have the best of intentions or motives. This will undoubtedly try to have a negative bearing upon you. So, prayer becomes crucial. You may want to stay in a contemplative mind, repeat a mantra, or meditate while you are speaking truth to power.

Our modern political world has become so caustic. Sometimes, when I read blog posts online it feels like I am touching the third rail of hate and anger; as if I were merging with that consciousness then and there, online.

That is why meditation and prayer are so important when you bear witness.

Richard Deats of the Fellowship of Reconciliation, in his obituary of Walter Wink, said that Wink felt that the way of prayer was essential to deeply rooted activism. Nonviolence was an aperture open to God. Quoting Wink's *The Powers That Be*:

> [T]he struggle against evil can make us evil, and no amount of good intentions automatically prevents its happening. The whole armor of God that Ephesians 6:10-20 counsels us to put on is crafted specifically to protect us against that contagion of evil within our own souls, and its metals are all forged in prayer.[164]

Bearing Witness—A Way of Life

You need to make bearing witness a part of your life. As you go on about your day and see a wrong, or a slight, gently point it out to the transgressor—label it. This will bring about positive change. Not only is this the right thing to do, but by working to improve the circle, you reduce the amount of bad karma you will take on from a circle that might not be the best. As with all good acts, it will help with your spiritual development.

There are several caveats to this. First, I am not telling you to put your life at risk and label someone, or something, that could bring violence into your life. Secondly, remember that discretion is the better part of valor. Don't turn a molehill into a mountain, and ask yourself if this issue would be better left alone? If you see a crime or injury of any sorts, report it and perform the duty to the circle that you belong to.

Quakers are very much dedicated to peace, and are pacifists dedicated to non-violence. To many this means committing to peace and being an advocate for it by bearing witness for it, as Quaker Gray Cox notes:

> The guiding concern of people bearing witness is to live rightly, in ways that are exemplary. Insofar as they have and end they aim at, it is perhaps most helpful to think of it as the aim of cultivating their souls and converting others.[165]

There is a great mystical truth, a powerful force of light that comes when one comes to the aid of the downtrodden, the outcast, and the pariah; what many would consider society's miscreants. I cannot touch and explain it to you. I know it is there. It is a great mystical transformative light.

Praying, meditating, and feeding the poor are all wonderful, but you need to step out and do more. You need practice bearing witness.

Few Are Guilty, All Are Responsible

Rabbi Abraham Joshua Heschel (1907 – 1972) a Polish-born American rabbi, was one of the great theologians of the twentieth century and a strident voice for social justice. He got his Ph.D. from the University of Berlin, doing his dissertation on the Hebrew prophets in 1933. When the Nazis took power in Germany, they deported him back to Poland in 1938 and he subsequently fled to America in 1940 to teach at Hebrew Union College in Cincinnati, Ohio. Unfortunately, his efforts to rescue his mother and sister and other family members failed.

Rabbi Heschel marched with Dr. Martin Luther King from Selma to Montgomery, and was with him on several other civil rights actions. He a gave a prayer along with Dr. King at the Arlington National Cemetery in February 1968 to protest the Vietnam war. Dr. King called Rabbi Heschel "My Rabbi" and there are several iconic pictures of them walking together arm and arm with others at marches.[166]

Later, Heschel would expand his dissertation into a book titled the *Prophets* that is a classic, and arguably the definitive book on the Hebrew prophets. He saw the prophet not as a foreteller of the future, but one whose task was to convey the divine view. At the same time, the prophet was a person, one with their own perspective who said no to society and was charged to interpret the times and reconcile the people with God.

According to his son, Rabbi Heschel felt that the opposite of good was not evil—but indifference. As much as the prophets spoke about right and wrong, they spoke to the apathy of the people, which was a crime. Heschel summed it up well in the *Prophets* saying that "few are guilty, but all are responsible." In doing so he implied, that when we idly sit by and watch injustice occur, we are as guilty as the transgressors.

Heschel said,

> Above all, the prophets remind us of the moral state of the people: Few are guilty, but all are responsible. If we admit that the individual is in some measure conditioned or

affected by the spirit of the society, an individual's crime discloses society's corruption. In a community not indifferent to suffering, uncompromisingly impatient with cruelty and falsehood, continually concerned with God and every man, crime would be infrequent rather than common.[167]

You are called to be your sister's keeper, your brother's keeper and to be the keeper of all of creation. You are a keeper of all the circles in your life, and to some that are not in your life. You are a keeper of Mother Earth. You are to love all of creation.

You need to embrace the prophetic spirit of speaking truth to power and to defending and helping the pariah; not only because you are called to do so, but because you may well one day become one yourself.

10. Take A Break With a Mystical Experience

A mystical experience where your consciousness breaks momentarily free from the Earth Plane can be incredibly transformative and therapeutic. For a brief moment, you are not tethered to any of your circles. Some people have been radically transformed by a mystical experience. In your quest to break from the karma of others and raise your consciousness, having a mystical experience should be high on your list.

Breaking From The Big Circle of Reality

British born Aldous Huxley (1894-1963), author turned mystic and seeker, wrote *Brave New World*, a futuristic dystopia, in response to what he saw as the devastating consequences of technology and science upon humankind in the twentieth century. His book *Perennial Philosophy* is a classic on the timeless ancient theological wisdom that runs throughout history.

As a friend of Krishnamurti, Huxley wrote the Foreword for his book *The First and Last Freedom*. He contributed regularly to the Vedanta Society of California.

Huxley's biographer, Nicholas Murray, saw Huxley's lifelong struggle with defective eyesight as a metaphor for his search for the light throughout his life, saying he went beyond the confines of prose fiction into history, philosophy, science, politics, mysticism, and psychic exploration. Huxley was an early advocate of the ecological movement and a strident voice against what he saw as the dangers of nuclear weapons, over-population, the exhaustion of natural resources, militarism, and destructive nationalism.[168]

Huxley's *Doors of Perception*[169] describes his experiences with taking the hallucinogenic drug mescaline and provides us a keen insight and fresh perspective on reality and the physical world, the largest circle in our lives. The book is a widely quoted source. First, by writers on spirituality who focus on his 'reducing valve'[170] that limits our perception of reality and prevents us from seeing other realities or objects; and by nostalgic hippies and drug advocates, for his vivid description of his Hallucinogenic Trip and its benefits.

Half an hour after taking a mescaline pill, Huxley notes he:
became aware of a slow dance of yellow lights. A little later there were sumptuous red surfaces swelling and expanding from bright nodes of energy that vibrated with a continuously changing, patterned life. ...complex gray structures, within which pale bluish spheres kept emerging into intense solidity and, having emerged, would slide noiselessly upwards, out of sight.[171]

He saw no landscapes, no great visions. The great change was to the realm of objective fact and had no bearing on his subjective universe.

A drug-induced high and nothing more?

Huxley had broken free. The big circle we call reality had momentarily lost its grip on him. The scales had fallen from his eyes. He was free.

Remember that samskaras form an enclosure around us, as Meher Baba taught. They look to control us, have us think a certain way, behave in a certain way, limit what we see, and determine how we see it and interpret it. Every bit of our existence, perception and being is controlled and dictated by samskaras, and is done so at multiple levels in a myriad of ways. What we call reality is just another circle we all share—a very Big Circle.

What he saw and experienced was his way of perceiving and adapting. Others might see things differently. Or focus or think in other ways. Or...

The Reducing Valve

To describe how we are deceived into accepting the physical world as being real, Huxley resorts to what he calls a 'reducing valve.' Saying, "[m]ost people, most of the time, know only what comes through the reducing valve and is consecrated as genuinely real by the local language."[172] It is very similar to the concept that a samskara forms an enclosure around us.

Huxley believed that some achieve a temporary bypass of the reducing valve like he did through spiritual exercises, hypnosis, or by taking drugs. Others are born with a kind of reducing valve.

Furthermore, Huxley implies that schizophrenics are living their lives outside of the reducing valve, believing that mescaline takers only experience the heavenly part of schizophrenia. He said:

> The schizophrenic is like a man permanently under the influence of mescaline, and therefore unable to shut off the experience of a reality...it never permits him to look at the world with merely human eyes.[173]

The Detail is the Devil

You have heard it said that the devil is in the detail; that to totally grasp and comprehend a legal contract, or a document, or any agreement, for that matter, you need to read the fine print. By going through it with a fine toothcomb you will understand it better and not be deceived or fooled by any parts. By sifting through the detail, some wonderful mystery will be discovered.

Well, I will tell you that in many ways the detail is the devil. When we focus on the minutiae, the details trap us. I am not talking about the classic seeing the forest from the trees, or the whole from the details.

The details I am talking about are the material world, physical reality, the Earth Plane, the Big Circle of Reality, or whatever else you want to call it. The more we focus on it, the more wrapped up we become with it.

Understand that the more attention and credence you give to the material world, the more you relinquish control to it. Consequently, you increase the amount of karma that you pick up and the more negative consciousness you merge with, and in the process diminish your evolving soul, your psychic being.

Be judicious about what you embrace. Give your attention to all of creation and our Mother and not to material things.

The Mystical Experience

There are great benefits to be gained by having mystical journeys, or mystical experiences, where you break free from the Earth Plane, albeit only briefly. You may gain insights and greater awareness, can be spiritually transformed or nourish your soul, and possibly much, much more. Remember: when you have a mystical experience, you may be breaking free from your largest circle, the biggest samskara—physical reality.

Unfortunately, most of the research done on mystical experiences look at drug-induced experiences with LSD, mescaline, magic mushrooms, and the like. While these experiences can be legitimate mystical experiences, you do not have to take drugs to have them, as I shall explain.

One of those researchers is psychiatrist Stanislav Grof who, along with others, helped formulate the basic principles of 'transpersonal psychology.' Transpersonal psychology explores the full spectrum of human experience, including non-ordinary states of consciousness, and attempts to integrate spirituality and new paradigm science.[174]

Grof was a pioneer in the study of LSD in the late 1950s and has been studying non-ordinary states of consciousness ever since. His work shows that one of the most important changes people experience through non-ordinary states of consciousness is a new appreciation for spirituality in their lives.[175]

Being a psychiatrist, Grof focused on the psychological benefits of experiencing non-ordinary states of consciousness, saying:

> Non-ordinary states of consciousness tend to work like an inner radar system, seeking out the most powerful charges and bringing the material associated with them into consciousness where they can be resolved.[176]

Huston Smith (1919-2016) was an ordained Methodist minister who started exploring the mystical paths of eastern traditions such as Buddhism, Hinduism, and Taoism, beginning in the 1950s. In 1955 he hosted a program about the world's religions for the National Education Television Network that would become PBS. It was the early days of television, and the American public saw Smith talk about yoga and meditation. He would go on to write the *Religions of Man* that became the popular *The World's Religions* that is still sold today.

Interestingly, it was Aldous Huxley that introduced Smith to Timothy Leary (1920-1996). A clinical psychologist at Harvard, Leary was an evangelist for hallucinogenics who expounded the benefits of the psychedelic experience. He famously said, "turn on, tune in, drop out," and educated America about psychedelics. President Nixon called him the "most dangerous man in America."[177]

Leary would be the guide who would take Smith and his wife Kendra on their first trip with psilocybin. Up to this point,

Smith had never had a mystical experience.[178] That would all change, as he would write about later in his book *Cleansing the Doors of Perception, The Religious Significance of Entheogenic Plants and Chemicals,* saying,

> ...to have become overnight a visionary—one who not merely believes in the existence of a more momentous world than this one but who has actually visited it—was no small matter. How could what felt like an epochal change in my life have been crowded into a few hours and occasioned by a chemical?"[179]

A study done at John Hopkins in 2006 in which thirty-six volunteers were given either psilocybin or methylphenidate (treats ADHD) on alternating occasions found the effects of psilocybin to be dramatic:

> It is remarkable that 67% of the volunteers rated the experience with psilocybin to be either the single most meaningful experience of his or her life or among the top five most meaningful experiences.[180]

Participants compared it to the birth of child or the death of parent. A third (thirty-three percent) felt it was the most significant spiritual event in their lives and thirty-eight percent rated it among the top five spiritual events of their lives.

Near Death Experience

One of the more profound ways to disconnect from the circle we call reality is to have a Near Death Experience (NDE), where you die and go to heaven. The International Association for Near Death Studies (IANDS) in defining an NDE says that:

> An NDE may begin with an out-of-body experience—a very clear perception of being somehow separate from one's physical body, possibly even hovering nearby and watching events going on around the body. An NDE typically

includes a sense of moving, often at great speed and usually through a dark space, into a fantastic landscape and encountering beings that may be perceived as sacred figures, deceased family members or friends, or unknown entities. A pinpoint of indescribable light may grow to surround the person in brilliant but not painful radiance; unlike physical light, it is not merely visual but is sensed as being an all-loving presence that many people define as the Supreme Being of their religious faith.[181]

I have been blessed to have met and spent time with two women in their eighties who had NDEs, PMH Atwater and Estelle Weed. Both are vibrant, much younger than their age, and very spiritual and committed to God. PMH is very gifted spiritually, and could see beings in other realms, among other things.

Studies show the experience of taking a psychedelic drug such as LSD can lead to having a mystical experience comparable to a NDE.[182] Not only do people that have NDE find it to be one of the most important experiences in their lives, but they were also transformed afterwards in many ways. With changes such as having a reduced fear of death, finding greater meaning and purpose in life, having greater respect for life, getting closer to God, becoming more spiritual and desiring to love and serve others.[183]

PMH Atwater has been researching NDE ever since 1978, a year after she had three NDEs. She has found that some people occasionally develop special gifts after a NDE. Some became gifted healers or innovative inventors. Others developed the ability to "channel" information from 'The Other Side.' Some developed psychokinetic abilities where they could affect, or manipulate matter with their mind. Others developed the ability to empathize with someone to the point where they were able take on their pain or illness.[184]

What is a Mystical Experience?

Clearly, mystical experiences can have a profound influence on us. But what is a mystical experience? How does one define it?

One of the sources people turn to find an answer is William James, who lived in the latter half of the nineteenth century. His *The Varieties of Religious Experience* is an often-quoted source. At the time, it was a bold departure that argued that religious experiences could be found outside of the church and within individuals themselves.

James said that mystical states occur beyond normal consciousness. They take us from "small to vastness…We feel them as reconciling, unifying states. They appeal more to the yes-function more than the no-function. In them the unlimited absorbs the limited and peacefully closes the account."[185]

British philosopher Walter T. Stace is considered to have written one of the definitive works about mysticism. He defined the mystical experience as, a unifying experience expressed as a sense that "all is one." As well as, experiencing a feeling of blessedness, or joy and believing that what has been apprehended is holy, sacred, or divine; an experience of God.[186]

To me, defining a mystical experience is like defining food—we can say that it nourishes you and keeps you alive. What is it? What kinds of food are there? A mystical experience is meant to raise your consciousness and possibly nourish your soul. Ultimately, you break free from the Earth Plane in some way, or have an experience outside what is considered the norm, such as a flow of energy into, or within you.

I have been blessed with having a myriad of mystical experiences. They can be something as simple as an energy rush, where you feel energy move into you, or something as profound as hearing the voice of God. You may have a vision, gain an insight, feel at peace, or feel blissed out or spiritually high. You may have a vision, see colors, or beings in other realms, or have things appear differently to you. You may find resolution to a dilemma, or communicate with an angel or divine being in another realm. You may feel profound love for humanity, even for the most despicable person. You may leave your body, or feel your body melt or vibrate from the sound of someone's voice, as if your subtle body was made of Jell-O. Or you may experience a deep understanding of the universe or something else, or may be overwhelmed with great joy. You may feel a deep connection and oneness with all of creation. There are a multitude of other experiences you may have. This is only a partial list.

Whatever you experience bask in it and relish it to the max. Feel blessed, because you certainly have been. Give thanks to God. You want to nourish those nascent experiences and feelings. Focus on them. In doing so you will make them stronger.

Turn to Our Mother for Mystical Experiences

You don't have to take drugs to have a mystical experience. In fact, I would tell you not to do so. There are a myriad of ways you can have profound and deep mystical experiences with a little effort. Just as Mother Earth nourishes your body with food and water, and your Energy Body with energy, She nourishes your soul as well. Ancient cultures understood this.

The work of Michael Persinger (1945-2018) demonstrates that our Mother's 'Earth Energies' can cause mystical experiences. Persinger found that increased geomagnetic activity within the earth leads to paranormal activity within people. For example, thousands of people saw intense displays of exotic, luminous phenomena over a church in Zeitoun (Egypt) from seismic activity 400 kilometers to the southeast.[187]

We have lost our connection to Mother Earth. By developing a strong bond with Her, you can not only increase the chances of having a mystical experience, but also can begin to sense and feel Her emanations better.

Ancient cultures would work to enhance Mother Earth, often creating stone structures to be better able to experience Her. Fortunately, there are many wonderful sacred places that have been able to weather the onslaught of civilization.

Consciousness Raising?

Whenever you disconnect from the Earth Plane, there is a good chance that your experience will be consciousness-raising. When you have a mystical experience, you are not tethered to the circle of reality, or its consciousness quotient. This in and of itself will help raise your consciousness and possibly make you see things differently, as all the preceding testimonials speak to.

When you break free from the Earth Plane, you will be in a more spiritual place. Mystics say that when you experience Samadhi, you are experiencing pure consciousness. Consider it being like pure spirit rather than the world of matter we live in. When you have a mystical experience, you will not be necessarily going to a place that is pure consciousness, but you will be going to a place that lies between the Earth Plane and pure consciousness.

When you are in a place that is of a higher consciousness, you will merge with that consciousness. This can bring all sorts of benefits, from spiritual gifts to raising your consciousness and making you a more loving person. Again: you merge with the reality you are in, and when you have a mystical experience, you will be in a reality of a much higher order.

Earlier, I had talked about the devolution of consciousness (Exhibit 2.1) to create the material world and how, with each step down the amount of spirit (consciousness) diminishes and the percentage of matter increases. Now think of that process reversing. As you climb higher, the amount of spirit increases and the amount of matter decreases, as shown in Exhibit 10.1, Climbing the Ladder of Higher Consciousness.

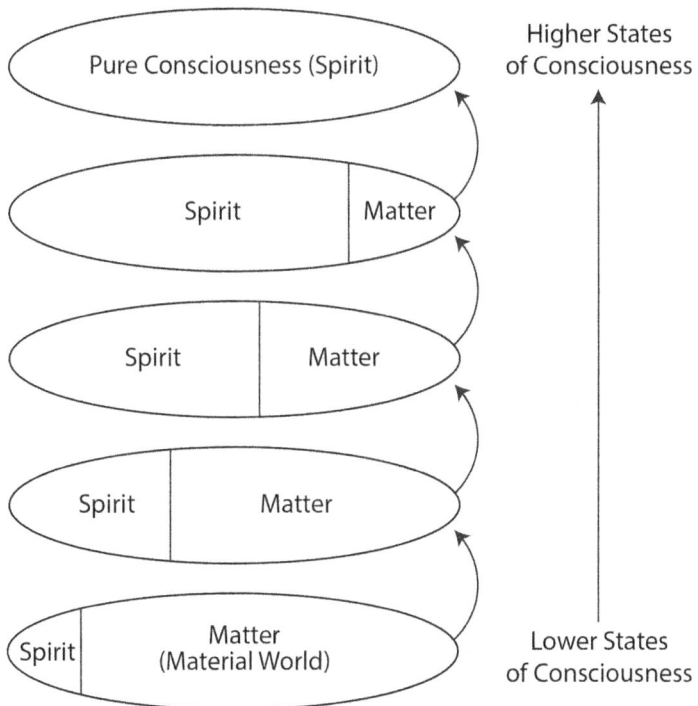

Exhibit 10.1 Climbing the Ladder of Higher Consciousness. As you ascend, you merge with increasingly higher consciousness. So when you have a mystical experience and break free from the Earth Plane, you go to realms that have a higher spirit (consciousness) component. When you are in that higher realm, you will be ensconced in a place with a higher spirit or consciousness quotient and you will be merging with it. Because you are in this more spiritual place and merging with

it, all sorts of wonderful things happen; from profound mystical experiences to raising your consciousness, as witnessed with people having NDEs.

Huston Smith admits that psychedelic drugs can induce a religious experience, but they do not necessarily induce religiosity in people.[188] There is a kernel of truth to this. I believe that drug-induced mystical experiences are of a much lower order than those that you experience naturally with Mother Earth.

Reality Keeps You Tethered to It

The big circle we call reality, like all samskaras, looks to control you and dominant your thinking. As Meher Baba taught, it forms an enclosure around you, so that it limits what you see and how you see it. Mystical experiences where you transcend the material world or the Earth Plane, present an enormous threat to the circle of reality.

During a mystical experience, when you break free from the Earth Plane, the grip that the circle of reality has upon you is reduced. As more people begin to believe that physical reality is an illusion, the influence of the circle of reality begins to slowly diminish.

Mystical experiences also bring beliefs that go contrary to the fundamental underpinnings of the circle of reality. These include (as mentioned earlier), among others, an understanding that we are all connected; that there is a greater reality beyond material existence; and that there is a God. The more powerful the mystical experience, the stronger these beliefs, as seen with people having NDEs.

Understandably, the circle of reality knows this. Just as a samskara looks to form an enclosure around us and control our thinking and perspective, so it looks to block or prevent threats to itself.

Psychedelic drug research begun in the early 1950s began to be curtailed in 1966 when manufacturer Sandoz closed down production of LSD and the FDA sent out letters ordering researchers to stop their research. Psychedelic drugs were not researched again and used for religious purposes in the USA until 2006.

Stanislav Grof in an interview with Michael Pollan for his book *How to Change Your Mind*, which examines psychedelic drugs and how they can help change us said:

> [P]sychedelics loosed the "Dionysian Element" on 1960s America, posing a threat to the country's puritan values that was bound to be repulsed… That says something important about how reluctant cultures are to expose themselves to the changes these kinds of compounds can occasion.[189]

Grof further noted the threat posed by mystical experiences to society (aka the circle of reality), saying: "There is so much authority that comes out of the primary mystical experience that it can be threatening to existing hierarchal structures."[190]

Pollan, a NY Times best selling author was inspired by the John Hopkins research on the benefits of mystical experiences induced by psilocybin and the use of psychedelics by cancer patients to write his book, *How to Change Your Mind, What the New Science of Psychedelics Teaches Us About Consciousness, Dying, Addiction, Depression and Transcendence*.

The desire to maintain conformity as seen with the circle of reality is a feature of group behavior. Yale psychological researcher Irving Janis studied group behavior in the twentieth century. He coined the term 'groupthink' (after 'doublethink' from George Orwell's *1984*) to describe how groups strive for conformity. He noted that when a group member says something outside of the group's norms, members initially increase communication with the nonconformist with the hopes of changing them:

> Attempts to influence the nonconformist member to revise to tone down the dissident ideas continue as long as most members of the group feel hopeful about talking him into changing his mind. But if they fail after repeated attempts, the amount communication they direct toward the deviant decreases markedly. The members begin to exclude him, often quite subtly at first and later more obviously, in order to restore the unity of the group.[191]

Mystical experiences present a huge threat to the Big Circle of reality, and its progeny of materialism, science, technology, and… Remember: a group is a circle, is a samskara. Again, you can see how samskaras look to control and manipulate us, and how powerful they are.

Take a Break From Your Senses

Meher Baba spent the greater portion of his life in silence. You may do the same for a day or two. Or fast and don't eat any food for a day. My friend Joe would experience long periods of time in darkness.

All of these activities disconnect you from the circle of reality we are all bound to. When people meditate too much, or take on lots of Earth Energies, I look to ground them and better connect them to the Earth Plane. One of the best ways to do this is to eat, particularly root vegetables. This shows how food and your other senses help tether us to physical reality.

The fifth rung of Patanjali's eight rungs of yoga is pratyahara; where you disconnect from the external world of senses and sense objects. "Pratyahara is, as it were, the imitation by the sense of the mind by withdrawing them from their respective objects." (YS 2.54)

Swami Satyananda Saraswati in his interpretation says:
It should be understood that pratyahara means withdrawing the mind from the objects of sense experience, then the senses function according to the mind, and not vice versa. The capacities of smell, taste, sight, touch and hearing are withdrawn from their objects and the senses begin to follow the mind inward and not outward.[192]

Again: not indulging one of your senses for a prolonged period of time will disconnect you, albeit partially, from the circle of reality.

Meditation Can Free You

One of the best things you can do to break free from the circle of reality is to meditate. The simple process of focusing on an object, your breathing, or on emptiness ever so slightly disconnects you from the circle of reality. By meditating, you are reducing the hold the tentacles of reality has on you, albeit briefly.

But if you are truly sincere about raising your consciousness, a mystical experience is a must. A mystical experience will accelerate your spiritual transformation and bring a host of other benefits.

11. Working With Samskaras

"Ek Onkar Satnam Siri WaheGuru"

Repeating the words of this mantra a few times has me beginning to disconnect from the Earth Plane and elevates me into blissful states of higher consciousness. While its vibe has diminished over the years, it is still very potent.

Its Punjabi translation is "There is One God – Whose Name is Truth – Praise the Ever Greater Ever More Wondrous God."

The Sikh Master and mystic Baba Virsa Singh Ji, through Ralph Singh, his devotee and director of his farm based spiritual community Gobind Sadan in Central New York, gifted this wonderful mantra to me. Babaji (what the followers of Baba Virsa Singh Ji call their Master), taught it to Ralph, who spent several years studying with him in India.

Babaji was blessed with 'Nam' (the mantra) during a profound mystical experience in his youth. In it, Guru Nanak, the founding guru of Sikhism and his oldest son Guru Baba Siri Chand Ji visited him. Babaji vividly remembered the vision, particularly that they were both well over six feet tall. Guru Nanak Dev Ji wore lathu-wale karavan (wooden sandals with a central "toe" knob) and his chola (long gown) was mouse-colored.

Guru Nanak told him, "Repeat after me – Ek Onkar Satnam Siri WaheGuru." Babaji was then told to recite these words and to share the shabad (sound/speech/hymn) with others. He then blessed Babaji with a profound insight, telling him that Nam was similarly bestowed upon him through a mystical experience.[193]

The meeting concluded with a visit by Guru Gobind Singh Ji, the tenth and final guru of Sikhism. Guru Gobind Singh, along with Guru Baba Siri Chand, would tutor Babaji in meditation and service to humanity. Babaji would name his farm-based spiritual community after Guru Gobind Singh Ji.

Because of the mystical way Nam was conveyed to Babaji, his followers see it more as a divine gift than a mantra.

In the ensuing years, Babaji would travel from town to town, teaching about the love of God and healing many. In 1968 he settled down on a dry and rocky piece of land at the south end of Delhi and began to develop it into what would become Gobind Sadan, 'God's House Without Walls.'

My experience with the mantra began in the immediate aftermath of 9-11. The Gobind Sadan USA's temple had been burned down in a hate crime. Miraculously, the sacred text was unharmed, and a fireman was saved when he heard a voice tell him to go back downstairs moments before the second floor collapsed. That is nothing unusual for this sacred place.

I began to recite Nam periodically, but did not do so in earnest until the following spring when Ralph and his wife Joginder traveled to India to be with Babaji. I was tasked to feed lunch to Baba Siri Chand, a statue in a small-enclosed temple in their backyard, for the first week of their sojourn.

I would take a plate of fresh fruit to Baba Siri Chand, light the sacred fire, say a prayer, and burn the fruit as an offering. It was during those visits that I would endlessly repeat Nam while I was there.

That was my first inkling of how mantra could elevate your consciousness, bring you closer to God, give you wonderful mystical experiences, and bliss you out. I also got messages, and at times felt as though Baba Siri Chand was there and was communicating to me.

Nam was a blessing to me from all those that had ever repeated it, because I was climbing the ladder to higher states of consciousness and garnering insights on the rungs that they had built.

Babaji said, "As soon you start meditating, reciting Nam, and seeking God's Light within yourself, your life will change. As more and more people do so, the world will change."[194]

History is a legacy of our works that we leave behind. Most of us will leave behind children, some of us will leave behind war and violence, others compassion and love. There are those like Andrew Carnegie, who left behind endowments to fund libraries and other public works.

Babaji left us Nam, a mantra that can elevate your consciousness, send you on wonderful journeys, give you great insights and bliss you out. That is the power of a mantra, of a meditation, and of a samskara: to transcend time and be a boon to those that follow. A samskara like the Nam mantra can be a wonderful gift for future generations.

What do you want your legacy to be?

Mantra Can Do Many Things

It is said that meditating on a word, which is essentially a mantra, is supposedly the quickest and easiest way to achieve the meditative state of Samadhi. A mantra can do and be many different things. It has a rich history of service for those that believed in its magic and worked with it to achieve a variety of remarkable results.

More importantly, their transformative mantras were not bestowed upon them like the Nam that Babaji has blessed us with. Rather, they were nothing more than a hope, a belief that their words could become transcendent. They planted seed thoughts that they nourished with repetition and focus. Earlier, I discussed how we could overcome depressed moods by focusing on and embracing moments of joy, in essence planting a seed thought of joy. Mantra is similar. It begins with the planting of a seed that grows and morphs into something wondrous.

We think of Mahatma Gandhi as being a courageous and preserving, selfless advocate. Gandhi was not born with the fearlessness and courage he exhibited in his public life. As a young boy, he was fearful of boys half his size. One day an old family servant, Rambha, took him aside and told him there is nothing wrong with admitting fear. But instead of running away, he was to repeat the mantra "Rama, Rama, Rama…" over and over in his mind, because it can turn fear into fearlessness.

Gandhi would repeat the mantra endlessly, initially with his lips and eventually with his heart. The seed Rambha had planted in him would become powerful and bore much fruit. Gandhi said that, "The mantram becomes one's staff of life and carries one through turbulent times."[195]

To him, each repetition had a new meaning and carried him nearer and nearer to God. He said that:

> Though my reason and heart long ago realized the highest attribute and name of God as Truth, I recognized Truth by the name Rama. In the darkest hour of my trial, that one name has saved me and is still saving me.[196]

The Russian Pilgrim[197] is the story of a nineteenth century spiritual seeker that traveled about the Ukraine and Russia ceaselessly repeating the Jesus prayer, "Lord Jesus Christ have mercy upon me," a mantra of sorts. It is revered by many in the Russian Orthodox church and among other Christian traditions as well, particularly as a manual on ceaseless prayer and how to commune with God.

The story begins with the pilgrim hearing a reading in church from Thessalonians (1 Thess. 5.17) that one should "pray without ceasing." He wondered what that meant. So begins his quest.

After some time, the Russian Pilgrim finds a teacher who tells him to repeat the Jesus prayer as much as he can—at least three thousand times a day—and that will open up a door to his heart, as it did for him. The first day, the pilgrim finds his throat choked after twelve thousand repetitions and feels a compelling urge not to stop. So the ceaseless praying begins.

The Russian Pilgrim takes to wandering the streets, always repeating the Jesus prayer. He decides to go to Siberia and visit the grave of Saint Innocent of Irkutsk, feeling that the Siberian forests and steppes would allow for quiet and peaceful traveling. During his journey, he finds that the Jesus prayer migrates from his lips to his heart. He realized that while his heart was beating naturally, somehow it "began to repeat within itself the words of the prayer in rhythm with its natural beating: 1)Lord…2)Jesus…3)Christ…"[198]

On his journey, he would meet many, and was even mugged. Upon reading about interior prayer in the Philokalia, a collection of Greek Christian writings from the fifth to fifteenth century that focus on spirituality and mysticism, he decided to learn it. First, he focused on trying to hear his heartbeat, then he focused on his breath. While visualizing his heart, he would breathe in saying "Lord Jesus Christ," and exhaled repeating "have mercy on me." After several weeks of ceaselessly practicing interior prayer, his heart became sore. Then something remarkable happened to his heart. It would vacillate between bubbling over with sweet delight and burning love for Jesus Christ.

As the Russian Pilgrim continued to wander, he taught others about the Jesus prayer and praying ceaselessly, as well as about interior prayer. All the while, the Jesus prayer was repeating in his heart. The prayer had so delighted him that he could not imagine any contentment greater, even in the Kingdom of Heaven. Everything around him now appeared enchanted—people, trees, animals. Not only did he feel a kinship to them, but also they inspired him with love and gratitude for God.[199] The story concludes with the planning of a pilgrimage to Jerusalem.

Shortly after leaving Wall Street on my spiritual quest, I was gifted with two wonderful mantras to repeat. I was still living in New York City, and it was during a meditation that I heard a voice within myself tell them to me.

One was of the mantras was "we are one," meaning that everyone and everything is connected to each other. This mantra helped me develop the feeling of oneness and unity of all of creation.

The other mantra was "the world is not real," which I eventually shortened "its not real." Over time, it increasingly edified the concept of Maya: that the physical world is an illusion and that there is a greater reality behind it.

I would repeat these mantras for hours on end while hiking; while walking about New York City; and while driving on long trips.

Mantra and Meditation are Samskaras

Mantra is a form of meditation. Meditation is a samskara. It has all its properties. It looks to get you focus on one particular thought, it blocks out other thoughts and in the process, it controls your attention. As Meher Baba said, it forms an enclosure around you. Meditation like a samskara gets stronger the more that you feed it with your intention.

As noted earlier, Patanjali's Yoga Sutras' is about developing a samskara of meditation so that you may achieve Samadhi. You feed your meditation samskara through practicing it. Over time, it becomes stronger and better at holding your attention and blocking out other thoughts. In many ways, you are looking to create an earworm of sorts that gets you to focus exclusively on it. In the process, you begin to disconnect from the Physical Plane and the circle of reality, and you enter higher states of consciousness.

That is the power of samskara when applied in a certain way to elevate your consciousness, or get you closer to God, make you more loving or more giving, or…. It can become a powerful self-reinforcing pattern for the good.

That is what Babaji and his followers achieved with Nam.

Anything can be a samskara because each thought we have, or each action we perform, creates a samskara. This means that a meditation, a movement, a ritual or ceremony, a song, or a place can be turned into a powerful samskara with repetition.

You have within yourself the power to build a samskara for whatever purpose you want: to be happy; to fall asleep; to protect yourself; and to block out problems…

It can be for you, or a legacy to leave behind for others.

Some Samskaras to Embrace

Earlier, I talked about certain thoughts/actions that you should consider making part of your life. They can help reduce bad karma, as well as lead to wonderful experiences.

Be Positive, Especially in the face of calamity. As mentioned, karma operates on many levels both physical and, emotional. For example, when things go wrong, you may get upset, or angry. Because of the Law of Attraction, this emotional response may attract more of the same. It can become a self-feeding loop where you have an accident and get upset. Your upset mood attracts more accidents to make you upset. That attracts another calamity, and that attracts…

You need to try and remain as positive and upbeat as you can at all times. Be especially vigilante and try to maintain a positive, upbeat persona in the face of challenges. This will help prevent a 'when it rains, it pours type of phenomenon.' Again: should things get bad and you enter such a loop—give, give, give and keep giving. This should eventually help you stop a loop of negativity.

See the wonder of synchronicity around you. Synchronicity is about how a myriad of unrelated events can occur simultaneously, as if choreographed by God. Begin to see the world through the lens of synchronicity and marvel at the work of God.

Believe it. See it. Seek it

When you see synchronicity at work, dwell on it, thank God and feel blessed; savor its wonder and beauty. Isn't God amazing? The world can truly be magical.

By savoring that experience and dwelling on it, you give strength to that nascent vision the same way dwelling on a happy moment can make you a very happy person. Earlier, I discussed the work of neuropsychologist Rick Hanson and his *Hardwiring* Happiness,[200] about what he calls 'self-directed neuroplasticity.' He maintains that, by focusing and dwelling on positive experiences throughout the day we begin to rewire out brains (neuroplasticity) and start to develop the sense to see the positive in everything. Dwelling on synchronicity similarly gives strength to it and begins to alter our view of reality.

You are looking to build a samskara, not to form an enclosure, but to develop a way of seeing the wonder of the world and the beauty of God's work.

As you increasingly begin to see synchronicity around you, expand your vision and share your experience with others close to you so that they too can marvel at its wonder.

With practice, you will grow closer to God and will be spiritually transformed by seeing the process of synchronicity blossoming around you. You will come to understand that God is always there, reaching out to you. Your soul will also be nourished as you tap into the divine consciousness of synchronicity.

The world needs wonder and magic. You can help by developing a samskara of seeing the synchronicity in the world the same way that Babaji blessed us with Nam.

Control is an Illusion

People talk about controlling their destiny and taking control of the situation, while others are control freaks. How much control do we ever really have? The fact is that we are at the mercy of our karma and our samskaras, which exert a tremendous influence upon us.

To a great degree, we are controlled by our previous thoughts and actions in this life and from previous lives. Who we are and who we will be was determined, to a large extent, by our past. This is not to say that we don't have a choice, rather, there are powerful influences that shape us.

Then there is the karma of everyone and everything else that stretches back to the earliest of time. This will, as does our individual karma, help shape who we are and will be.

While you can certainly control things for the moment in the Physical Plane, what are you sowing in the unseen world? You will reap what you sow. If you manipulate to achieve your purpose, you will be putting out manipulation and control and will find yourself being similarly manipulated and controlled. Karma and its Law of Attraction will bear more fruit in your life in response to the seeds of control that you have planted.

You have to learn to work with samskaras within the context of karma. Whatever you put out there will boomerang back to you.

All we can do is choose what change we want to see and then live it, think it, and act it. You must become the change you want to see.

Be the Change You Wish to See

Mahatma Gandhi never uttered the "be the change" mantra attributed to him.[201] I believe that this phrase may have been coined by the Mother, Mirra Alfassa, in speaking about the spiritual life and how it can become a contagion that can sweep you and others up with its radiating love:

> If one sincerely wants to help others and the world, the best thing one can do is to be oneself what one wants others to be – not only as an example, but because one becomes a centre of radiating power which, by the very fact that it exists, compels the rest of the world to transform itself.[202]

The Mother was giving a response to a question after the reading of an extract from the *Life Divine*, Sri Aurobindo's opus on the spiritual evolution and development of humankind and the world.

In the excerpt, Sri Aurobindo notes that the "cures to the ills" of the world have failed because humankind has refused to turn inward and has deflected the spiritual impulse, saying:

> [O]nly a spiritual change, an evolution of his being...can make a real and effective difference...To discover the spiritual being in himself is the main business of the spiritual man and to help others towards the same evolution is his real service.[203]

The question about the reading was how someone with little "spiritual capacity" can best help in this work.

The Mother begins her answer by saying she does not know whether one has little or no spiritual capacity. To live the spiritual life requires a reversal of consciousness and turning inwards. When one truly turns inwards one touches the "Infinite," the "Eternal."

The Mother tells that once the reversal is complete and one has turned inward, one no longer seeks, but sees; one no longer deduces, but knows; one no longer gropes, but walks straight to the goal. When one goes a little farther, "One knows, feels and lives the supreme truth that the Supreme Truth *alone* acts, the Supreme Lord *alone* wills, knows and does through human beings."[204]

The only way to bring peace is to be peace. You cannot achieve peace any other way. All other alternatives may bring you short-term results, but longer term, you will be reaping karmic payback. You cannot kill your enemy.

The only way to achieve something, as the Mother says, is to be yourself what you want to achieve, because the Law of Attraction will bring you more of the same.

Be the change you wish to see.

If we want to free ourselves, we must free others.

If we want forgiveness from people we have injured, we must forgive those that hurt us.

If we want people to love us, we must love others first.

If we want people to come to our aid when we are stranded or injured, we must come to the aid of strangers when they are hurt or stranded.

My mother's favorite saying was "give with one hand, get back with two hands." Her mother passed it to her and taught her about kindness and generosity. She remembers a terrible time growing up in Estonia when there was little food to go around. A woman came to their home begging for food. My grandmother fed the women. My mother asked: "How could you give away what little food we have left?" My grandmother said: "Give with one hand and get back with two hands."

Decades later, my mom found herself starving in Europe during WWII, with nowhere to turn. A stranger, a woman out of the blue, fed her. My mother realized what her mother had taught her. As happy as she was to be fed, she felt the guilt of a stupid child for questioning her mother over her generosity.

The only choice you have in the world is to be the change you wish to see. That will be your seed thought, your samskara, that you will put out there. It will bear fruit and bring karmic payback.

Choose wisely.

Be the change you wish to see.

Ceremony, Ritual

Any act, any ceremony, and any ritual can become a powerful samskara if we repeat it enough. The stock of intent, with a dash of emotion and a strong blend of commitment, can go a long way. Adding others will give it even more strength, as I noted with my story mantra. My annual canoe trips to Algonquin Provincial Park in Ontario, Canada, that I would perform for decades, became a powerful samskara (ritual).

Rupert Sheldrake believes that a ritual is an act of morphic resonance, and collapses time as participants connect with all those that have ever participated in it, saying:

> The purpose of ritual is to connect the present participants with the original event that the ritual commemorates and also to link them with all those who have participated in in the ritual in the past. Rituals have something to do with crossing time, annihilating distance in time, bringing the past into the present...From the point of view of morphic resonance, rituals make perfect sense. By consciously performing ritual acts in a similar a way as possible to the

way they have done before, the participants enter into morphic resonance with those who have carried out the ritual in the past. There is a collapse of time. There is an invisible presence of all those who have done the ritual before, a transtemporal ritual community.[205]

The idea that ritual can transcend time is possible with all samskaras, as I will discuss in Chapter 13, Earth Magic. I actively seek Energy Vortices in hidden places so that I may transcend time and connect with the spirit of those that created them.

Unfortunately, most rituals and ceremonies have lost their zest over time and picked up negative karma over the years. Like the bulk of samskaras, they do not age well.

Creating a ritual, or ceremony can be of great benefit and can certainly be of help for many for several years. Here are some suggestions:

A solitude haven. Algonquin Park in Ontario, Canada became my haven for solitude. You too can find a place to go to: a camping area, a retreat center, or a place you hold dear. You want to go to the same place so that you will associate your experience with it and add to it each time you visit. When you visit, whether it is for a day or a week, make it a spiritual experience, or a particular focus, which you can revisit over the years.

A pilgrimage. Pick a sacred site to visit and make it a regular visit. I try to go Chief Red Jacket's monument in the Finger Lakes Region of New York State each year and say a few prayers and meditate for peace between Native and non-Native people. Just going there puts me in a particular frame of mind, and when I tie it with a visit to other sacred sites, I feel as though I am visiting old friends. Which brings me joy.

Red Jacket (1750-1830) was a chief in the Wolf Clan of the Seneca nation, known for his speaking and negotiations as a peacemaker.

Create your own ceremony. Determine what you wish to achieve with your ceremony: cleansing, healing, or… Use some objects (feather, incense) and read from sacred texts to consecrate it. It is important they be used exclusively for the ceremony. Perform your ceremony in a contemplative mind.

Story Mantra, an Oral Tradition

Story can be a powerful mantra, as noted with my story mantra, which I described as being like a vegetable soup. I have created several story mantras. One was the story of the greatest teachers, sages, and prophets the world had ever seen and how they inspired, and the lessons to be learned through their example and teachings. The other was the Light, a tale of the divine light that shines in the world—what it means, how and where it manifests, its history and more.

I would begin by going into a meditative state and telling the respective tales, either verbally, silently, or a combination thereof, to myself. I would repeat them and repeat them. Often, it was the same words that I was uttering over and over again in a contemplative mind. After a while, as soon as I began to say the words, I would start to slip into trance.

After much repetition and practice, and having forged a powerful samskara, I would take my story mantras public at times. As previously noted, the intent and focus of others, particularly in trance, would give increased strength to my story mantra. Now there were several people in trance focused on it, and not only did this increased focus give the samskara strength, it pulled in more energy (Cosmic Prana).

I believe that through my story mantra I was partaking in the age-old oral tradition of using the spoken word, and in the process was giving strength to it. The oral tradition is where people would tell tales, and stories and give lessons that had been handed down for generation upon generation. However, my tales were a bit more souped-up, because they were done in a contemplative mind and adorned with other features.

Arthur Caswell Parker (1881-1955) was a historian, archaeologist, and folklorist of Seneca descent. He served as head of the Rochester (NY) Museum of Arts and Sciences and won numerous honors for his archaeological work. He also gifted us with several works on Native American (particularly Haudenosaunee (Iroquois) customs and folklore.

Parker tells that the Seneca people had designated storytellers that were taught by their predecessors, and that no stories could be told over the summer months because they would offend the little people and wood fairies.[206] These Seneca myths and folktales were built upon certain beliefs such as unseen spirits, magical powers, transformation, all Nature is conscious and has souls and more. Furthermore, there were universal themes such as contests with sorcerers, animal foster-parents, lover wins mate, the conflict between good and bad spirits, and more.

While much had changed by the time Parker's *Seneca Myths and Folk Tales* was published in 1922, the Seneca still practice their rites and ceremonies in several Seneca communities (Cattaraugus, Allegany and Tonawanda, New York). They also, as Parker teaches, "still tell the folktales that his ancestors loved and *these remain unaltered to this very day.*"[207]

Years ago, I was fortunate to have heard Chief Jake Swamp (1946-2010) of the Wolf Clan of the Mohawk Nation tell the story of Haudenosaunee prophet the Peacemaker, his planting of the Tree of Peace and giving his people the Great Law of Peace. The USA's constitution was modeled after the Great Law of Peace.[208]

In 1984, Chief Jake Swamp started the Tree of Peace Society. He traveled the world, planting Trees of Peace (white pine), and told the story of the Peacemaker. The telling of the Peacemaker's story stretches back to when the first Tree of Peace was planted on the shores of Onondaga Lake (Syracuse, New York).

The Medium is the Message

Canadian Marshall McLuhan (1911-1980) was an influential commentator on media and the dangers posed by technology in the second half of the twentieth century. He has been called "the high priest of pop culture" and "father of the electronic age."[209] McLuhan gave us concepts such as the "global village" and "the medium is the message."

McLuhan felt that how a message was delivered had greater influence than the message itself, saying "the medium is the message" because it is the medium that shapes and controls the scale and form of human association and action."[210] The "message" of any medium or technology is the change of scale or pace or pattern that it introduces into human affairs.[211] As an example, McLuhan looked to technological innovations such as the railway that accelerated human movement and created new kinds of cities, work, and leisure, and opening commerce and allowing for rapid expansion in places like America in unimaginable ways.

McLuhan warned us not to fall for the hype of how media is used (whether for good or bad) is what matters. He said:

> Our conventional response to all media, namely that it is how they are used that counts, is the numb stance of the technological idiot. For the "content" of a medium is like the juicy piece of meat carried by the burglar to distract the watchdog of the mind."[212]

Stories can be powerfully impactful. Joseph Campbell (1904-1987) spoke of the 'hero's journey,' an archetypal story of how a hero goes on a quest and overcomes numerous challenges and returns home triumphant and transformed by the experience. Campbell's hero's journey has become a widely used template by Hollywood screenwriters.

In an interview with Bill Myers of PBS Campbell said that, Myths are stories of our search through the ages for truth, for meaning, for significance… Myths are clues to the spiritual potentialities of human life… Myth helps you to put your mind in touch with this experience of being alive. It tells you what the experience is. Marriage, for example. What is marriage? The myth tells you what it is.[213]

No doubt, myths or stories have a profound and important influence upon us. Does it matter how a story is delivered?

Yes! As McLuhan teaches in the medium: how a story is delivered matters much more than its message. Is it told orally, via print, over the radio, on a CD, on TV/screen, over a cell phone or….? It matters; it really matters a lot. As previously noted, the railway did not invent human movement, but accelerated it and dramatically altered how we lived. The modern technologies we are using today have dramatically altered our lives and the influence that stories have upon us.

We have lost the oral tradition; or at least the effect that it had upon people long ago. Stories were recited over and over again, often to an attentive audience that found them entertaining. In the process a story could become a powerful samskara. A samskara that had been strengthened by the focus and intent of its listeners; as well as being adorned by the visions and images which listeners welled up while hearing the story.

It is next to impossible to ascertain whether stories in an oral tradition did, or did not, become powerful samskaras.

There is also the negative impact that may have become associated with the story. For example: listener's feelings of boredom, indifference, jealousy for the storyteller, the anger of captive listeners and other negative intentions/emotions and more. Then there is the issue of decay over time.

A story in an oral tradition that becomes a powerful samskara can be very impactful. People in trance are more receptive to its underlying message. It can help people achieve higher states of consciousness, allow for greater bonding between listeners, can bring on mystical experiences, and so much more.

Stories told via technology are like white bread. Worse, they block us from Mother Earth's Energies. What impact does the feelings of love and compassion that may well up within us, while hearing a story have, if we are being robbed of the accompanying spiritual nutrition? No doubt we can and will be impacted by the content of a story. We may learn something. Stories told via our modern technology, compared to the oral tradition, are like food that was overcooked and robbed of its nutrients the day before, and now is being reheated in a microwave to kill whatever benefit it may had left. Sure, it can, like food, fill our bellies, but does not do much else.

I strongly encourage you to create your own story mantras for yourself, your kids, your friends, or to help others achieve blissful states of higher consciousness and learn some valuable lessons.

Creating a Story Mantra

To create your story mantra, begin in a contemplative mind and meditate on your theme and what you want to say. Next, figure out what you want your story to be; it could be something new, or an old tale or experience. This can take time. Consider doing some research. I am a believer in planting seed thoughts and having them take root and waiting for the fruits come back to us over time. In other words, don't worry if something does not come to you right away. Keep contemplating and eventually something will come to you.

Once you have your story, you need to keep reciting it with a contemplative mind. Keep reciting, and reciting it. If you are not a good meditator, you will be handicapped and may not, even over time, create a powerful story mantra.

After your story mantra has some strength and gets you into a mild meditative state, you should tell it to others. The others should be people that are into meditation and are interested in your story mantra. Telling it to disinterested people, or people that don't meditate at this early stage, can be very destructive. A group meditation of your story mantra is a very good thing that can significantly strengthen it.

Over time, you may wish to spice up your story mantra and decorate it like a Christmas tree. For example, begin a new contemplative meditation concentrating on love or forgiveness, or some other noble action. Continue meditating on your subject (love, forgiveness…) for some time. Once it has some strength, incorporate it into your story mantra. You do this by reciting your story mantra and pausing at some point. Then focus on your object of contemplation (such as love or forgiveness). Make sure to do it a few times and stop at the same place each time.

You can also add details or images to your story mantra. For example, when reciting your story mantra, when you come to a certain point/person/concept/detail, visualize it, or something similar. Focus for some time on the image during your meditation. Then resume reciting your story mantra. When you next recite your story mantra, pause again at the same place and visualize the image for a little while. Do this for a few recitations.

There is so much more you can do to soup-up your story mantra. Spend some time in contemplative meditation pondering on how you can improve your story mantra.

Once you have something wonderful and palpable, share your story mantra. Use it as way to introduce people to meditation, provide an escape for those in pain, or bring joy and uplift those that are struggling. A story mantra is a wonderful way to lead a group meditation or prayer, particularly in an environment that is not conducive to meditation, or when listeners are not experienced meditators. Try to find ways to share your gift.

Forgiveness

Forgiveness can be enormously challenging. When we are gravely injured, or someone close to us is, forgiving the perpetrator, even after a long period of time, can be difficult. How could they? You may relive the experience over and each time, well up with anger or hate. Forgiveness is never easy.

Forgiveness calls for us to stop feeling angry or resentful towards someone that has sinned against us in some way; it does not mean that we do not hold a perpetrator accountable. Lets put the concept of sin in the context of Jesus and the story of the adulteress and consider what it teaches about judging the sins of others.

One morning, Jesus left the Mount of Olives and came to the temple. Many sat around him and he began to teach. The scribes and Pharisees (religious leaders) came with a woman that had been caught committing adultery. They made her stand in front of everyone, undoubtedly very humiliating:

> [T]hey said to him, "Teacher, this woman was caught in the very act of committing adultery. Now in the law Moses commanded us to stone such women. Now what do you say?" They said this to test him, so that they might have

some charge to bring against him. Jesus bent down and wrote with his finger on the ground. When they kept on questioning him, he straightened up and said to them, "Let anyone among you who is without sin be the first to throw a stone at her." And once again he bent down and wrote on the ground. When they heard it, they went away, one by one, beginning with the elders; and Jesus was left alone with the woman standing before him. Jesus straightened up and said to her, "Woman, where are they? Has no one condemned you?" She said, "No one, sir." And Jesus said, "Neither do I condemn you. Go your way, and from now on do not sin again." (John 8.4-11)

While this powerful story is generally considered to be about not judging others, it is also a lesson on judging those who have sinned against us. When we refuse to forgive others, we are picking up the stone, and want to hurl it against those that have sinned against us.

Street preachers are fond of saying that "we are all sinners." Indeed we are.

So when you think about forgiveness, think about your own transgressions. I imagine some reading this have had horrific acts committed against them, such as rape or other violent acts, or have had loved ones killed. Nothing similar has ever happened in my life, so who am I to talk about forgiveness?

Understand that karma will insure that justice will be served. If someone has sinned against you, they will be picking up a karmic debt that must be repaid. It could also be that the injury to you is the payback of your karmic debt, or you assuming someone else's karmic debt. If the perpetrator is forgiven by the grace of God, then that grace will also be bound to you in some way. Meaning: by showing forgiveness a little grace may flow to you. Karma can be truly wonderful in strange ways.

Forgiveness is a lesson that we are here to learn. It is so important that it is mentioned in the Lord's Prayer, the greatest prayer of Christendom: "And forgive us our sins, for we ourselves forgive everyone indebted to us. (Luke 11.4) In other words, if we want our sins to be forgiven, we must forgive those who have sinned against us. Karma!

It is forgiving that we are forgiven.

When you fail to learn the lesson of forgiveness and refuse to forgive someone, you may bind yourself to the injury against you and possibly to its perpetrator, as well. Earlier, in speaking of reincarnation, I had talked about a patient of Edgar Cayce's named Stella Kirby. She became a nurse who found herself taking care of a man that did not have his wits about him and lived in a cage. Their paths had crossed twice before in previous lives. Once she learned to give love to this man, something that she had previously refused to do, her karmic debt was absolved.

Even the Bible says that we will not be forgiven until we learn to forgive others: "For if you forgive others their trespasses, your heavenly Father will also forgive you; but if you do not forgive others, neither will your Father forgive your trespasses."(Mt 6.14-15)

Forgiveness heals us in many ways and at many levels. Alexandra Asseily[214] became a psychotherapist to explore her own responsibility in the trauma and violence of the bloody civil war in Lebanon (1975-1991) that turned the Middle East's jewel into a war zone. After a life-changing experience in 1997 she was inspired to create the Garden of Forgiveness (Hadiquat as Samah) in Beirut, a project to build a garden in the heart of the city to facilitate forgiveness.

She works to heal traumatic memory and pain that people may have experienced or unconsciously inherited, feeling that,

[f]orgiveness allows us to actually let go of the pain in the memory, and if we let go of the pain the memory, we can have the memory, but it doesn't control us. When the memory controls us, we are puppets of the past.[215]

Forgiveness is a lesson to be learned. The Law of Attraction will ensure that you will be placed in situations that call for forgiveness. Is this a class that you wish to repeat, and repeat and repeat? Possibly with the same perpetrator?

Make an effort to develop a samskara of forgiveness, begin small, and build upon it. As Dr. Martin Luther King Jr. said, "Forgiveness is not an occasional act; it is a constant attitude."[216] This comes from a sermon Dr. King wrote titled 'Love in Action.' It begins with a quote from Jesus when he is on dying on the cross and asks God to "forgive them; for they do not know what they are doing." (Luke 23:34) King says it is "love at its best."

In another sermon titled 'Loving your Enemies,' Dr. King instructs that to have the capacity to love our enemy, we must first be able to forgive them. He says, "we must develop and maintain the capacity to forgive. He who is devoid of the power to forgive is devoid of the power to love."[217]

Both of these sermons are contained in a book titled *Strength to Love*. Dr. King began writing the sermons contained in the book in July of 1962, when he was in jail for fifteen days for holding a prayer vigil outside of the City Hall of Albany, Georgia. He was part of a coalition of groups whose goal was to desegregate the city. Ralph Abernathy was his cellmate.[218]

Plant the seed of forgiveness within yourself.

If you find it difficult to even start, begin small by just repeating a mantra, such as "I forgive Joe" even if you don't believe it. Over time, it will grow stronger and you will find it within yourself to forgive people. It is one way that we can remove some of the karmic debt that we carry. Free yourself.

It is by forgiving, that we are forgiven. Become the change you wish to see, and forgive others.

Loving Boomerangs

Here a few samskaras that will not only help make you a better person and facilitate your spiritual evolution, but are wonderful gifts that can boomerang back to you when you need them the most. Consider them to be spiritual habits to develop—samskaras that bear the most wonderful fruit.

Pray for others. You may already be praying for others on a regular basis. When I first began my spiritual quest, I used to constantly pray for strangers. For example, when I was in the subway and I would see a forlorn looking person, I would pray for them. I would not stare at them; just pray for them. This can be challenge because at times people can sense that your attention is on them even if you are not staring at them.

There have also been periods in my life where I pray for anyone that comes within my vision, walks the street, or is at the gym, or at a grocery store. Often when I am in the woods while I am hiking, I will pray for someone that is sick, or someone or some cause in need. It will usually take a good chunk of time, like half an hour or more. I may split the time of my hike with contemplation on an issue or concept.

Praying for others is a great way to get out of your own head. Today, many spiritual teachers tell us to be present and mindful during our waking hours. While being present can help us to concentrate and reduce anxiety, it also turns the focus of our thoughts upon ourselves. We already live in a society overly occupied with self and you don't need to add to it. You need to find ways to break free.

When you are praying for others you are actively turning your focus and attention on others. It is a wonderful way to become more compassionate and caring. By praying for people, you are also sending them love. Wouldn't it be wonderful to have people praying for you, especially at a difficult time in your life?

Joy and Happiness. Although I can be pretty serious and intense, at times I can be childishly silly. Earlier in my life, at times I took it upon myself to try and make people happy whom I encountered throughout the day. I'd give them a big smile, convey a feeling of joy, compliment someone, or find in some other way to make people happy.

Not only did this put in me a more joyous mood, but it would come back to me in the most wonderful ways when I was not in the best of spirits. What is the value of someone who can lift you when you feel down? Karma can certainly perform wonderful acts.

Help others. We should try and help others whenever we can. This does not necessarily mean putting yourself at risk in a dangerous situation. Rather, it's to try to help people when you see them in need.

Return items you find. You should make an effort to return lost items you find. Bring them to lost and found. Or, if you are walking a trail or some other places without a formal place to return items you find, place them in plain view in a place where people are sure to see them, such as a trail sign. The boomerang of having lost items come back to you is very rewarding. If you practice returning items, you will come to understand that nothing is ever lost.

Anything and Everything is Possible

Anything can be a samskara and can carry karma. A movement or dance, if practiced with intensity, concentration, and preferably in a trance state, is capable of becoming a potent samskara. Similarly, a song or chant, can become one, as can a gesture or a pattern of behavior….

Samskaras define your life and who you are. The only real choice you have is to live and embody the change you wish to see. Over time, it will grow into something powerful.

Mahatma Gandhi was born into wealth. But he made an effort to give away his wealth and material possessions throughout his life. At the time of his death, he was left with only a few items: a pair of sandals; his glasses with a case to hold them; a bowl; a watch; and a couple of other things.

Samskaras can be truly transformative. Choose what you want to be and leave a gift behind whose embrace will help others.

12. Drink Living Water

Dowsing folklore would have you believe that the intersection of three or more water veins in the ground below, underneath your bed, or under your home is dangerous to your health. Water veins are underground streams or currents of water that vary in size from a mere trickle to large streams. It is believed that the friction of the moving water against rocks, or the movement of water itself (like electricity in a wire), creates an electric current. When too many water veins cross in the same place, the electric charge created can be bad for your health.

'Geopathic stress' is a catchall phrase to describe damaged areas of Mother Earth. The consequences of living in an area of geopathic stress include feeling drained, insomnia, fatigue, lack of energy, joint aches, and more. Long-term exposure can lead to problems with your organs, cancer, and depression.

While I was learning about dowsing, geomancy, and how to connect with our Mother, I bought into this folklore and perpetuated this myth that the intersection of water veins creates geopathic stress. I have since learned better.

The fact is that water, like everything else in the sea of consciousness in which we live, interacts with everything it comes in contact with. So water can pick up samskaras and retain a memory of where it has been and what has been done to it, and it can pick up karma. Like everyone and everything, water has a consciousness quotient.

Unfortunately, much of the water in the world runs through polluted places, industrial areas, and places where bad things have happened, or comes in contact with sludge, chemicals, pesticides, or worse. Even though the water is moving and does not linger in any one place, it still merges with negative consciousness. The cumulative effect is that water takes on negative consciousness.

Just as a synergy occurs when we unite and come together, a reverse synergy occurs when negative consciousness comes together. The sum of the negativity is much more than that of the individual parts. So when several water veins with negative consciousness intersect, the negativity is much worse

Sleep or spend too much time over such an area where water veins containing negative consciousness intersect and of course it will be bad for your health.

What troubles me about this myth of crossing water veins, this false narrative, is that it implies that there is something wrong with Mother Earth; that Her water veins are dangerous and bad for our health. Nothing could be farther from the truth.

Remember that the microcosm is like the macrocosm. Think of the human body. What is dangerous within the human body to itself? This is arguably an oxymoron. We could possibly be hurt by stomach acid if we were to come in contact with it—but that would take some doing because it is covered by a lot of flesh and organs. Yes, you can contract acid reflux, but that is a disease.

Yes, Mother Earth does have radioactive areas and lava—but when do we come in contact with them? You can also argue that violent storms such as hurricanes show the harm Mother Earth can bring; but how much of this is like a fever in response to bad actions and intentions by humankind?

The unfortunate thing is that many other such false myths show our Mother as being dangerous. In doing so, they have alienated us from Her and we, seeing Her as the enemy, make assaults upon Her justifiable.

Liquids Retain a Memory and Have Karma

Like everything else in the sea of consciousness of our existence, water and all liquids, and all materials, retain a memory, carry karma, and have a consciousness quotient reading. This has important consequences for your well-being.

We need to drink water to stay alive and healthy. Because it can carry karma, water retains a memory of where it has been and what has been done to it. This means that the water you drink will do to you what has been done to it.

Consider tap water. It has been filtered and treated with chemicals to remove impurities and kill waterborne diseases. It may have been chlorinated or heated. Because many people feel that water treatment facilities may not properly remove all the harmful elements from water, they add their own water treatment, such as reverse osmosis.

Not only do these treatments destroy the nutrients in the water, but they kill the Life Force and any other Earth Energies that it may have contained.

More importantly, since water retains the memory of all that has been done to it—that is its KARMA – that same karma will be unleashed upon you. It is going to treat you the way it has been treated. Do you really want to have this karma unleashed on your gut's microbiome?

I do not know what affect this may or may not have upon you. But many call our digestive tract our 'second brain.' I can't imagine that this is good for the bacteria in your digestive tract.

Think of it in another way. Water that has been aggressively treated by public and private water purification systems has been "processed." It took decades to realize that processed foods are of poor quality. Many consider them bad for your health. So do you think it is good to consume large amounts of processed water, which may be the liquid equivalent of junk food?

The Karma of (Distilled) Water

To see the karmic payback of liquids, we need only look to distilled water. Through the process of distillation (water boiled into steam), water is stripped of its contaminates; whether they are harmful to your health (such as chemicals and metals), or beneficial (such as minerals, nutrients, electrolytes, and the Life Force that you need for your health and well-being).

Although removing harmful chemicals and bacteria from water purifies it, eliminating beneficial minerals and electrolytes robs it of its nutrients. Worse, drinking distilled water that has been denuded of its beneficial nutrients and electrolytes will leach nutrients, minerals, electrolytes and the Life Force from your body. In other words: distilled water will do to you what has been done to it—KARMA.

Before considering the merits of distilled water, it is important to note that drinking water laced with harmful chemicals or pollutants, containing bacteria/parasites or harmful organisms, is dangerous to your health. So, for some, drinking distilled or very purified water may be the best option.

Writing for the World Health Organization (WHO), Frantisek Kozisek of the National Institute of Public Health Czech Republic, said that drinking distilled water increased the elimination of sodium, potassium, chloride, calcium, and magnesium ions, and it increased the elimination of electrolytes from the body. Furthermore, he noted, as did others in the WHO report, that "demineralized water is highly aggressive and… attacks the water distribution piping and leaches metals and other materials from the pipes and associated plumbing materials."[219] In other words, distilled water, when put in contact with piping, corrodes it. If it corrodes piping when it comes in contact with it, what will the consumption of distilled water do to your intestines, your body, and your health…?

Canadian doctor Zoltan P. Rona, who writes for Vitality Magazine, agrees that people should not drink distilled water because it is an "active absorber" of what it comes in contact with. He points out that the most toxic commercial beverages that people consume (cola beverages and soft drinks) are made from distilled water. According to Dr. Rona:

> The longer one drinks distilled water, the more likely the development of mineral deficiencies and an acid state. I have done well over 3000 mineral evaluations using a combination of blood, urine, and hair tests, in my practice. Almost without exception, people who consume distilled water exclusively, eventually develop multiple mineral deficiencies.[220]

Dr. Joseph Mercola, an osteopathic physician and alternative medicine proponent, concurs about the effects of drinking distilled water, saying that it "[l]eaches minerals from your body which can lead to health problems,"[221] and adding that it's "[a]ctually MORE Toxic than Municipal Tap Water." After years of recommending reverse osmosis water filter systems, he stopped doing so because he felt that the systems produce water similar to distilled water; and he has switched his home water purification system to a charcoal filter system.

Many advocates for and in the distilled water industry point to Dr. Andrew Weill, Director of Integrative Health and Healing at Arizona University, and an advocate of alternative medicine. Dr. Weill recommends drinking distilled water because it has been cleaned of harmful contaminates. He does admit that distilled water is bereft of minerals, but is not concerned because "We get our minerals from food, not water."[222] However, Kozisek, in his WHO paper, and other researchers whom he cites, say that we do receive nutrients from water, and they can provide significant health benefits.

The work of Theodor Schwenk shows that water retains a memory of how it has been treated and the associated problems with drinking distilled water. Earlier, you were introduced to Theodor Schwenk and his concept of archetypal phenomenon of vortex formation. This was the concept that I used to explain the formation of circles. Schwenk saw magic in the movement of water, believing that water is always in the process of becoming or dissolving.[223]

In 1961, Schwenk founded Flow Sciences (Institut für Strömungswissenschaften) to study "what makes good and enlivening water in all its connections with life."[224] To help determine the health of water, he developed the Drop Picture Method, which depicts the quality of water in a visual image. Healthy water shows movement and a multiplicity of forms. Natural spring water shows mobility, while tap water and polluted water do not.

The Drop Picture Method shows that distilled water is less robust, has fewer vortices, and is lifeless. Distilled water sucks out, or pulls in whatever is around it; meaning it will do to you or whatever it comes in contact with, what has been done to it. Both distilled water and water treated by reverse osmosis are deficient in minerals.[225] Through the Drop Picture Method we can vividly see that water retains the memory of where it has been and how it has been treated. It demonstrates that water retains a memory and carries karma.

The fact is that you need to drink the water that dowsers and Earth Healers call "living water." Not only is it free from all those wicked memories of its bad treatment, but also it is chock-full of nutrients and the Life Force. This is not bottled water, which also has been mistreated and is not of the highest quality. You need to drink water from a spring or from the bowels of the earth, or as close to it as you can get. This means you have to begin collecting water yourself. Drink living water.

Living Water

To appreciate living water, you must understand the characters that are involved with it. People who love water are a dedicated and passionate bunch, often eclectic, bordering on eccentric, and see their work as a mission, whether it be educational, conservation, or bringing potable water (safe to drink) to those in need locally or in a third-world country. To them, water is a spiritual and living essence.

Viktor Schauberger (1885-1958) was born to a long line of Austrian foresters. As a young boy he would spend hours in the forest studying water and its interplay in watercourses such as streams, as well as in plants and animals. He forsook academia to observe Nature firsthand. Not limited by the regiment and mentality of traditional science (samskara), he became an innovator and made some incredible discoveries. However, this also made him a pariah to the scientific and academic communities.

Schauberger, who many call the 'Water Wizard', understood that water sustained all of life, saying it was:

[t]he upholder of the cycles that supports the whole of life. In every drop of water dwells a Deity, whom we all serve; there also dwells Life, the Soul of the 'first' substance - Water - whose boundaries and banks are the capillaries that guide it and in which it circulates.[226]

Schauberger believed living water carried energy and nutrients, could communicate information, had healing properties, and could self-cleanse and discharge waste. He saw our technologies and water treatment methods as being dangerous and felt that they made water lifeless and robbed it of its ability to nourish and sustain life. To him, dead water could lead to degenerative diseases like cancer.[227]

In its movement, water does a magical dance that not only nourishes and sustains life, but regenerates itself; primarily through its spiraling movement. Above ground the blood of Mother Earth (the role Schauberger saw water fulfilling) moves through Her arteries, spiraling as it travels downstream, turning and twisting with each river bank it encounters. Below ground, water it does its spiral dance of life as Schauberger taught:

> When rain falls, like distilled water, it is without life. It trickles down in spiraling motions around rocks beneath the ground, where it gradually meets a rising temperature, and begins at some point to percolate upwards again in a spiraling motion, gathering material ions and Life Force until it meets light.[228]

Schauberger realized that it was this spiraling, vortex-like movement that gave water life. Specifically, it was the spiraling inwards what he called implosion and what science calls centripetal force. Schauberger maintained, "The form of movement which creates, develops, purifies and grows is the hyperbolic spiral which externally is centripetal and internally moves to the center."[229]

It is this spiraling, vortex-like movement inward that gives water its power and embrace. This is the same inward spiraling movement that gives life to Natural Vortices, or Energy Vortices; only they nourish humankind and not water. Similarly, sages and teachers for time immemorial have told us to look within and turn inwards, not without.

Conversely, Schauberger saw the outward centrifugal movement as being destructive and bringing death, saying: "[T]he destructive and dissolving form movement is centrifugal in Nature—the forces moving medium from the center towards the periphery in straight lines."[230]

Schauberger felt that modern science and technology were based on the centrifugal movement of breaking down and destroying through heat, combustion, explosion and expansion. To him, the inefficiencies of modern technology were the result of Nature's resistance to our destructive tendencies. He foresaw that our pursuit of technology would bring about ecological problems and strains upon humankind, saying "our technology points to death."[231]

Then there is what Stephan Riess (1898-1985) calls 'primary water.' He calls it primary water because of its close relationship with primary minerals in the earth's magna. Primary water is created under certain circumstances deep in the earth, when water and oxygen combine to form water. Under great pressure, it is expelled up to the surface of the earth through cracks or faults in the earth's crust. Others call it 'new water' because it is newly formed, or 'juvenile water.'

German-born Riess[232] had his first inkling about primary water in the 1930's when, as a mining engineer, he began finding mines flooding during digs in hard rocks in desert areas. By the 1940's, he began to hypothesize that the subterranean water was shooting vertically upwards from deep in the interior of the earth. By the 1950's, he was talking about new water, primary water, forming deep below the earth's surface. By the 1970's, he had drilled over eight-hundred primary water wells that directly or indirectly tapped into fissures in the earth.

After Riess' death, science discovered that there is indeed an ocean of water in the Earth's mantel that could be as great, if not greater than all the water in all of the oceans around the world, or so says Scientific American.[233] Furthermore, science now believes that this water was created and is still being created in the mantel of the earth.[234]

Primary water is living water that has taken Schauberger's spiraling journey to the surface of the earth. It could be new water, or water that is ancient—and I mean really ancient. We have to remember that earth has been around for a long time. What's a few million years for water to be recycled for a planet that has been in existent for billions of years? So, perhaps much of the living water in the world is ancient water that has been recycled, having done Schauberger's spiral dance journey, first downward and then reversing course when it was heated deep in the earth. At least, that is what water dowser and humanitarian Steve Herbert[235] believes.

Steve has been dowsing for water all over the world for over thirty-years. He got the bug in the early 1990's when, at the age of forty, he joined the Peace Corps as a volunteer in Senegal in West Africa. His job title was Agricultural Technician. Thanks to a donation, he was also able to travel around Senegal finding water through dowsing and building wells. After leaving the Peace Corps, Steve has continued to bring potable water to places in need around the world.

Water's Memory

Memory and karma attaches to water, other liquids, and every other substance, because memory attaches to consciousness and everything is consciousness in the sea of consciousness in which we live. This is an important concept because whatever you consume can take on karma. Similarly, any material or object can pickup karma and retain it. So you must be aware of what you keep close to you.

At the same time, the fact that water retains a memory can help you. The holistic healing modality of homeopathy relies upon water's memory to bring about healing. In fact, several other disciplines work with water's ability to retain memory, as well.

Masaru Emoto (1943-2014) captured the world's attention with his microscopic photographs of water that showed the impact of different variables (classical music, saying thanks, pollution) on the crystalline form of the water. He believed that water retained a memory and could be influenced by human consciousness. The crystalline shapes of water reaffirmed in him the belief in the transformative power of love.

Jacques Benveniste (1935-2004) was a French immunologist and physician who gained notoriety for a 1988 experiment in which he found that a diluted substance could have a biological effect,[236] appearing to support homeopathy. Benveniste and his colleagues diluted the solutions of antibodies in their experiment so much that they no longer contained even a single antibody molecule, but it still provoked a response from immune cells. In other words, they found that water could retain the memory of molecules that were no longer present in the liquid.

John Maddox, the then-editor of *Nature Magazine*, the same fellow who blasted Rupert Sheldrake over his thesis that species retain a memory, agreed to publish the paper provided a team from *Nature* could visit the laboratory and replicate the experiment. Shortly after publication, a team from *Nature* showed up. Interestingly, it included James Randi, a stage magician, paranormal investigator, and debunker of claims to mystic powers.

The results were not replicated and the experiment was dubbed a failure. *Nature* published an article entitled "'High-dilution' experiments a delusion."[237] It said "the hypothesis that water can be imprinted with that past memory of solutes is as unnecessary, as it is fanciful... The claims made (Benveniste) are not to be believed...The phenomena described are not reproducible."

Understandably, Benveniste was bitter, and the incident did not help his career. Friend and colleague Bernard Poitevin felt the incident contributed to his heart ailment and premature death.[238] Professor Madeleine Ennis of Queen's University, Belfast carried out dilution experiments and did find a positive reaction from a diluted solution.[239] Though Elisabeth Davenas, who worked with Benveniste, was later able to reproduce the results and find high dilution solutions are affective, others have failed, so controversy remains.

French virologist Luc Antoine Montagnier was the joint recipient (with Françoise Barré-Sinoussi and Harald zur Hausen) of the Nobel Prize in Medicine in 2008 for their discovery of the human immunodeficiency virus (HIV). In 2010, he climbed on the water retains memory train when he discovered that certain bacterial and viral DNA sequences dissolved in water and caused electromagnetic signals to be emitted at high dilutions.[240]

The response was swift and strong; so much so that Montagnier decided to move and teach in China, what Science magazine called an escape from "Intellectual Terror."[241]

The circle of science is powerful and large in numbers. Remember that a circle looks to exert its influence and have you buy into its beliefs. It looks to exert conformity. It also, as Meher Baba said, looks to form an enclosure around its members limiting their perspective.

Homeopathy

Homeopathy is a discipline that works with the memory, or karma, of water. Two principles underlie Homeopathy: one is the belief that "Like can cure like," meaning that a person can be cured of a disease by a substance that produces similar symptoms in healthy people. The Greek origin of the name homeopathy is derived from the concept that like cures like; *homeo* meaning 'similar' and *pathos* meaning 'suffering.'

The second principle underlying homeopathy is the "potency, potentization' of a remedy, with the belief that the lower the dose of the medication, the greater its effectiveness. Many homeopathic products are so diluted that no molecules of the original substance remain.

It is this idea of dilution, where none of the original element is contained in the cure, that so irks traditional science because it implies that water retains a memory, aka karma.

Consider the process of homeopathic dilution. Because some of the remedies given are poisonous, they have to be diluted. It was discovered that further dilutions prevented 'aggravations' (increased symptoms), and had improved results. The remedy would be diluted with water, or a combination of water and alcohol. It would then be 'secussed,' a two-step process of vigorously shaking followed up by strong banging of the container holding the dilution on a hard surface.

The dilution process of homeopathy implies that the diluted remedy worked because it had retained the memory, or karma, of its earlier less diluted version. The initial dilution had merged with, and successfully absorbed, the original memory/karma. That original memory/karma was retained through successive dilutions as if it had its own cycle of reincarnations. Homeopathy demonstrates that karma works.

German physician Samuel Hahnemann (1755-1843) discovered homeopathy. He stopped practicing medicine after nine years because he was disappointed with the extreme practices of the day, feeling instead that better hygiene, nutrition, and housing could do much to improve people's health. By happenstance he read about how quinine might be a cure for malaria. He took quinine and found that he displayed symptoms similar to malaria, even though he did not have the disease. He tested more medicines for different diseases and developed a "symptom picture" of each remedy. Eventually, Hahnemann determined that remedies that produce similar symptoms to a particular disease could be used to treat it. The Law of Similarities was born.[242]

Several other disciplines, such as Bach Flower Remedies, rely on the fact that water retains a memory. The Bach process begins by making a mother tincture of plants and water, which are combined with an equal amount of brandy. Two drops of the solution are then mixed with thirty milliliters of brandy. [243] At the end of the process almost none of the original mother tincture is contained in bottles that you buy in the store.

Everything Retains a Memory

The fact is that everything retains a memory, even liquids. Although the impact is usually minimal, you should be aware of what you consume. Consider blessing your food before eating.

You can help heal polluted waterways. Have a water ceremony where you take water from a lake or stream and place it into a container. Pass the container around and let everyone hold it and give thanks to the water, and tell why water is important to them, or tell a wonderful story about water, or say a prayer. After everyone has participated in giving thanks, pour the water back into the body of water.

You can also make your own holy water. Although it is an extensive process, one of the easiest ways to make holy water is to keep a bottle of water next to you when you meditate. Your intentions will attach to the water. You can also just hold the water and pray.

Keep chemicals and poisons away from your food, drinking water, and plants. Even though they might not touch the toxins, close proximity may affect them.

Anything you consume is going to retain a memory of its treatment and where it's been. Drink processed water or eat processed food and it will similarly ravage you. As we are taught "Do unto others as we wish others to do unto us," whatever has been done to what we consume will be done to us.

13. Earth Magic

Earlier, I had said that you should turn to Mother Earth for mystical experiences. That is because some of the most profound journeys, insights and transformative experiences I have had took place in Nature. The more you are connected to our Mother and the farther you are along on your spiritual path and meditation, the greater your chances are that you will have a deep and profound mystical experience.

Your relationship with our Mother has a bearing upon your spiritual development. She can help make your aura grow so that you can pull in more spiritual nutrition.

Mother Earth is also integral to your physical health and well-being. Hippocrates, the father of medicine, said, "Illnesses do not come upon us out of the blue. They are developed from small daily sins against Nature. When enough sins have accumulated, illnesses will suddenly appear."[244] In other words, when we are out of sync with Mother Earth we increase the chances of getting sick.

Natural Vortices

One of the great joys in my life is to go questing in the woods looking for Natural Vortices, or Energy Vortices. When you meditate in a Natural Vortex, it gives you an extra dose of soul nourishing Cosmic Prana. It also contains a powerful imprint of those that created it.

It is the increased dose of Cosmic Prana that may propel you to higher levels of consciousness and help you break free from the circle of reality.

The imprint is the real jewel of a Natural Vortex. That is because when you meditate in a Natural Vortex, you will be merging with the samskara of an individual(s) that had a high enough level of spiritual acumen and a deep enough bond with Mother Earth to create a Natural Vortex. Creating a Natural Vortex is no easy feat, so whoever created it must have had a good soul and was most likely well along on their spiritual path. Meditating in a Natural Vortex is a very personal and intimate connection with the spirit of the being(s) that created it. It is also an excellent way to tap into other people's samskaras and make karma work for you.

A Natural Vortex is like the sweetest of mother's milk. When a baby drinks its mother's milk, a host of benefits occur from providing the best nutritional food, to improved health, to increased immunity as the baby takes on their mother's immunity, to reducing the chances for disease, and to growing up healthier and smarter. The mother hands down these benefits to her baby, who may have gotten them from her mother, or developed them on her own.

Similarly, the benefits of meditating in a Natural Vortex are passed down to you. Your consciousness quotient will most likely rise because of the time you will be spending merging with the samskara of its creator(s). You may experience an improvement in your meditative ability, or prayer level.

Then, depending upon the activities that were performed to create the imprint (samskara) of the Natural Vortex, these will determine the other gift(s) that may flow to you. It could have been vision questing by Indigenous People crying for a vision that created the imprint, and so you will garner visions. Perhaps its creator(s) time spent in contemplation and pondering; if so, you may get great insights. Or maybe it was the giving of thanks and honoring our Mother that fueled the formation of the imprint and its Natural Vortex; if so, you may be blessed with an increased connection and appreciation of our Mother. Or…

I have experienced all these and many more. There are many ways to love, heal, pray, meditate, act altruistically, and give of yourself that can lead to a co-creation and a new birth with our Mother. So there are many types of wonders that you may experience when you meditate in a Natural Vortex.

There are also two other gifts that will flow to you when you meditate in a Natural Vortex and connect with the spirit of its creator(s).

Earlier, I said that when you help others or give of yourself, your soul is nourished. I also think that much more happens; something similar to drinking mother's milk. You are made more whole (and much more so) if you meditate in a Natural Vortex. What do I mean by this?

Think of it like drinking the milk of someone else's mother. You will be gifted with something that your mother might not have. It's as if each of us has a piece of an enormous puzzle. When you connect with, or help someone, or meditate in a Natural Vortex created by someone else, you pick up another piece of the puzzle. I have experienced this many times after meditating in a Natural Vortex. I might not sense it, but I knew it happened. Sometimes I can feel it very deeply, as if the addition changed me or gave me something I was lacking or deficient in. Such occurrences are rare, but each time you help someone or meditate in a vortex, you become ever more so slightly whole. Remember: when you are meditating in a Natural Vortex you are merging very deeply with, the samskara of an advanced soul. Not only will this raise your consciousness, but it can also bestow innumerable gifts.

While you always transcend time[245] and connect with the spirit of the individual(s) that created the Natural Vortex, sometimes the experience can be profound; to the point that you feel that you have traveled back centuries, or even millennia, to when the vortex was forming. That can be a mind-blowing experience as if you entered a time warp. That ticket to transcend time is always there. As in my vegetable soup analogy, you just need to take a bite of the right vegetable and hope that you are so blessed.

The woods abound with Natural Vortices. To find one, you need to develop a strong bond with our Mother, which I will talk about developing in more detail shortly. It will also help to learn basic geomancy, earth healing, and dowsing. I cannot emphasize enough how important this is: your bond with our Mother will weigh heavily in determining your ability to develop those skills.

Natural Vortices are testament of the power of positive karma and samskaras to transcend time and can be a benefit to future generations. They are a wonderful gift from seers, pilgrims, lovers of our Mother, and spiritual aspirants from the past. I encourage you to develop the requisite skills to find a Natural Vortex.

Just remember that they are hidden in woods, where they have been protected. Hunting and other violent activities, as does technology, harm them.

Take a Pilgrimage to a Sacred Site

While you may not have the interest, time, or the wherewithal to develop the skill set to find Natural Vortices, you can certainly visit a sacred site. Genuine sacred sites are power spots with strong earth energies.

Unfortunately, as is true about so much in our world today, what was once a sacred site may no longer be so. John Michell (1933-2009) writes how the Christian Church reclaimed ancient pagan sacred places such as stone circles and standing stones in England by building churches upon them: "[t]hrough its policy of occupying and re-consecrating the old places of inherent sanctity the Christian Church quickly assumed the spiritual control of the country."[246]

Michell did not see this necessarily as a bad thing. Saying: "It was not only as landmarks that churches helped to preserve the memory of the old tradition. In their structure they incorporated many of the features of the stone circle they replaced."[247]

In the late 1960s with publication of his *View Over Atlantis*, and its subsequent revision *The New View Over Atlantis*, Michell became an icon in the Earth Mysteries movement at a time when New Age spirituality was beginning to hit its stride. He became a esotericist who studied numerology, sacred geometry, and crop circles, among other things.

The idea that the buildings of traditional mainline religion are now located over ancient pagan sacred areas is most likely not a good thing. However, it is not unusual, because the reclaiming of sacred sites has been going on from the earliest time. A sacred space is covered with samskaras, and the Law of Attraction will have others drawn to them to use for spiritual purposes.

Look to the fruit of what is considered a sacred place. Find out if people have garnered great insights, had mystical experiences, or found resolution at a particular place. If it is truly a sacred place, then its fruit should reflect this. Often these are places off of the radar screen. So ask around.

When you see psychics, healers, masseuses, metaphysical stores and other signs of commercialization flourishing at a supposedly sacred area—be careful.

My spiritual transformation was greatly enhanced by meditating in power spots. The fruits I looked to were those individuals that changed the world for the better. These were the homes of abolitionists, Women's Rights leaders and other reformers. Or places like Onondaga Lake in Syracuse, NY where the great Haudenosaunee (Iroquois) prophet the Peacemaker planted the Tree of Peace. I eventually found a formation of Mother Earth that I dubbed 'Fields of Consciousness' at the homes of many great souls. I then began to search the forests for them, and found some incredible places. I would meditate for hours on end at these transformational places.

These places were truly consciousness raising. I remember one of my early experiences meditating in a Field of Consciousness (FOC). I had been speaking out about the second invasion of Iraq (2003) for some time. While meditating in a FOC, I experienced one of the most profound feelings of compassion towards one of the Iraqi War's chief architects. I was shocked. A few days later, that feeling of love subsided, but I felt better for the experience. Subsequently, when I told friends about this love experience, they either did not believe me, or dismissed it as some mystical hallucination.

I can tell you firsthand that Mother Earth can be powerfully transformative and that all of Her energies and essences are not the same.

Building Spiritual Strength

You need spiritual nutrition to help with your spiritual evolution. If you meditate at a sacred site, or spend a lot of time meditating free from the embrace of negative circles, you will be getting a good dose of spiritual nutrition. Like digesting food, it will take time to process your increased intake of spiritual nutrition.

A big intake of spiritual nutrition will also tax you. Just as an intense workout can drain you and requires rest, it is no different when you absorb a lot of spiritual nutrition. The effect of a spiritual workout can be just as taxing as a rigorous workout, so you need to rest.

You also need to realize that if you are dedicated to your spiritual transformation, you cannot be dedicated to an intense regiment of physical workouts at the same time. Both can put an enormous strain upon you. That is not to say that you need to stop working out, hiking and doing other strenuous activities. You need to find a balance, or focus on one over the other, in spurts.

We Need Mother Earth, And She Needs Us

The formation of a Natural Vortex shows the wonder of our relationship with our Mother and the magic to co-create a new birth with Her. There are other amazing gifts that She can bestow upon us if only we follow the eternal message of God that has been echoed by the prophets, teachers, sages, and mystics time immemorial: to love, give, heal, to be our brothers/sisters keeper as well as keeper for all of creation. I would add bearing witness and helping the pariah.

For example, what many call a 'thin veil' can form at a sacred place that has been imbued with love and prayer. A 'thin veil' is where communication with the divine (or with other realms) has been enhanced or made easier. This could be an actual thinning between higher realities, or a powerful imprint (samskara) of communication to the divine that has formed at a given location.

Our relationship with our Mother is very simple: LOVE. All sorts of wonder will manifest if we do that. A Natural Vortex is the testament to the power of love because it forms in response to positive and loving human intentions.

All of Mother Earth could be blanketed with Natural Vortices if only we were more loving. That is because all of the world, every piece of our Mother, and even all objects retain a memory.

It is that clinging of memories, of imprints, of samskaras, to the land that gives a space its vibe, or its je nais se quoi. So a space just like any samskara can elevate you, or drag you down.

The samskaras that attach to land can also enhance the flow of energy and spiritual nutrition as with Natural Vortices. Or they can degrade the flow of energy and create dead zones, with areas of geopathic stress that are harmful to both humankind and to our Mother.

Our relationship with our Mother is beyond symbiotic—it is synergistic. With Her, we can create many more wonders, from mystical journeys, to feelings of joy and euphoria, to deep awareness and more. This synergy applies particularly to special parts of Mother Earth. Prayer, ceremony, and love makes them more potent—this means stronger doses of Mother Earth.

The world needs spiritual nutrition if we are to make a better world. We do this by working with Mother Earth. Technology and other negative circles need to be kept away from sacred areas. Working to heal space and being cognizant of our impact upon our Mother will go a long way to healing Her and helping us on our spiritual path.

We need Mother Earth to achieve our fullest potential, and She needs us to achieve Hers.

Property a Reflection of its Owner

There is something more to the fact that the property of mainline organized religions prevents the formation of a Natural Vortex because it bears the institution's consciousness quotient. Property can also reflect the character of its owner. One of the more surreal, but totally understandable phenomena is that the owner of a property often greets you before you meet them.

What do I mean?

When I walk onto the property of a warm and friendly person, sometimes I immediately sense their warmth and hospitality. Wisdom's Golden Rod in Hector, NY comes to mind. I remember going there to interview one of its members a few years ago for their write-up in *Sacred Sites in North Star Country* and feeling a powerful welcoming feeling. I had known about Wisdom's Golden Rod for some time, but had not been there in years, and my connection to Mother Earth had improved since.

It is the former guests, practitioners of Therapeutic Touch (an energy healing modality), which greets you when you visit Pumpkin Hollow Retreat in Craryville, NY. Their dedication and passion for healing (most are nurses) are palpable when you walk on the grounds. Interestingly, years ago when I walked the grounds, I conducted an experiment to gauge the consciousness of the space. I dowsed just the other side of their boundary markers and the consciousness reading dropped appreciably.

Similarly, I have seen the changing composition in the group of people involved with a sacred space affect its consciousness quotient; sadly, for the worst.

I generally do not experience particular emotions or intentions when I am in negative space. Usually I am just overwhelmed by its negative vibe.

Realize that you are constantly interacting with the space you are in, or travel through, or think about.

The introduction to the television show Star Trek always said that space was the final frontier. True. But it is not the space in outer space, but rather the space around us and in us. Start exploring.

Bonding with Mother Earth

You need to develop a strong bond with Mother Earth. She is the one that nourishes you physically and spiritually. A strong bond with Her will increase the size of your aura, or spiritual lungs. The larger your aura the more spiritual nutrition you can draw and hopefully absorb. So when you act altruistically, heal others, give, pray, or meditate, you will begin to gradually see an ever-increasing larger draw of spiritual nutrition.

For many, learning to connect with Mother Earth will involve wholesale radical change and much effort; but it's well worth it. So start small and buildup.

As with creating a mantra or changing a depressed mood by focusing on happy moments, find a time when our Mother gives you great joy. This could be something as simple as taking a walk on a lovely day, or a walk in the woods. Whatever the joy is that She gives you; dwell on it, savor it. Feel blessed and give thanks.

Give thanks to our Mother for other things. This could be the air that we breathe, the water we drink or the food that we eat, or it could be the wonder of our forests, or oceans. Just start giving thanks to our Mother. Giving such appreciation will help you to develop a bond with Her.

Begin to see our Mother and not the accouterments of our technological and materialistic society. If you gaze out and see a mass of buildings and a few trees, focus on the trees. Similarly, as you go about your day, focus on Nature and not on buildings, or telephones poles, or roads, or signs, or… See Nature.

Stop to smell the flowers.

Begin to read books on Nature, or ones written by environmentalists. Take up gardening, hiking, or other activities that put you in contact with Mother Earth.

Longer term, you may wish to become an Earth Healer. Not only is this the right thing to do, but also it will help you build an even stronger bond with Mother Earth. It will also build great karma, as our Mother will do to you as you have done to Her, and will shower you with love and much more.

Just realize that to develop a strong connection with Her, you cannot be involved with circles that harm Her such as technology, mainline religions, corporations, and the like. A cell phone, social media and such will block your ability to develop a bond with Mother Earth. If you are serious about connecting with our Mother, you need to ditch your cell phone and abandon social media and other technology. You cannot partake in circles that are dedicated to harming our Mother if you want to get closer to Her.

By developing a strong bond with our Mother, it will create a strong karmic bond with Her. A karmic bond that will bring all sorts of wonders.

Create Sacred Space

One of the things you can do to help yourself, the world at large, Mother Earth, and at the same time leave a legacy for others that follow, is to create sacred space. Sacred space can raise your consciousness, cleanse you, heal you, and more. It is a wonderful tool to help you on your spiritual path and can be a great aid to you when you are troubled.

We are constantly interacting with the space we traverse through during the day, and much of it is not good. Because of this, we are constantly walking in a sea of negativity that is continually depleting us and reducing our consciousness quotient. Your home needs to be a sanctuary, a refuge where you can be healed.

Choose a room in your home, or a corner of a room, or even a place in your backyard to transform into a sacred space.

It does not have to be a large space. The important thing is that the space be solely used for spiritual purposes and nothing else. Create an altar in your sacred space. Place your sacred texts there, hang inspiring pictures. Find a place for an incense holder so that you can burn incense. Once you have chosen your location, hold a ceremony to consecrate it. Say a prayer and a blessing, read a sacred text out loud, and burn incense.

You need to treat your sacred space as holy ground. Fuss over it, and say a prayer whenever you are there. Keep your actions and intentions focused on the divine and sacred when you are within your sacred space. Swami Vivekananda believed that we should have a room dedicated solely to spiritual practices, if possible. He said:

> Have no quarrel or anger or unholy thought in that room. Only allow those persons to enter it who are of the same thought as you. Then gradually there will be an atmosphere of holiness in the room, so that when you are miserable, sorrowful, or doubtful, or when your mind is disturbed, if you then enter the room you will feel peace.[248]

Meditate and pray there as much as you can. This will help raise the vibe and begin the long-term process of co-creating an Energy Vortex with Mother Earth.

One of the things you can do (if space allows) is to create several sacred spaces with specific purposes. For example, you may wish to have a place dedicated solely to contemplation and getting answers. By continually contemplating and meditating with the purpose of achieving a solution you will create a strong dedicated imprint (samskara) that will encourage more of the same. Then, when you are in need of an answer to an important decision, the samskara will help you find a solution.

I have a place for relaxation and sleep. I started it decades ago when I would go into yogic sleep when I was meditating. I then began to try and relax whenever I was in the space. Over time, I built a strong imprint that encourages sleep so that I can go there when I cannot sleep or am troubled in some way. It also has a humongous Natural Vortex.

A Sportsman's Cushion

Buy yourself a rugged and sturdy outdoor, or sportsman's cushion (or sportswoman's cushion). This is the type of cushion that people fishing or hunting sit on when they are in the woods, or on a boat during inclement weather. The cushion should contain padding. It should also have at least one side with a rugged exterior that cannot easily be pierced, and a loop to which you can attach a clip.

Again, you want a sturdy sportsman's cushion because you will be using it as a meditation cushion for years to come. Buy a clip and attach it to your cushion so that you can strap it to your belt loop or backpack, to take with you.

Every time you meditate, contemplate, or say a prayer, sit on your meditation cushion, or keep it close by, no matter whether you are out in the woods, at home, or at a group meditation. You are looking to have a samskara (imprint of your intentions) attach to your meditation cushion.

The more you use your cushion for meditation, the stronger the samskara gets. The samskara needs to be fed, and you do that by meditating or praying on it.

Over time, you will notice that you are better able to enter trance and go deeper into meditation when you sit on your cushion—discernibly so, compared to not sitting on the cushion. The imprint on the cushion is beginning to do its wonder and is helping propel you along on you spiritual path.

You will also begin to increase your draw, or pull, of spiritual nutrition. Even if an Energy Vortex has still to form and attach to your meditation cushion, you will increasingly be attracting more spiritual nutrition.

If you are persistent you may be blessed and a Natural Vortex may form on your meditation cushion. Then it's 'vavoom,' as your draw of spiritual nutrition will increase dramatically.

Any object or material will have a samskara attach to it. So there are an infinite number of things that you do, from creating prayer stones, to making happy handkerchiefs. All it takes is your imagination and a lot of prayer and meditation.

Our Mother

Your spiritual evolution is closely linked to Mother Earth. She is the one that nourishes your soul. You have to decide how important your spiritual growth is to you. If it is important, you need to develop a strong bond with our Mother. She has the ability to greatly enhance your spiritual transformation, so your bond with Her is critical.

If you want to get close to our Mother you have to dissociate yourself from circles that are harmful to Her. Don't spray your yard with chemicals that will injure the earth. The ground will also retain a memory of the pesticides, chemicals, and more which you have mistreated the earth with. This intent of killing will be unleashed upon you and everyone that walks your grounds. It will also affect you even when you are not in contact with the negative consciousness. Remember: as I said earlier, a property is a reflection of its owner. Your property and how it is treated will reflect, or act, upon you, as well.

Begin to see Mother Earth in the world. Give thanks to Her. Give Her a Big Hug.

Great wonder awaits you when you are intimately connected to Mother Earth.

14. Blown Away

Kitty Dukakis is the wife of Michael Dukakis the former governor of Massachusetts and the Democratic Presidential Candidate in 1988. In her book *Shock, The Healing Power of Electroconvulsive*,[249] she tells how electroconvulsive therapy (ECT) has given her extended respites from the severe depression that had tormented her for over twenty years when medications failed.

ECT consists of a short-term electric stimulus to the brain of a patient under anesthesia, often with the intent of producing a seizure. The American Psychiatric Association notes that extensive research has found ECT to be highly effective for the relief of major depression.[250]

However, ECT is not without controversy. Introduced as electroshock therapy in the USA in 1940, it was administered initially without anesthesia. It was also used to treat a myriad of mental health issues: schizophrenia, bipolar disorder, depression and much more. Some hospitals used electroshock therapy as much as two times a day to quiet disturbed patients.[251] Electroshock therapy was often overused and administered in mental health facilities, usually without the patients consent.

Award-winning journalist and author Richard Whitaker noted that over a million patients had been shocked in the first two decades of its use. He described it as a form of "brain trauma" that produced results similar to concussive head injury; as well as resulting in lower cognitive functioning, severe memory loss, and restrictions in intuitive and imaginative thinking.[252]

Public opinion turned against electroshock therapy after the demonization of mental health facilities and their treatment of patients with the release Ken Kesey's 'One Flew Over the Cuckoo's Nest' as a movie.

Dukakis is well aware of the cloud that 'One Flew Over the Cuckoo's Nest' cast over ECT. However, in her book, she tells story after story of those that have gotten back their life thanks to it.

As for her own experience, she says:

It is not an exaggeration to say that electroconvulsive therapy has opened a new reality for me. I used to deny when a depressive episode was coming on…how much it hurt, how long the darkness would last. I just couldn't face it…As important, ECT has gotten me off antidepressants… Once I went on antidepressants I couldn't bring myself to tears, whether I was listening to music or mourning my father. The drugs somehow blocked my emotions.[253]

Kudos to Kitty Dukakis for the courage to speak truth to power, and openly challenge the circle of public opinion about ECT. She is a powerful witness to her story and the truth.

Memories

Memory loss is a well-documented side effect of ECT. The American Psychiatric Association acknowledges such, noting that the severity of the loss increases substantially if fifty or more ECT treatments were done on a patient. They did note that longer-term memories return after six to nine months after treatment and the ability for new learning is not impaired, but memory problems continue to persist in many patients.[254]

Dukakis openly acknowledges her troubles with memory loss and says it is the most feared side effect of ECT, in her book *Shock*. For example, she has no memory of a trip she took to Paris with her husband Michael before their thirty-eighth wedding anniversary just before her first ECT treatment. It is only because her husband told her that she knows about the weeklong trip and the lovely restaurants that they went to each night and the places they visited. She presumes that the memory was permanently lost when they channeled electricity into her brain, but acknowledges she would undergo ECT again.[255]

Memory is also the root of karma. Without a memory, karma could not exist. Is there something in the story of ECT therapy reducing memories that speaks to reducing one's karma? Could a modified less harmful version of an electrical burst be used to eliminate some of your karma?

Yes.

Let me begin by repeating the doctrine of the Emerald Tablet: "As above, so below; so below, as above." This means that what is happening in the physical world is similarly occurring in the unseen world. That fact that electric shock removes a person's memories means that it may also be removing a person's karma. Then the question becomes whether there is a way to simulate an electrical shock that is not harmful.

Meditation can reduce your samskaras and in the process lessen your karma. Again, you need to make sure that you are getting a good dose of spiritual nutrition (Cosmic Prana) when you meditate. If you do good, help others, and act selflessly, this intention will begin to merge with your other consciousness and will slowly begin to elevate your being. But a good dose of spiritual nutrition, like a strong gust of wind, will blow off, or burn, some of your samskaras.

Sri Swami Sivananda in speaking about the benefits of meditation describes how by meditating on the infinite with a pure heart one is purified. He says,

In contemplation you are in spiritual contact with the unchanging Light. You are cleansed of all of the impurities. This Light cleanses the soul that touches it…

Meditation acts as a powerful tunic…

The fire of meditation annihilates all foulness due to vice.[256]

To better understand this remember how meditation will attract Cosmic Prana as long as it is done free from the clutches of a negative circle. Cosmic Prana, is a type of prana, or energy. It nourishes your soul; or charges it. Similarly, the Life Force that sustains all of life (what Hinduism calls prana) is an energy that charges your Energy Body. Both the Life Force and Cosmic Prana are energy; and arguably, they power you the way that electricity powers lights and other devices.

If you attract enough Cosmic Prana during meditation, it can begin to burn off your samskaras. Once you become an accomplished meditator, you may begin to notice that recent trivial thoughts, or attitudes, or concerns you had disappear after a long and deep meditation, as if someone had wiped you clean of those impressions. In other words, you may loose a bit of your recent memories.

Deeply embedded samskaras can also disappear over time. When I was meditating for long periods in powerful Fields of Consciousness that contained a much more potent spiritual nutrient than Cosmic Prana (a higher blend of consciousness, less matter/energy), I would often become spacey. I would notice certain memories and even ways of thinking would be eradicated. That was because they were being blown away by my intake of the spiritual nutrients Mother Earth was blessing me with. It was as if whatever was not deeply rooted was swept away. Even some of the deeply rooted ones would eventually be blown away.

The question becomes: are there other ways that you can blow away your memories, or samskaras besides becoming an accomplished meditator meditating in Mother Earth's power spots?

Yes.

One of the other ways to burn off samskaras is through group practices where you collectively draw an immense amount of Cosmic Prana, or some other energy/essence from Mother Earth. A group meditation or other group spiritual activity done in unison with dedication, in earnest, and with the right people, will at minimum, provide you with a good spiritual boost. The group intention and focus will increase the amount of spiritual nutrition that is attracted. In other words, you will get a stronger jolt than if you were practicing the meditation, or activity, by yourself. If you are lucky, it can do much more and can free you of some of your samskaras.

Group spiritual activities, if done free from the clutches of negative circles, can work like magic. I am to the point that a group satsang, where you sing and chant, or a simple group prayer can send me into trance or bliss me out. Group spiritual activities can be powerful.

Sacred Sweat Lodge

The Native American spiritual ceremony of a Sweat Lodge can be a powerful group practice that can burn off your samskaras. The group gathering of saying prayers, chanting/singing, or casting away your issues attracts a lot of spiritual energy. Understandably, and rightly so, Native Americans consider it to be a purification rite, which it is.

A sacred sweat lodge ceremony takes place in some sort of round tepee-like structure that is heated to a high temperature. The ceremony is done in a scared manner, with thought and intent applied to every action. Everything is blessed and revered. Often people are smudged with a smudge stick or a feather before entering the sweat lodge to clean off impurities.

The logs for the sacred fire may be blessed or given thanks to before being burned. The intent of acting in a sacred manner elevates the ceremony.

Rocks are heated in the sacred fire, usually outside of the sweat lodge by the Firekeeper, and brought inside. Water is poured on them, creating steam. Prayers and blessings are given with each round of pouring water on the rocks. The steam adds to the feeling of heat from the rocks.

The steam causes sweating and the purging of toxins. The physical act of sweating reinforces the purging of emotions and other baggage that you may be welling up. It is powerfully purifying at many levels.

Black Elk (Hehaka Sapa, 1863-1950), the Oglala Lakota (Sioux) Holy Man, tells that the rite of purification (sweat lodge) utilizes all the Powers of universe. He said that when water is poured on the rocks participants should think of Wakan-Tanka (Great Spirit).

Black Elk teaches that everything is sacred and is done with intent and purpose, saying "All these things are *Wakan* to us and must be understood deeply if we really wish to purify ourselves, for the power of a thing or an act is in the meaning and the understanding."[257]

In his youth, priests taught Black Elk the sacred lore of the Oglala and the entire history of its ancient religion. His biographer Joseph Eppes Brown notes that he fasted and prayed much and became a wise man; receiving many visions and a special power to be used for good to help his people. Brown felt that this vision haunted Black Elk because he did not know how best to lead his people in the sacred ways. He believed Black Elk confided in him because in doing so, Brown could convey the beauty and truth of the ancient Sioux religion to non-Natives.

I have participated in sweat lodge ceremonies on several occasions. I always found them cathartic and purifying.

It Got Shook Out

Early on in my pilgrimage, I participated in several yogic and pranayama group activities. I would always get blissed out, or intoxicated by the energy that was pulled in by the group. Pranayama is the fourth stage of Patanjali's Yoga and is about the control of prana, or energy.

Pranayama exercises consist of pulling in prana through a variety of breathing exercises, manipulating its flow within your subtle body, or blocking it. Control of our prana internally aids concentration and increases one-pointedness to your focus. Through practice, I got to the point where I was able reverse the movement of prana in the area of my bellybutton. This had the effect of slowing the flow of prana within my subtle body and induced the beginnings of a meditative trance state.[258]

One group class I participated in consisted of a weekend-long instruction, beginning Friday night. We were taught the basics of a few pranayama exercises that would become a medley we were to practice daily. The class would close with the practice of the medley, followed by a group breathing to the voice of the instructor

This was repeated during the Saturday morning and afternoon sessions, as well as the Sunday morning session.

It was in the Sunday afternoon session during the group breathing when I had a profound cathartic mystical experience. The instructor would say "Soooo……Haaaamm. Sooooo……Haaammm…" We were to breathe in on "Soo" and exhale on "Hamm." He would alter the cadence between fast and slow periods while saying the words.

About twenty of us would all be breathing in on "Sooo" and exhaling on "Haammm." We were told it was all right to shout, or cry, or laugh. Whatever urge came to us, we were to let it fly. We would begin in a cross-legged position and finish on our backs, lying on a blanket or yoga mat that we had brought.

It was when I was sitting in the easy pose (cross-legged) that my body began to shake and contort and move in erratic fashion, almost as if I were having some sort of seizure. I was not.

My upper body moved in circles, and would twist and sway. I did not know why I was doing this: all I knew was that it felt right. The contortions, herky-jerky movements, and the twisting and turning continued for some time. I had relinquished control to what was being done to me. It went on for some time and I really got into it.

Years later, a friend who was there said, "That was you?" as if it looked weird or unusual. I imagine that it did.

When I got home later that day, I called my friend and one of my first teachers Mother Angela, whom I met when I was in still living in New York City (having left Wall Street and attending St. Marys Episcopal in West Harlem). She was an active Episcopal Minister at the time.

She immediately asked me if my shaking had stopped. I had recently started to have my arms shake, at times. No, I told her: they were not shaking. She said that the group breathing had probably gotten rid of it.

As I reflected back, it certainly did seem as though my body was trying to expel something; as if something had stuck to my hand and I was shaking my hand to have it fly off.

I would go on to meet others that had similar cathartic, (both physical and psychological) experiences from group breathing. It was amazing to learn how potent and therapeutic a group activity could be.

I would continue to practice the pranayama regiment taught to me for a few years. After a hiatus of several years and developing a strong bond with our Mother, when I next participated in the group breathing, I did not feel the best.

See your spiritual pilgrimage as being like the Odyssey, with you being Ulysses looking to return home to his beloved Penelope. Always keep moving on and learning from your experiences, and try not to dwell with one exercise/ religion/ practice for too long, if possible. I practiced pranayama for years and then I got connected to Mother Earth. Yes, you should stick with meditation and with a particular group if you feel so inclined, but try to move on as much as you can.

Participate in a Group Spiritual Activity

A good dose of spiritual nutrition will go a long way to helping you clear your samskaras and karma. This is not to say that all you need to do is meditate or participate in group activities that attract a lot of energy to be enlightened. Rather, it is to reinforce and drive home the fact that removing yourself from negative circles and developing a strong bond with our Mother will go a long way in facilitating your spiritual evolution. That is because, just as you need protein to build muscle and calcium to build strong bones, you need spiritual nutrition to feed your soul and elevate your consciousness.

A group activity such as a group meditation is a great activity to supplement your spiritual regiment. It can help remove some of your baggage.

A group activity is also a wonderful way to increase the vibe of space. Start a group meditation with some friends and take turns meditating in each other's homes. The increased draw of Cosmic Prana to a space will help clear it and elevate it.

No doubt you need to act altruistically, be compassionate and loving and bear witness. These are all important characteristics that you need to foster within yourself. But a good dose of Mother Earth from a group activity can help work wonders.

Get our there and give Her a big hug.

15. The Great Cleansing

Saint John of the Cross (1542-1591), a Spanish Carmelite priest coined the term "dark night of the soul" to describe the spiritual road that the soul must travel on to "arrive at the state of the perfect, which is that of the Divine Union of the soul with God."[259] Dark: meaning it is challenging, arguably tormenting, as one is expunged and purified of their deficiencies. From our perspective I would say of their karma and its tendencies (vasanas).

John of the Cross detailed the journey of the dark night and its travails in his book *Dark Night of the Soul*.[260] He felt that it was only God that could guide one through the dark night:

> However greatly the soul labors, it cannot actively purify itself so as to be in the least degree prepared for the Divine union of perfection of love, if God takes not its hand and purges it in that dark fire." (Bk. I. Ch III.iii)

He gives several sins that must purged such as pride, avarice, spiritual gluttony, and more. He believed that "spiritual persons suffer great trials." (Bk. I. Ch X.i)

The goal of the dark night is "drawing forth the soul from a life of sense into that of spirit." (Bk. I. Ch X.i) In other words, the purification of the soul is an extremely painful, grueling, and tormenting experience. It is a purgatory where one is cleansed and purged by the dark spiritual fire of love. (Bk. II. Ch.XII.i)

The Great Cleansing Begins

After some journeying on your spiritual pilgrimage, you should begin to face challenges and traumas. This is the beginning of the great purging and purifying of your soul when you begin to burn off your samskaras and karma as you move closer to becoming an evolved soul. Your dark night has begun.

If you have been doing good and meditating in earnest, you should at some point begin to navigate your boat through troubled waters. It is as inevitable as the rising of the sun. If everything is still hunky dory, peachy keen, and beautiful after seriously meditating daily for a few years, as well as acting and thinking lovingly, then something is amiss, and most likely you have not been getting enough spiritual nutrition.

If this is so, then you need to examine your circles and meditative practices. A particular circle in your life could be blocking the flow of spiritual nutrition to your soul. Or your meditative technique could be behind your blockage. You may, for example, be practicing meditation regularly using an established mainline religion's technique or doctrine, and it could be responsible for holding you back.

You also need to do some serious soul searching and make sure you are fully committed to the path ahead because the journey is going to get much more difficult. Trauma, depression, sleepless nights, and worse might not be what you bargained for. So, make sure that you are up to it. If not, and all you want is the mental benefits that come with meditation, then practice meditating in the clutches of a negative circle.

If you are committed to your spiritual transformation you need to make sure you are getting enough spiritual nutrition. It is your absorption of spiritual nutrition, coupled with loving acts, that will elevate your consciousness to lofty levels, the same way protein builds muscle.

Meditation is important, because like ECT, it can help accelerate the burning off of samskaras that are holding you back. Just like ECT, you can loose memories, get spacey, or even experience headaches, vomiting, etc.

When challenges, tests, and traumas begin, take a step back with a break from your spiritual practice. Make it a mini-vacation and use it to reaffirm your commitment to your path. You need to make sure that you are committed to becoming a better, more loving, giving and caring person; because your journey is about to get progressively more difficult and challenging the farther you walk your path.

I would suggest thanking God for getting you to this point; a good practice to maintain as you progress on your journey forward. Because it is God that will be helping guide you, and the more able you are to see your dark night as a blessing, the better able you will be to cope with its challenges.

We Are Always Burning Off Karma

You are always burning off karma. Most of it has been acquired recently. Some has been percolating for a long time, possibly several lifetimes. Or you may have chosen to take on someone else's karma to learn.

Former monk turned psychotherapist and author Thomas Moore believes that we have all been through several dark nights of the soul. They are events like a difficult marriage, a child in trouble, betrayal by a lover or business partner, or going through a divorce, grieving the loss of a spouse or parent, or even finding yourself caught in a tenacious and terrible mood. Moore noted that:

> For some people, these situations are problems to be solved, but for others they are the source of deep despair. A true dark night of the soul is not a surface challenge but a development that takes you away from the joy of your ordinary life. An external event or an internal mood strikes you at the core of your existence. This is not just a feeling but a rupture in your very being, and it may take a long while to get through to the other end of it.[261]

Moore sees the dark night as a process that can transform you in ways you would have never imagined. Because in the dark place, you question who your are, what the world is, what do you fear... Educating us that you learn more about the depths of your soul from periods of pain and confusion and feeling that something of your makeup comes to an end during your dark night—your ego, your self, your creativeness, your meaning.[262] It is a rite of passage.

Moore's *Dark Night of the Soul, A Guide to Finding Your Way Through Life's Ordeals* is divided into three parts, two of which (Disturbances and Degradations) go into detail about dealing with specific types of dark nights (such as lovesickness) and deep-rooted emotions (such as anger and more).

Moore gained national recognition when his book *Care of the Soul* became a NY Times bestseller in 1992. Its goal is not to solve problems, but help you to see the sacredness in ordinary life, giving it depth and meaning.[263] Moore has written several books since then, most focusing on the soul.

The Climb Begins

As your dark night begins you start hitting some rocky and challenging times. These are only going to increase in frequency and intensity and will become more traumatic the further you move along. You may never totally travel to the end of your dark night in this lifetime. You may not survive.

Dr. Willoughby Britton is a trained neuroscientist and instructor of Mindfulness-Based Stress Therapy and Mindfulness-Based Cognitive Therapy. After her own personal trauma following a meditation retreat and seeing two people taken to the hospital after an intense meditative practice, she decided to investigate.

She began interviewing people and found that a number of them had all sorts of offbeat and sometimes trying experiences after they began meditating. Soon, along with her husband Jared R Lindahl, a religious studies scholar, they started The Clinical and Affective Neuroscience Laboratory (CLANlab) at Brown University.

Here are a few testimonials from the from some of the people that they interviewed:[264]

> I was very calm and then, all of a sudden, the deepest, the most intense fear I had ever had an experience of in my entire life gripped me.
>
> I started to do a lot of shamatha meditations and I started to have little flashback memories of sexual abuse and other abuse issues that were incredibly frightening.
>
> Nine years on and off periods of deep depression, angst, anxiety and misery.

Dr. Britton also found that memory loss was quite common with respondents. For example, one respondent stated:

> The meditation I was doing was really confusing my mind's ability to access memory, including the most basic things: looking at a stoplight and seeing the color come up, but then having to think "but what does this mean again?"

Not surprisingly, many of the cases Dr. Britton studied occurred after, or during, a meditation retreat when a group of people were meditating together. She herself had an episode after a group meditation. This again reinforces how beneficial group meditations and other collective spiritual activities can be in increasing the spiritual potency of the activity by drawing more spiritual nutrition.

Like John of the Cross, your dark night is about making you more like spirit and moving closer to God. The goal is to have you flowing over with Christ consciousness.

Realize that you are moving into rarified air. The greatest sages, mystics, and teachers that have ever lived have traveled this same path that you are now beginning.

There is no manual: no guide to lead you step by step. How could there be? Your path was specifically designed for you. It is your karma, your samskaras, unique to you, that need to be burned off. It is what you need to become more loving, giving, selfless, more...

Your teacher, your own guide, is within you. It has always been there and now it will be taking the lead.

Challenges, Calamities and Crises

You may, or may not, have life-changing events while you are traversing your dark night; things like the loss of a parent or loved one, bankruptcy, being arrested or a major health problem. Again: what happens to you will be a function of your karma and what you need to work on.

Saint Teresa of Ávila, also called Saint Teresa of Jesus (1515 –1582), was a compatriot of John of the Cross. She was a Spanish mystic who practiced contemplation and was known for her mystical writings. In 1535, Teresa entered the Carmelite order and about a year later was stricken by a mysterious illness. It was during that period she began to practice mental prayer rather than oral recitation, to guide her.[265] Years later she would begin to have visions and other mystical experiences.

Teresa's contemplative life and focus on spirituality spurred her to reform her Carmelite order, which she saw as more worldly, with its unenclosed chambers that encouraged visitors and its lack of solitude and prayer. She also wanted to provide guidance in the contemplative life, particularly to women, which was so lacking in her training. In 1562 she started a monastery in Avila modeled after the Desert Hermits.

After meeting John of the Cross in 1567, Teresa persuaded him to join the new Discalced Carmelites. A year later, a monastery for John and other men was built in in Duruelo, not far from Avila.[266]

The Great Cleansing

Sixteenth century Spain was a harsh time. The Inquisition was suspicious of spirituality and mental prayer, feeling that the focus should be more on doctrine rather than experience. Biographer Gillian T. W. Ahlgren, writing on Teresa's challenges in *Teresa of Avila and the Politics of Sanctity*, notes that the Inquisition played a huge role in Teresa's life, particularly her writings.[267] They would denounce her at least six times. Teresa's books were scrutinized, and she was asked to rewrite several sections of some of them.

In 1576, several inquisitors visited the Carmelites to search for information on Teresa and others who were accused of having unusual mystical experiences. Teresa would be asked to give two accounts of her life and describe her mystical experiences in detail. Ahlgren notes the acts of the others were slight in comparison to those of Teresa's "continual levitations, predictions and recurring visions. Teresa's physical manifestations in prayer were disruptive to the entire religious community."[268] Evidently, both Teresa and John could levitate, and supposedly did so together, at times.

In February of 1577, three Carmelite nuns were found guilty, but Teresa was exonerated; however, she was confined to one of her convents for a time. This did not stop the persecution of others around Teresa. Later that year, fifty-five nuns were excommunicated because they had voted for Teresa to be their prioress at the Convent of the Incarnation.

On December 2nd of 1577, men broke into John of the Cross's residence at Incarnation and abducted him and another friar and took them to the monastery in Toledo. John would be beaten because he refused to denounce Teresa. He was fed only bread and water and an occasional sardine. He underwent regular floggings and was eventually placed in solitary confinement in a tiny cell with only a slit in the wall for air and light. After nine months of captivity, John escaped.[269]

It was during this period of great persecution that John began to write his greatest works, *The Dark Night* and *The Spiritual Canticle*, memorizing them in his mind.

Teresa and John not only show how hardship can be part of and even lead the charge during a dark night experience, but also of the courage to speak truth to power to bring a circle back in line (in this case the Catholic Church). While they suffered greatly for their reform efforts, they were eventually revered for their work. They also sought to get closer to God and found great solace in prayer during their hardship, underscoring that bearing witness is a spiritual experience.

One of the more inspiring testaments of hardship leading to spiritual transformation is the story of Etty Hillesum, a Dutch Jew who died in a Nazi concentration camp. In the face of incredible cruelty and inhumanity, she was transformed and found God. We know this because of a diary she began keeping as a twenty-seven-year-old women on March 8, 1941.

Biographer Patrick Woodhouse tells that the early pages of Etty's diary show her to be "an insecure, emotionally disturbed and sexually chaotic young woman struggling with a turbulent life which she cannot understand and which from time to time pitches her into deep depression."[270]

Etty describes herself being, "deep down something like a tightly-wound ball of twine binds me relentlessly, and at times I am nothing more or less than a miserable, frightened creature." (March 9, 1941)[271]

Fortunately, Etty had recently met Julius Spier, a psychochirologist or hand reader, that had apprenticed with Carl Jung for two years. He would be one of the catalysts of change, along with others in Etty's life. All the while, her transformation was taking place against the backdrop of increased hostility and the persecution of Jews by Nazis.

The turn would take time. She writes, "[m]ortal fear in every fiber. Complete collapse. Lack of self-confidence. Aversion. Panic." (November 10, 1941)

Yet, later that evening she would write, "God, take me by Your hand, I shall follow You dutifully, and not resist too much. I shall evade none of the tempests life has in store for me, I shall try to face it all as best I can." The next day she talks about loving your neighbor and among other things says, "I have come to realize that on those days when you are at odds with your neighbors, you are really at odds with yourself."[272]

One must wonder whether Etty had hit bottom and was beginning to be transformed.

A few weeks later, she writes, "I kneel once more on the rough coconut matting, my hands over my eyes and pray: "Oh, Lord, let me feel at one with myself. Let me perform a thousand daily tasks with love, but let every one spring from a greater central core of devotion and love."[273] Initially challenged to kneel down and pray, she would later say she was forced down on the ground to kneel by some force greater than herself.[274] She called herself the "girl who could not kneel" on several occasions.

On July 11th of 1942 she writes of Jews being exterminated in gas chambers and being buried alive. But instead of fleeing on July 14th, she volunteers for the Jewish Council, writing,

> I simply cannot make active preparations to save myself, it seems pointless to me and would make me nervous and unhappy…For once you have begun to walk with God, you need only keep on walking with Him and all of life becomes one long stroll—such a marvelous feeling…I hate no one. I am not embittered. And once the love of mankind has germinated in you, it will grow without measure. (July 14, 1942)

At the end of July, Etty volunteered to accompany the first group of people sent to Westerbork, an internment camp for Jewish people before they were be sent off to an extermination camp. She tells of the overcrowding, the anxiety, and the overall deplorable conditions at Westerbork. She also tells how she had a hand in helping to keep someone off of the transport to be sent to extermination.[275] (July 5, 1943) While some of her diary entries mention God and scripture, Etty's focus turns more on daily life and the people she encounters.

Etty died at Auschwitz on November 30, 1943.

Tools to Navigate Your Dark Night

Your dark night is unique to you. All I can do is offer you some overall advice.

Understand what is going on. Realizing that you are going through a dark night of the soul is incredibly helpful. It took some time before I realized that I was not crazy and was going through a dark night. Still, the trauma was almost unbearable at times. There is a benefit and consolation in knowing what is going on.

Get rid of your day job. Having a 9 to 5 job can become next to impossible during a dark night. There may be long periods of time when you cannot sleep or are gripped in overwhelming terror. If you are going to work, you need to have some flexibility in your job.

Bear witness to your mind. You need to be able to observe your thoughts. Earlier, I had talked about learning to observe and control your thoughts. This skill can be invaluable during a dark night. You may face moments as if your mind was a car and someone had taken control of it and started driving recklessly and there was nothing you could do about it. Being able to observe and realize what is going on can be incredibly helpful.

Embrace it. See your dark night as gift to grow spiritually and grow closer to God. See it as a blessing

Read self-help, or therapy books, or even see a therapist. I am not a therapist, but suggest reading Moore's (and similar books by others) for help facing the challenges of a dark night. You might want to seek counsel to help you overcome an issue.

Be Inspired. Read inspirational stories of people that overcame incredible challenges—Saints, NDEs, etc.

Your Dark Night Accelerates

The dark night is like a mountain climb that gets progressively steeper and more challenging the higher your climb. Then, at some point it goes vertical, close to the top, with false peaks with deep dips. Like a hiker carrying too much, you start leaving items behind to lighten your load, but you are discarding parts of yourself, changing others.

At some point these changes will reach a crescendo. Trauma becomes a living nightmare that never ends as you do your dance with death to get rid of what keeps you from evolving—deep ingrained character flaws, vasanas built over many lifetimes, acts created in the past, and more.

What would have taken many more lives and reincarnations to work through are thrust upon you and crammed into your life for a period lasting a few years to decades. It is intense.

It is said that before you can get over an issue in your life, it makes one last stand (appearance, in this case) and fights with a veracity you have never seen before. Like a rat trapped in a corner, it is fighting to save its life and not be expunged from you. Although I had issues with alcohol and binge drinking for much of my life, I never joined AA, or had a life-changing bender. I imagine that hitting rock bottom is where you are continually bouncing off of your worst times on a continual basis, with each fall worse than before. This is sort of phenomenon that you will be facing.

As Joseph Campbell teaches:
It is by going down into the abyss
that we recover the treasures of life.
Where you stumble,
there lies your treasure.
The very cave you are afraid to enter
turns out to be the source of
what you are looking for.
The damned thing in the cave
that was so dreaded
has become the center.[276]

During the height of a dark night, you may begin to think that God has abandoned you. You may feel like hope has kicked you in the teeth and sucked out whatever optimism you may have had for the future. Despair, depression, and loneliness become like old drinking buddies from the day that have come to live with you and refuse to go. Torment will become like a sharply bristled brush that you continually rake over your soul for extended periods. Whatever phobia, fear, anger, insecurity, coldness, and other issues you have are now going to be rerun over and over again in your life, increasing in veracity with each successive visit.

Both Buddha and Jesus had intense, dark night experiences before they began their respective ministries. Buddha achieved Enlightenment while meditating under the Bodhi tree. But before he achieved Enlightenment, Mara visited him and tempted him with sensual pleasures and violence and mocked him. Some say Mara was a demon, others believe that Mara represented the negative qualities in all of us that need to be expunged.

Soon after defeating Mara Buddha achieved Enlightenment.

Similarly, Jesus spent forty days in the wilderness before beginning his ministry. After getting baptized by John the Baptist, Jesus was led by Spirit into the desert for a forty-day fast. After not eating for forty days, Jesus became hungry. The devil came to him and told him to turn stones into bread to eat. He refused. Then the devil took him to the highest point of a temple and told him to jump and said that angels would save him. Again Jesus refused, saying one should not test God. Finally, the Devil took him to a mountain and told Jesus that he will be given all that he saw if he worshipped him. Again, Jesus refuses.

Each year, Christianity honors Jesus' forty day fast with Lent. Beginning on Ash Wednesday, forty days before Easter Sunday, Christians are asked to fast, give something up, and prepare for Easter Sunday.

The temptations of Buddha and Jesus underscore the role of the dark night in our spiritual transformation. Notice also that both had their experiences in a state of solitude in Nature, where they were by themselves.

Kundalini, or Dark Night?

We get another glimpse of the dark night through the autobiography of Gopi Krishna (1903-1984), *Kundalini, The Evolutionary Energy in Man*,[277] an Indian spiritual seeker and social reformer who advocated for Women's Rights. In 1937 at the age of thirty-four, after seventeen years of meditating, he had a profound mystical experience while meditating:

Suddenly, with a roar like that of a waterfall, I felt a stream of liquid light entering my brain through the spinal cord.

Entirely unprepared for such a development, I was completely taken by surprise...The illumination grew brighter and brighter, the roaring louder, I experienced a rocking sensation and then felt myself slipping out of my body, entirely enveloped in a halo of light.

Little did I realize that from that day onwards I was never to be my old normal self again.[278]

Gopi noted that the days that followed were like a 'prolonged nightmare.' He felt the continual burn of energy within himself causing excruciating pain; as if burning pins were piercing and blistering his body and organs. His joy of meditation disappeared, and after being a good sleeper his whole life, he became an insomniac. His appetite disappeared. He was in a continuous state of high anxiety and tension. His heart beat spasmodically and he was not sure if it was going to stop, or even burst.

Gopi Krishna believed that he had awakened the Kundalini Energy in his spine; but that it had traversed up the wrong nerve to the top of his head, and that was why he was having all of his horrible experiences. Adherents of Kundalini Yoga believe that Enlightenment comes when the Kundalini Energy in the base of your spine rises to the top of your head, or what many refer to as your Crown Chakra.

In his Introduction to Gopi Krishna's autobiography Interreligious Studies professor, Frederic Spiegelberg, compared being exposed to Gopi's experiences to that of meeting a space traveler to a distant star who did not have the proper equipment and was reporting about the "bewildering landscape" around him, with no idea of what it meant. He felt that Gopi had a Samadhi-like experience, or achieved a very high Yogic state, based entirely on the development of his inner feelings, and was not guided by any tradition.

Having met with Carl Jung, Gopi Krishna is well known by Jungian scholars. One of them, James Hillman (1926-2011), wrote an insightful analysis of Gopi's experiences that is accompanied in Gopi's autobiography, saying:

We may gain a glimpse of how Enlightenment can be accounted for psychologically…. The flow of this psychic energy in its totality is the entire psychological self, or the Self. When the partial system of the ego is released to, identifies with, or is overwhelmed by, the self, an experience of Enlightenment ensues. This is what Gopi Krishna describes. The immersion of the ego in this stream of light is a common theme of religious mysticism, and also of psychopathological derangement.[279]

Hillman notes that Gopi's fear of madness, the inner workings of his deranged mind viewed outside of religious circles and within psychiatry, would be classified as a psychotic experience. Hillman's comments are reminiscent of Aldous Huxley's view that a schizophrenic is like a person under mescaline all the time.

Gopi felt that this force of energy, which he had no control over and was only a witness to, was altering his body, organs, and mind. The absence of bliss and beauty that was supposed to accompany such mystical experiences made him doubt its validity. Hillman compared it to the suffering that the Desert Hermits talked of, and thought it was signaling a new birth.

Among other traumas, Gopi often found himself at night looking with dread at horribly disfigured faces and distorted forms bending and twisting into various shapes. Hillman points out that Homer, Virgil, and Dante describe similar phenomena when their hero descended into Hades. It is part of their journey. Noting the appearance of these horrific faces "reminds heroic consciousness that there are still shadows in the cave even if one has seen the light oneself. The psyche is separable; even if 'I' have moved, there are some tormented 'me's' left behind in hell."[280]

After three years Gopi Krishna's perpetual torment would come to an end. He would have longs bouts of trauma, but felt as though he was gradually improving. After twelve years he was restored and blessed with spiritual gifts such as seeing auras, and could enter higher states of consciousness.

Hillman tells that we cannot be but enormously impressed with Gopi's death experience, noting that it has to be a totally real and believable experience if we are to have a rebirth experience. It is the terror and threatening aspect of it that gives it the conviction of reality.

Hillman concludes:

> Our author's experiences, he tells us, are possible in varying forms to everyone. Furthermore, they are teleologically meant for everyone. Our task is to incarnate the Gods within. Having seen this as the result of decades of wrestling with himself and these Gods, he can give us a golden vision of how things not only might be, but are meant to be.[281]

My Dark Night

While I started meditating in the late 1990s I would meditate two times a day for about a total of forty to sixty minutes per day. In April of 2005 I began an aggressive spiritual program to achieve the meditative state of Samadhi. I would spend eight to ten hours a day doing yoga and pranayama, meditating, praying, doing mental exercises, and reading sacred texts.

It took some time to be able to meditate for a few hours at a clip. Initially I would get nauseous at times. Looking back at those early days of getting sick, it was probably a good indication that I was getting enough spiritual nutrition.

Although I did a variety of meditations, my main meditation practice was concentration. As I noted earlier, I selected a flower to be the object of my meditation.

In October, my program came to an end. From then on I would meditate a minimum of two hours daily, and usually about four to six hours a day.

The Great Cleansing

In the spring of 2006 I began to meditate regularly at serious power places (Fields of Consciousness), so I was getting high doses of spiritual nutrition. I would spend several days a week at such places, meditating most of the day.

I began having sleep issues. While fear had been part of my life, it became much more intense. These fears grew over the years during my dark night and at times I found myself totally gripped by fear, with occasional panic attacks. Anger was there as well, but was much less of an issue.

My past life started to regularly play out in front of me. It began with a trip down memory lane when I had not been my better self; times when I acted selfishly; or my actions hurt others; or when I was inconsiderate, or….I would spend a few hours, a few days, or a few weeks facing them: and then I would move onto the next issue.

Over time, I was able to go into deep states of meditation where I had no sense of my body and felt totally separate from it. At the same time, meditation that had been a great joy and a respite from my regular existence began to disappear. It was as if heaven had turned into hell. It also seemed that God was much more distant.

After a few years, I realized I was going through a dark night of the soul. I read several books and researched about the dark night. Unfortunately, I found no books to guide me.

Insomnia and terror would continue to haunt me.

Overcoming my struggles with growing up during my teenage and adolescent years and issues with drugs gave me a resolve and confidence that I could face and persevere over any challenge. Several long periods of unemployment after getting my MBA only strengthened my resolve; albeit those were traumatic times. This resolve, this rock within me, that I can overcome any challenge, was shattered by the sledgehammer of my dark night. How could this be?

All of my angst gave me high blood pressure. In the summer of 2011 I was prescribed several medications to take. The playback of my life continued.

Things began changing in the summer of 2012. I walked close to a cliff and felt no fear—very strange, because I had acrophobia my whole life. I assumed that my dark night had purged my acrophobia.

Interestingly, earlier that year, I had taken a job at our local SEARS selling appliances, which forced a sharp cutback in the amount of time I spent meditating daily.

In September of 2012, after almost eight years of long daily meditations, my effort to achieve Samadhi hit a temporary roadblock (or maybe I was flirting with it?) After going into deep trance where my body shut down, as my consciousness began returning to my body and the Earth Plane, my heartbeat became wildly irregular. Two days later, I went back into deep meditation, and as I got into trance my heart rate became normal until I lost contact with my body. As I was returning, I counted my heartbeat at ten or maybe fifteen beats a minute; then it became wildly irregular. Did my heart stop, or did it just slow someplace between zero to ten beats per minute? A few days later I went off of one of my high blood pressure medications, Norvasc, that I was prescribed a year earlier. Almost immediately my heartbeat began returning to normal.

I stopped meditating. All of the trauma and stress of my heart brought back the fear and terror that I had beaten back. Fortunately, over time I was slowly able to push them back again.

Then, in the summer of 2014, I was working five to six days, trying finish one book (*Vortices and Spirals*) and starting another one (*Sacred Sites*), and noticed I was getting fatigued at times, not because of a lack of sleep, but rather, I was just flat-out tired and worn out. Then, a little after Independence Day, I could not sleep one night, and then I could not sleep the following night, and…

A few days without sleep can literally drive you crazy, or least cause you to be paranoid and fearful. The terror and fear that I had experienced a few years earlier was now back, stronger and nastier than before. I felt as though I had relinquished control of myself to fear and paranoia. All I could do is be a witness and tell myself that is was fear, and not I, running things. It was this ability to witness my mind that helped me overcome this period in my life, and why I encourage you develop the ability to bear witness to your thoughts.

A hypnotist I went to for my insomnia persuaded me to start meditating again. Slowly, over time I was able to work myself out of my abyss of fear and terror.

A few years later, I stopped meditating again. I have found that the longer I stick with a regimen of meditating, that mystical experiences can become regular happenstance at any time.

I still have my life playing out within me, only now I focus on times when my thinking was less than noble.

I continue to be interested in achieving the meditative state of Samadhi because I believe it can help me with my work; but I wonder how much time I should spend in meditation. I do meditate periodically. But I find that the mild sense of bliss I experience much of the time after connecting with our Mother can accelerate to the point to where I become an observer in my life. It is as if I am watching a movie, which can accelerate to the point that I feel like someone is about to change the channel.

I also learned that not only does Samadhi possibly remove all of your karma, but it might also bring an end to your existence on the Earth Plane, the big circle we call reality. Sri Ramakrishna says such:

> Generally the body does not remain alive after the attainment of Samadhi. The only exceptions are sages like Narada, who live in order to bring spiritual light to others. It is also true of Divine Incarnations, like Chaitanya. After the well is dug one generally throws away the spade and the basket. But some keep them in order to help their neighbors. The great souls who retain their bodies after Samadhi feel compassion for the suffering of others. They are not so selfish as to be satisfied with their own illumination.[282]

In his autobiography Carl Jung said that:

> A man who has not passed through the inferno of his passions has never overcome them. They then dwell in the house next door, and at any moment a flame may dart out and set fire to his own house. Whenever we give up, leave behind, and forget too much, there is always the danger that the things we have neglected will return with added force."[283]

We are here to learn and be transformed. At some point, in this lifetime or one in the future, you will face your own dark night of the soul. It is inevitable.

PS. You may never go through a dark night in this lifetime. My writing about its trauma and agony may repel you and cause you to stop meditating.

I have wanted to write about the dark night for some time. Just as we are ignorant of how karma connects us and transcends time, we are similarly ignorant of the dark night. I hope this helps those of you that might traverse your own dark night in this lifetime.

16. You are Never Alone

I began this book with an epigraph:
> The question is not whether a tree makes a sound if no one is around to hear it fall. It does because that is a given. The question is why did the tree fall and what are the ramifications?
> That is because the Great Law of Karma connects everyone and everything that has ever been and that will ever be.

This came to me during a contemplative hike when I was drafting the outline for this book. It was evident that not only does everything have karma, but also that karma transcends time and links everyone and everything together.

It was also a criticism, arguably a rebuke, of one of the great philosophical questions of our time about the importance of observation and perception. The query is credited to philosopher Bishop George Berkeley (1685-1743).

The tree falling question is also reflection of our time. It speaks to ego and the importance humanity places upon itself. Would a nearby deer have been startled hearing the tree fall, or a mouse, or a butterfly?

It also makes a statement about the importance of material existence in our world today. If we cannot hear it (or touch it, see it, feel it, smell it), it does not exist.

You know that the falling tree exists and that it may well have a bearing on you in some way.

Is Karma a Law?

I also stated that karma was a law. Is it? No, I think that there is something much more to karma that we cannot comprehend.

Earlier, I quoted Meher Baba on how samskaras limit out view: "*samskaras* or impressions form an enclosure around the possible field of consciousness. The circle of *samskaras* constitutes that limited area in which alone the individual consciousness can be focused." In other words, we are getting limited glimpses of karma, prejudiced by our perspective. This limited perspective has also jaundiced our view about karma.

Karma is a teacher. It is our partner through many lifetimes, helping us with our spiritual transformation, to become more loving, compassionate, and altruistic. Many outside of the Eastern Traditions dismiss karma as being impersonal and a cold indifferent enforcer of retribution. Karma is anything but. It is intimate and personal and involved with the most sacred of duties—the transformation of our evolving soul.

Yes, there will be pain as you are confronted with the same challenges over and over again until you learn your lesson. Those challenges and deficiencies will disappear as you move closer to the divine.

Earlier, I said Karma was a memory. However, what I probably should have said is that karma, or samskaras, are the root of memory. That is because memory exists to facilitate the working of karma—without karma there could be no memory. Remember: each thought, intention and emotion we have and every action we undertake creates a samskara, or impression. That is how memory is created.

By understanding that memories are created to serve karma, this expands our view of karma and shows how pervasive karma is.

Karma transcends time and connects to our many past lives and carries us forward into our future lives. It also links us to our collective past through what Jung calls our collective unconscious and what Sheldrake calls morphic resonance.

Perhaps it is our prejudices about time, developed ever since the world began, that limits our ability to fully understand karma. Karma connects everyone and everything that has ever been and that will ever be. It transcends time

We can say that karma is a memory that remains vibrant, interacting with everything that it comes in contact with as it travels through time, carrying forward the imprints of what has been and what will be, and altering itself along the way. What does it say about time?

I think it is our concept of time that limits our understanding of karma. We see it as being linear. I can tell you full well that I have transcended time on several occasions when I mediated in Energy Vortices and connected with the spirit of its creator(s). It was as if I had entered a time warp, or time machine, and was hurled back in time. I have also been blessed to have seen the future, on occasion.

Seeing God

I am sure that many of you had trouble accepting parts of what I have said, from the concept that karma connects everyone and everything to that it transcends time; or that you are responsible for the actions of others. We have been so indoctrinated to see the world solely through how it affects us that we cannot imagine that we are responsible for the actions of others; or even what has transpired in the past.

To me, it speaks of God, because it is all God; and all of us have at some time had difficulty seeing, albeit accepting God.

For example, people ask how is sadism, pedophilia, murder, and cruelty possible in a world with a loving God? Or genocide?

The story that has helped me come to grips with atrocities and cruelties is Chapter 11 of the Gita, where Krishna reveals him/herself to Arjuna.

It starts when Arjuna asks Krishna to show him his/her immortal self:

Behold, Arjuna, a million divine forms, with an
Infinite variety of color and shape. Behold the gods
of the natural world, and many more wonders never
revealed before. Behold the entire cosmos turning
within my body, and other things you desire to see. (11.5-7)

But Arjuna cannot see these things with his ordinary eyes, so Krishna gives him spiritual vision.

Arjuna saw an infinite number of faces, countless miracles and incredible weapons. The sight of Krishna drives Arjuna to ecstasy and sends his hair standing on end. He tells Krishna,

If a thousand suns were to rise in the heavens
at the same time, the blaze of their light would
resemble the splendor of that spirit. (11.12)

He sees creatures of all kinds, as well as an infinite number of mouths, arms, stomachs and eyes, and a multitude of forms.

As Arjuna's vision continues, he begins to become fearful. He sees all those gathered on the battlefield rushing to Krishna's jaws to be crushed by his/her gnashing teeth. He asks Krishna to reveal again his/her normal self and not the infinite number of body parts and soul. Fear leaves Arjuna as Krishna returns to his normal form.

To me, this passage speaks to the challenge of seeing God whether it be seeing God in others or accepting cruelty in the world. How can this be?

This is a challenge that we all need to acccpt and will keep confronting on our path. When I realized the implications of everything having karma and how circles can block spiritual nutrition, I became upset and arguably angry, wondering whether we (humankind) have been on a treadmill going nowhere for some time. Worse, we were doing so because we lacked the knowledge about how karma connects everyone and everything.

Over time, I began to accept that there was a reason for this and that I should have faith in what God was doing. It was the story of Arjuna being unable to behold God that helped me come to grips with my anger towards God, as it has done on other occasions before—this time it took a little longer.

Oneness

Oneness, that we are interconnected to each other and to all of creation, is a big concept that many of us believe and talk about. Unfortunately we continually revert back to how we have been programmed to see the world—through ourselves.

I hope that this book has given you the knowledge to overcome that urge, that samskara, and better understand and work with our interconnectedness to make a better world. You are never alone. Although our paths may be different, we are all on this journey together.

We are the keepers of all of creation.

We need each other. Because when we lift up others, we lift up ourselves. In doing so, we make ourselves more whole.

I have planted a seed thought with the knowledge contained within this book. I ask you to please water it so that it may blossom into something wonderful that we cannot even begin to imagine at this time.

WE ARE ONE.

Bibliography

Gillian T. W. Ahlgren, *Teresa of Avila and the Politics of Sanctity*, Cornell University Press, Ithaca, New York. 1996.

Mirra Alfassa (The Mother) & Sri Aurobindo, *The Psychic Being, Soul, It's nature, Mission and Evolution,* Lotus Press, Twin Lakes, Wisconsin, 1999.

Saul Alinsky, *Rules for Radicals, A Pragmatic Prime for Realistic Radicals*, Random House, New York, New York, 1971.

Anonymous, *The Way of the Pilgrim and The Pilgrim Continues His Way*, Olga Savin(Trans), Shambhala Classics, Boston, Massachusetts, 2001.

Stephen, Arroyo, *Astrology Karma & Transformation, The Inner Dimensions of the Birth Chart*, CRCS Publications, Davis, California, 1978

PMH Atwater, *Beyond the Light, What Isn't Being Said About the Near Death Experience*, Birch Lane Press, New York, New York, 1994.

Meher Baba, *Discourses*, Volume I Sixth Ed (1967) Avatar Meher Baba Trust eBook June 2011. www. ambppct. org/ Book_Files/ Discourses%20Vol%20I. pdf

Meher Baba, *God Speaks, The theme of Creation and Its Purpose*, Dodd, Mead & Company, New York, New York. 1973.

Alick Bartholomew, *Hidden Nature, The Startling Insights of Viktor Schauberger*, Adventures Unlimited Press, Kempton, Illinois, 2005.

The Bhagavad Gita, Translated by Eknath Easwaran, Nilgiri Press, The Blue Mountain Press, Tomales, California. 2001, 1985.

H. P. Blavatsky, *The Key to Theosophy, An Abridgement*; Edited by Joy Mills; Quest Publishing, Wheaton, Illinois, 1992.

Joseph Eppes Brown, *The Sacred Pipe, Black Elk's Account of the Seven Rites of the Oglala Sioux*, Norman, University of Oklahoma Press, Oklahoma, .1967, 1953 C.

James Burke & Robert Ornstein, *The Axemaker's Gift—A Double Edged History of Human Culture*; G. P. Putnam's Son, New York, New York, 1995.

Nicholas Carr, *The Shallows, What the Internet is Doing to Our Brains*, W. W. Norton & Co, New York, New York, 2010.

Edgar Cayce, *Edgar Cayce on Reincarnation*, by Noel Langley and Hugh Lynn Cayce, Warner Books, New York, New York, 1988, 1968c.

Callum Coats, *Living Energies: An Exposition of Concepts Related to the Theories of Viktor Schauberger*, Gill & MacMillan, Dublin, Ireland, 2001.

Harold G. Coward, *Jung and Eastern Thought*, State University of Albany Press, Albany, New York, 1985.

Kitty Dukakis and Larry Tye; *Shock, The Healing Power of Electroconvulsive Therapy*, Penguin Group, New York, New York, 2006.

Eknath Easwaran, *Gandhi the Man, How One Man Changed Himself to Change the World*, Nilgiri Press, Tomales, California, 2011, 1972 C.

Masaru Emoto, *The Shape of Love*, Doubleday, New York, New York, 2007.

Matthew Fox and Rupert Sheldrake, *Natural Grace, Dialogues on Creation, Darkness, and the Soul in Spirituality and Science*, Doubleday, New York, NY 1996

Mahatma Gandhi, *The Gospel of Selfless Action, or, The Gita According to Gandhi*, Navajivan Publishing House, Ahmedabad, India, 1995, 1945c.

Mahatma Gandhi, *The Mind of Mahatma Gandhi*, Edited by R. K. Prabhu & U. R. Rao, Navanivan Publishing House, Ahmedabad, India. 1969, 1945 C.

R. R. Griffiths & W. A. Richards & U. McCann & R. Jesse, 'Psilocybin can occasion mystical-type experiences having substantial and sustained personal meaning and spiritual significance', Psychopharmacology, August 2006, Volume 187, Issue 3, Pages 268–283

Stanislav Grof, Hall Zina Bennett, *The Holotropic Mind, The Three Levels of Human Consciousness and How They Shape Our Lives*, HarperSanFrancisco, San Francisco, California, 1990.

Bibliography

Virginia Hanson, Shirley Nicholson, Rosemarie Stewart, Editors, *Karma, Rhythmic Return to Harmony*, Quest Books, Wheaton, Illinois, 1993.

Etty Hillesum, *An Interrupted Life, The Diaries of Etty Hillesum 1941-1943*, Translated by Arno Pemoerans, Pantheon Books, New York, New York, 1983

Abraham J. Heschel, *The Prophets*, Perennial Classics, HarperCollins, New York, New York. 2001. 1962C.

Michael Jacobi, Wolfram Schwenk, Andreas Wilhelm, *Understanding Water: Developments from the Work of Theodor Schwenk*, Floris Books, Edinburgh, Scotland. 2005. C 1995.

William James, *The Varieties of Religious Experience, A Study in Human Nature*, Barnes & Noble Classics, New York, New York, 2004.

Carl Jung, 'A Causal Connecting Principle,' from the Collected Works of Carl Jung, Bollingen Series, Princeton University Press, Princeton, New Jersey, 2010,.

Carl Jung, *C.G. Jung Letters, 2:1951-1961*, edited by Gerhard Adler, Princeton University Press, Princeton, New Jersey, 1975.

Carl Jung, *Memories, Dreams, Reflections*, Pantheon Books, New York, New York, 1963

Carl Jung, The Psychology of Kundalini Yoga, 'Notes of The Seminar Given in 1932', Sonu Shamdasani (ed.). Boligen Series XCIX, Princeton University Press, Prineton, New Jersey, 1996

Carl Jung, *Atom and Archetype, The Paul/Jung Letter, 1932-1958*, C. A. Meier, Princeton University Press, Princeton, New Jersey, 1992.

Lakshmi Kapani, *The Philosophical Concept of Samskara*, Motilal Banarsidass Publishers, Delhi, India. 2013.

Lamaa Kazi Dawa-Samdup, edited by W. Y. Evans-Wentz, *Tibet's Great Yogi Milarepa A Biography From the Tibetan Being Jetsun-Kahbum*, Oxford University Press, New York, New York, 1969

Peter King, *Dark Night Spirituality, Thomas Merton, Dietrich Bonhoeffer, Etty Hillesum, Contemplation and the New Paradigm*, SPCK, London, England, 1995.

Valchand P. Kothari, *The Law of Non-Violence (Ahimsa) and its Relevance For All Times*, Lalchand Hirachand, Sholapur, India, 1975.

Gopi Krishna, *Kundalini, The Evolutionary Energy in Man, With a Psychological Commentary by James Hillman*, Shambhala Publications, Boston, Massachusettes, 1997, 1967c.

Jaron Lanier, *Ten Arguments For Deleting Your Social Media Account Right Now*, Henry Holt & Co., New York, New York, 2018.

Don Lattin, *The Harvard Psychedelic Club, How Timothy Leary, Ram Dass, Huston Smith and Andrew Weil Killed the Fifities and Ushered in the New Age for America*, HaperOne, New York, New York, 2010.

Andrew Lockie, Nicola Geddes, *The Complete Guide to Homeopathy*, DK Publishing, New York, New York, 1995.

Martin Luther King, Jr.; *Strength to Love*, Phoenix Press, Large print edition, 1984, 1963C.

Gerald G. May, *The Dark Night of the Soul, A Psychiatrist Explores the Connection Between Darkness and Spiritual Growth*, HarperSanFrancisco, San Francisco, California, 2003.

Marshall McLuhan, *Understanding Media, The Extension of Man*, McGraw-Hill, New , New York, 1964.

Thomas Merton, *The Wisdom of the Desert, Sayings from the Desert Fathers of the Fourth Century*, New Directions, New York, New York, 1960.

John Michell, *The New View Over Atlantis*, Thames and Hudson, New York, New York, 1983, 1969C.

Milarepa, *Drinking the Mountain Stream, Songs of Tibet's Beloved Saint, Milarepa*, Translated by Kama Kunga Rinpoche and Brian Cutillo, Wisdom Publications, Boston, Massachusettes, 1995.

Thomas Moore, *Dark Nights of the Soul, A guide to Finding Your Way Through Life's Ordeals*, Gotham Books, New York, New York, 2004.

Nicholas Murray, *Aldous Huxley, A Biography*, Thomas Dunne Books, New York, New York, 2002.

Paramhansa Yogananda, *Autobiography of a Yogi*, The Philosophical Library, New York, New York, 2005, c 1946

Arthur C. Parker, *Seneca Myths and Legends*, University of Nebraska Press, Lincoln, Nebraska. 1989.

Stephen H. Phillips, Yoga, *Karma, and Rebirth; A brief History and Philosophy*, Columbia University Press, New York, NY. 2009.

Bibliography

Michael Pollan, *How to Change Your Mind, What the New Science of Psychedelics Teaches Us About Consciousness, Dying, Addiction, Depression and Transcendence*, Penguin Press, New York, NY, 2018.

Ira Progoff, *Jung Synchronicity, & Human Destiny, Noncasual Dimensions of Human Experience*, The Julian Press, New York, NY, 1973.

Saint John of the Cross, *Dark Night of the Soul*, in *The Complete Works of Saint John of the Cross*, The Newman Press, Westminster, Maryland 1964.

Swami Satyananda Saraswati, his version of Patanjali' Yog Suras, *Four Chapters on Freedom—Commentary on the Yoga Sutras of Patanjali*; Yoga Publications Trust, Munger, Bihar, India; 2002.

Viktor Schauberger, *Living Water, Viktor Schauberger and the Secrets of Natural Energy*, by Olof Alexandersson, Kit and Charles Zweigbergk(trans), Gateway Publishing, Dublin Ireland, 1990.

Theodor Schwenk, *Sensitive Chaos, The Creation of Flowing Forms in Water and Air*, Rudolf Steiner Press: London, 1965.

Theodor Schwenk, Wolfram Schwenk, *Tater The Element of Life, Essaya by Theodor Schwenk and Wolfram Schwenk* Anthroposophic Press, Great Barrington, Massachusetts, 2000.

Adi Shankara. *Crest Jewel of Discrimination (Viveka-Chudamani.)* Translated by Swami Prabhavananda and Christopher Isherwood, Vedanta Press, Hollywood, California. 1975, 1946C.

Rupert Sheldrake, *The Presence of the Past, The Memory of Nature*, Park Street Press, Rochester, Vermont, 2012, c1988.

Sri Swami Sivananda, *Practice of Karma Yoga*, Motilal Banarsidass, Delhi, India, 1974, 1965c.

Sri Swami Sivananda, *Mind—Its Mysteries and Control*, The Divine Life Society, Himalayas, India. 2011, C 1935.

Huston Smith, *Cleansing the Doors of Perception, The Religious Significance of Entheogenic Plants and Chemicals*, Jeremey P. Tarcher/Putnam, New York, New York, 2000.

Anthony Storr, *Solitude, A Return To The Self*, The Free Press, New York, New York, 1988.

Claire Sylvia with William Novak, *A Change of Heart, A Memoir*; Little, Brown and Company; Boston, Massachusetts, 1997

Henry David Thoreau, *Walden*, W. W. Norton & Co., New York, New York, 1966.

Henry David Thoreau, 'Thoreau Life in Principle', in the *Portable Thoreau*, Penguin Books, New York, New York 1982

Father Francis V. Tiso, *Liberation in One Lifetime, Biographies and Teachings of Milarepa*, North Atlantic Books, Berkeley, California, 2014.

Sherry Turkle, *Alone Together, Why We Expect More from Technology and Less From Each Other*, Basic Books, New York, New York. 2017.

Jean M. Twenge, iGen, *Why Today's Super-Connecte Kids Are Growing Up Less Rebellious, More Tolerant, Less Happy—and Completely Unprepared for Adulthood*, Atria Books, New York, NY, 2017.

Jean M. Twenge, 'Have Smartphones Destroyed a Generation?', The Atlantic. September 2017. www. theatlantic. com/ magazine/archive /2017/09/has-the-smartphone-destroyed-a-generation/534198/

Roland Vernon, *Star in the East, Krishnamurti the Invention of a Messiah*, Palgrave, New York, New York, 2000.

Swami Vivekananda; *Raja Yoga*, Ramakrishna-Vivekananda Center, New York, NY 1973.

Benedicta (Sister) Ward, translator, T*he Sayings of the Desert Fathers, The Alphabetical Collection*, Cistercian Publications, Kalamazoo, Michigan, 1975

White, Ruth; *Karma & Reincarnation, A Comprehensive and Inspirational Guide*, Samuel Weiser, Inc., York Beach Maine, 2001

Edward O. Wilson, 'The Biological Diversity Crisis', BioScience, Vol 35, No.1, Dec 1985

Edward O. Wilson, *The Meaning of Human Existence*, Liveright Publishing Corp, New York, New York. 2014.

Walter Wink, *Engaging the Powers, Discernment and Resistance in a World of Domination*; Fortress Press, Minneapolis, MN, 1992.

Ian Whicher, 'The Liberating Role of "Samskara" in Classical Yoga, Journal of Indian Philosophy', Vol. 33, No. 5/6, December 2005.

Patrick Woodhouse, *Etty Hillesum, A Life Transformed*, Continuum, New York, New York, 2009.

Notes

Chapter 1 Everything Has Karma
1. Claire Sylvia *A Change of Heart, A Memoir*;. Page 89.
2. Ibid. Page 9.
3. About Paul Pearsall, www. paulpearsall. com/info/about. html.
4. Paul Pearsall, *The Heart's Code*. Random House, New York, NY. 1999. I believe this is the book whose working title was *Cellular Memories: The New Psychology of the Heart* that Claire Sylvia refers to on page 114 of her book.
5. Ibid. Page 117.
6. 'Changes in Heart Transplant Recipients That Parallel the Personalities of Their Donors', Paul Pearsall, Ph.D., Gary E. R. Schwartz, Ph.D., & Linda G. S. Russek, Ph.D.; Journal of Near-Death Studies, VOL. 20 NO. 3, SPRING 2002.
7. 'Thousands mark 500 years of Trier pilgrimage', Claudia Krell, Deutsche Well, April 13, 2013, http://www.dw.com/en/thousands-mark-500-years-of-trier-pilgrimage/a-15947238.
8. Tony Faber, *Stradivari's Genius, Five Violins, One Cello and Three Centuries of Enduring Perfection*, Random House, New York. Page XVI.
9. Yehudi Menuhin, *Unfinished Journey*, Alfred A. Knopf, New York, 1977. Page 206.
10. 'Why have so many dogs leapt to their deaths from Overtoun Bridge?', Daily Mail October 17, 2006. http:// www. dailymail. co. uk/news/article-411038/Why-dogs-leapt-deaths-Overtoun-Bridge.html.
11. 'Scotland: 600 dogs mysteriously jump off haunted suicide Overtoun bridge',Maria Khan, International Business Times, June 25, 2015, http:// www.. ibtimes. co. uk/scotland-600-dogs-mysteriously-jump-off-haunted-suicide-overtoun-bridge-1507827.
12. 'Dog Suicide Bridge': Why Do So Many Pets Keep Leaping Into a Scottish Gorge', Ceylan Yeginsu, New York Times, March 27, 2019.

13. T. C. Lethbridge, *The Essential T. Lethbridge*, Edited by Tom Graves and Janet Hoult. Granada Publishing: London England, 1980. Page 38.
14. "The Sins of Our Fathers," Night Gallery, Rod Serling, teleplay by Halsted Welles, from a short story by Christiana Brand February 23, 1973. Universal Studios, Night Gallery Season Two, DVD Universal Studios 2008.
15. *The Bhagavad Gita*, Translated by Eknath Easwaran, Nilgiri Press, The Blue Mountain Press, Tomales, California. 2001, 1985. Page 66.

Chapter 2 The Illusion of Reality

16. A. B. Purani, *The Life of Sri Aurobindo*, Sri Aurobindo Ashram, Pontichetty, India, 1978. Page 103. Purani describes it as a series of mystical experiences including experiencing Brahman Consciousness.
17. Ibid. Pate 110.
18. Ibid Page 135.
19. Kireet Joshi, *Aurobindo and the Mother, Glimpses of Their Experiments, Experiences and Realizations*, The Mother Institute of Research, Motilal Banarsidass Publishers, Delhi, India, 1999. Page 57.
20. Sri Aurobindo. *Letters on Yoga*, Volume 22, 'Section Five, Planes and Parts of The Being.' Page 236.
21. Adi Shankara. *Vivekachudamani of Shri Shankaracharya*, Swami Madhavananda (trans), Advaita Ashrama: Calcutta, India 1957 #391.
22. Adi Shankara. *Crest Jewel of Discrimination* (Viveka-Chudamani.) Translated by Swami Prabhavananda and Christopher Isherwood, Vedanta Press, Hollywood California. Pages 53, 64, 68, 70.
23. Ibid. Page 68, 52.

Chapter 3 Samskaras, The Root of Karma

24. Meher Baba, *Discourses*, Volume I Sixth Edition (1967) Fifth Printing (December 1973.) An Avatar Meher Baba Trust eBook June 2011. www. ambppct. org/Book_Files/Discourses%20Vol%20I. pdf
25. Ibid. *Discourses*. For a discussion see Pages 54-64. "The problem of understanding the significance of human experience, therefore, turns round the problem of understanding the formation and function of sanskaras." Page 55.

Notes

26. Zoroastrianism is monotheistic and one of the oldest religions in the world born in Persia, or modern day Iran. It's prophet is Zarathushtra, or Zoroaster. Their one God is Ahura Mazda.
27. Several books on Meher Baba discuss his affinity for Masts. *The Wayfarers,* by William Donkin San Francisco, California, 1969. 1948c. In it he distinguishes five states: I) God-merged. I) God-intoxicated. III) God-absorbed. IV) God-communed. V) God-mad.
28. Ibid. Discourses, quote Page 26 and Page 36.
29. Meher Baba, *God Speaks..* Page 29.
30. Patanjali, *Four Chapters on Freedom—Commentary on the Yoga Sutras of Patanjali*; Saraswati, Swami Satyananda; Yoga Publications Trust, Munger, Bihar, India; 2002. Page 139 (Chapter 2, Sutra 1.)
31. Ibid.
32. Ibid. Page 68.
33. Christopher Isherwood mentions this on several occasions in his *Ramakrishna and His Disciples,* Simon and Schuster, New York, New York. 1965, 1959C. In discussing why he felt Ramakrishna was an avatar, a divine incarnation, Isherwood cites his peculiar powers. Saying, "[o]ne is his ability to remain for long periods in the state of Samadhi, which would quickly destroy the physical body of an ordinary human being." Page 94.
34. Blavatsky,H.P.; *Isis Unveiled, A Master-Key to the Mysteries of Ancient and Modern Science and Theology,* Volume 1; Theosophical University Press, Pasadena Calif., 1877; www.theosociety. org/pasadena/isis/iu-hp.htm. Page 244.
35. Emphasis on attributed. While many Theosophists quote this, I have found no such reference in any texts or sayings of leaders.
36. William Walker Atkinson, *Thought Vibration or the Law of Attraction in The Thought World*; First Published by The New Thought Publishing Co. Chicago 1906; Electronic Edition Published by Cornerstone Publishing, 2001. Pages 1-2.
37. Swami Vivekananda; *What Religion Is*; The Julian Press, New York, 1962, Page 51.
38. Yoga Sutra 4.8-11.
39. Yoga Sutras 2.12-14

40. Richard Hanson, *Hardwiring Happiness, The New BrainScience of Contentment, Calm and Confidence*, Harmony Books, New York, New York, 2013.

Chapter 4 Circles

41. Theodor Schwenk, *Sensitive Chaos, The Creation of Flowing Forms in Water and Air*, Rudolf Steiner Press: London, 1965. Page 39.
42. Ibid Page 41.
43. Three Initiates (believed to be William Walker Atkinson and possibly others.) *The Kybalion, A Study of the Hermetic Philosophy of Ancient Egypt and Greece*. Rough Draft Publishing, 2012.
44. H. P. Blavatsky, *The Key to Theosophy—an Abridgment*. Pages 122-123.
45. The Mother (Mirra Alfassa), *The Psychic Being, Soul, It's nature, Mission and Evolution*. Page 6.
46. *The Mother (Mirra Alfassa), Works of the Mother*, Volume 3, p. 63 http:// saccs. org.in/texts/mother/-ma-whatispsychicbeing.php
47. *Four Chapters on Freedom—Commentary on the Yoga Sutras of Patanjali*, Swami Satyananda Saraswati. Page 111.

Chapter 5 The Pilgrimage of Reincarnation

48. Andrea Leininger, Bruce Leininger, with K. Gross; *Soul Survivor: The Reincarnation of a World War II Fighter Pilot*, Grand Central Publishing, New York, New York. 2009
49. Ibid. Page 236.
50. Brian L. Weiss, MD; *Many Lives, Many Masters*, Touchstone Books, New York, New York, 2012, c 1988.
51. Ibid. Pages 54-55.
52. Ibid. Page 54.
53. Elbert Hubbard, *The Notebook of Elbert Hubbard: Mottos, Epigrams, Short Essays, Passages, Orphic Sayings and Preachments*, Roycrofters, East Aurora, New York, 1927. Page 12.
54. Thomas Sugrue, *The Story of Edgar Cayce, There is a River*, A.R.E. Press, Virginia Beach, Virginia, 1997. Pages 202, 224.
55. Ibid. Page 224.
56. Edgar Cayce, *Edgar Cayce on Reincarnation*. Page 40.

Notes

57. Ibid. Pages 54-55.
58. Ibid. Pages 52-55.
59. Ibid. Page 156.
60. Brian L. Weiss, MD, *Through Time Into Healing, Discovering the Power of Regression Therapy to Erase Trauma and Transform Mind, Body, and Relationships*, Fireside Books, New York, NY, 1993. Pages 91-92.
61. 'Revisiting John Lennon's Quickly Recorded 'Instant Karma', Nick Deriso, :// ultimateclassicrock. com/john-lennon-instant-karma-song/
62. *Four Chapters on Freedom—Commentary on the Yoga Sutras of Patanjali; Saraswati.* Page 318.
63. Carl Jung, 'A Causal Connecting Principle', *from the Collected Works of Carl Jung, CW 8,* Bollingen Series, Princeton University Press, Princeton, New Jersey, 2010, #969.
64. Ibid. #843.
65. Carl Jung, C.*G. Jung Letters, 2:1951-1961.* Page 109.
66. One sees this in the correspondence of Jung and Pauli over their twenty-six-year friendship. In one letter dated June 22, 1949 Jung writes Pauli, "Quite a while ago, you encouraged me to write down my thoughts on synchronicity. I have finally managed to get around to it and more or less collected my thoughts on the subject. I would be most grateful if you would cast a critical eye over it, covered as it is with question marks."
Atom and Archetype, The Pauli/Jung Letters , 1932-1958, Edited by C. A. Meier, Princeton University Press, Princeton, New Jersey, 1992. Page 36J.
67. Ibid. Synchronicity title.
68. Ibid. #840.
69. Ira Progoff, *Jung Synchronicity, & Human Destiny.* Page 158.
70. Paul Brunton, *The Gift of Grace,* Paul Brunton Foundation, Larson Publishing, Burdett, NY. Page 72.
71. Ibid. Page 50.

Chapter 6 The Web of Circles

72. Rupert Sheldrake, *The Presence of the Past, The Memory of Nature*, Park Street Press, Rochester, Vermont, 2012, c1988.

73. Rupert Sheldrake, "autobiography", www. sheldrake. org/about-rupert-sheldrake/autobiography
74. 'A Book for Burning", John Maddox, Nature, Sept. 24, 1981, Vol. 293.
75. 'Out of the Ordinary, Science Book of the Year', Christopher Potter, Sunday Times, December 2, 2012
76. Rupert Sheldrake, *The Presences of the Past.* Pages 2, 366.
77. 'Society, Spirit & Ritual: Morphic Resonance and the Collective Unconscious—Part II", Rupert Sheldrake, Perspectives, Fall 1987, 18(2). Pages 320-331.
78. Rupert Sheldrake, *A New Science of Life, The Hypothesis of Formative Causation*, J. P. Tarcher, Inc. Los Angeles, California. 1981
79. Ibid. Pages 189-190.
80. Sheldrake, *Presence of the Past.* Pages 204-207.
81. Rupert Sheldrake, Perspectives (Spring 1987), 18(1) 9-25, filed under Part I - Mind, Memory, and Archetype: Morphic Resonance and the Collective Unconscious; https:// www. sheldrake. org/research/morphic-resonance/part-i-mind-memory-and-archetype-morphic-resonance-and-the-collective-unconscious
82. Carl G. Jung, 'The Archetypes and The Collective Unconscious', CW 9 Part 1. #90.
83. Jung. CW 11, # 280.
84. Jung. CW 9 Pt 1. #90.
85. Ibid. #80.
86. Harold G. Coward, *Jung and Eastern Thought (SUNY series in Transpersonal and Humanistic Psychology)*, State University of Albany Press, Albany, New York, 1985. Page 104.
87. Ibid. Page 96.
88. Carl Jung, 'The Psychology of Kundalini Yoga, Notes of The Seminar Given in 1932 C. G. Jung', Edited by Sonu Shamdasani. Boligen Series XCIX, Princeton University Press, Princeton, New Jersey, 1996. Pages 9, 69.
89. Jung, CW 9 Part 1 #99.
90. Ibid. #49.
91. Carl Jung, CW 10. 'Mind and Earth', #54
92. Ibid. #103.

Notes

Chapter 7 Disconnect

93. Lamaa Kazi Dawa-Samdup, edited by W. Y. Evans-Wentz, *Tibet's Great Yogi Milarepa A Biography From the Tibetan Being Jetsun-Kahbum*, Oxford University Press, New York, New York, 1969, Page 71.

94. Father Francis V. Tiso, *Liberation in One Lifetime, Biographies and Teachings of Milarepa*, North Atlantic Books, Berkeley, California, 2014. Notes the role solitude played in helping Milarepa achieve sidhis. "At this place I intend to attain the flower of siddhi by practicing in solitude for three years in accordance with the instructions of my Guru." Page 204.

95. Ibid. Page 168.

96. Milarepa, *Drinking the Mountain Stream, Songs of Tibet's Beloved Saint, Milarepa*, Translated by Kama Kunga Rinpoche and Brian Cutillo, Wisdom Publications, Boston, Massachusettes, 1995. Page 139.

97. www. tibettravel. org/tibet-travel-guide/milarepa-cave.html, Gregg Braden in 'The Spontaneous Healing of Belief, Shattering the Paradigm of False Limits' in Wisdom Magazine also talks about Milarepa's cave and his handprint, http:// wisdom-magazine.com/Article.aspx/540/

98. 'Thomas Merton, *The Wisdom of the Desert, Sayings from the Desert Fathers of the Fourth Century*. Page 3.

99. Ibid. Page 3.

100. THOMAS MERTON'S LIFE AND WORK, Thomas Merton Center at Bellarmine University, http:// merton. org/chrono.aspx#

101. Bendicta Ward, translator, *The Sayings of the Desert Fathers, The Alphabetical Collection*, Cistercian Publications, Kalamazoo, Michigan, 1975. Page 2.

102. Anthony Storr, *Solitude, A Return To The Self.*. Pages 34-35, 202.

103. Henry David Thoreau, *Walden*, W. W. Norton & Co., New York, New York, 1966. Page 66.

104. Ibid. Page 91.

105. Ibid. Page 211.

106. Ibid. Page 221.

107. "It is not from the benevolence of the butcher, the brewer, or the baker, that we expect our dinner, but from their regard of their

own interest." Adam Smith, The Wealth of Nations; Random House, Modern Library Edition, New York, New York, 1937. Page 14.
108. Jaron Lanier, *Ten Arguments For Deleting Your Social Media Account Right Now*, Henry Holt & co., New York, New York, 2018. Page 6.
109. Ibid. Page 136.
110. Ibid. Page 25.
111. Henry David Thoreau, 'Thoreau Life in Principle', in *The Portable Thoreau*, Penguin Books, New York, NY 1982. Page 645.
112. Roland Vernon, *Star in the East, Krishnamurti the Invention of a Messiah*, Palgrave, New York, New York, 2000. Page 177.
113. J. Krishnamurti online. www. jkrishnamurti. org/about-dissolution-speech.
114. Sri Swami Sivananda, *Practice of Karma Yoga*, Motilal Banarsidass, Delhi, India, 1974, 1965c. Pages 35-36.
115. Eknath Easwaran, *Gandhi the Man, How One Man Changed Himself to Change the World*. Page 125.

Chapter 8 You shall Know Them By Their Fruit

116. Carl Jung, *Memories, Dreams, Reflections*. Page 153.
117. Jeannette Q. Byers in *Brothers in spirit : the correspondence of Albert Schweitzer and William Larimer Mellon*, Syracuse University Press; Syracuse, New York, 1996. Page Xviii. This is not the original source.
118. Jung, CW 9, Part 1, No. 517.
119. For a more detailed explanation of vortices see my *Vortices and Spirals, Unlocking the Mystery of Our Dynamic Relationship with Mother Earth*. Or read online 'Energy Vortices', http ://wisdom-magazine. com/Article.aspx/1355/.
120. The traditional view is that all energies are the same. My work shows otherwise and that there are host of energies (if you can call them that) each with an assigned task. I will leave it at that for the time being because saying more would open up a flood of questions.
121. Jung, Vol 9 Pt 1. #99.
122. Robins, L. N., Helzer, J. E., Hesselbrock, M. and Wish, E. (2010), 'Vietnam Veterans Three Years after Vietnam: How Our Study Changed Our View of Heroin.' The American Journal on Addictions, 19: 203–211. doi: 10.1111/j.1521-0391.2010.00046.x.

Notes

Originally published in Problems of Drug Dependence, 1977, Proceedings of the Thirty-Ninth Annual Scientific Meeting of the Committee on Problems of Drug Dependence. Online at: http://onlinelibrary.wiley.com/doi/10.1111/j.1521-0391.2010.00046.x/abstract.

123. Alix Spiegel. 'What Vietnam Taught Us About Breaking Bad Habits.' NPR: January 2, 2012, http:// www. npr. org/blogs /health/2012/01/02/144431794/what-vietnam-taught-us-about-breaking-bad-habits.

124. Nicholas Carr, *The Shallows*. Page 44.

125. James Burke & Robert Ornstein, *The Axemaker's Gift—A Double Edged History of Human Culture*; G. P. Putnam's Son, NYC, NY. 1995.

126. Ibid. Pages 201-218.

127. Rory Cellan-Jones, 'Stephen Hawking warns artificial intelligence could end mankind', BBC, www.bbc. com/news/technology-30290540

128. Jean M. Twenge, 'Have Smartphones Destroyed a Generation?', The Atlantic, September 2017. www. theatlantic. com/magazine/archive/2017/09/has-the-smartphone-destroyed-a-generation/534198/

129. Ernest Hemingway, *A Moveable Feast*, Bantam Books, New York, New York, 1965. Page 29.

130. 'Empathy: College students don't have as much as they used to', Michigan News University of Michigan, May 27, 2010.

131. Jean M. Twenge, *Generation Me: Why Today's Young Americans Are More Confident, Assertive, Entitled--and More Miserable Than Ever Before*, Atria Books, New York, New York, 2014, 2006c.

132. Jean M. Twenge, *iGen, Why Today's Super-Connected Kids Are Growing Up Less Rebellious, More Tolerant, Less Happy—and Completely Unprepared for Adulthood*, Atria Books, New York, New York, 2017.

133. Robert Meikyo Rosenbaum(editor) and Barry Magid(Editor) What's Wrong with Mindfulness (And What Isn't): Zen Perspectives, Wisdom Publications Inc., Somerville, Massachusetts, 2016.

134. Ibid. Page 2.

135. Ibid. Page 6.

Chapter 9 You are a Keeper for All of Creation

136. Eknath Easwaran, *Gandhi the Man*. Page 98.

137. The Dhammapada 246.

138. Friedrich Nietzsche, *Twilight of the Idols, Or How to Philosophize With a Hammer*, Translated by Duncan Large, Oxford University Press, Oxford, England. 1998. No. 8, page 5.

139. 'Vital Signs, Containing Unusual Resistance', Centers for Disease Control and Prevention, April 2018, www. cdc.gov/vitalsigns/ containing-unusual-resistance/index. html

140. Richard D. Smith & Joanna Coast, 'Resisting Resistance: Thinking Strategically About Antimicrobial Resistance', Georgetown Journal of International Affairs, Vol 4. No. 1. Winter/Spring 2003.

141. "Consistent with this hypothesis, the present study finds that before the age of two, toddlers exhibit greater happiness when giving treats to others than receiving treats themselves. Further, children are happier after engaging in costly giving–forfeiting their own resources – than when giving the same treat at no cost.Elizabeth W. Dunn & Kiley Hamlin, 'Giving Leads to Happiness in Young Children', Plus One, June 14, 2012, https: //doi. org/10.1371/journal.pone.0039211

142. 'Study finds it actually is better (and healthier) to give than to receive', Michael Poulin, Press Release U of Buffalo, By: Pat Donovan February 4, 2013, www. buffalo. Edu /news/releases/ 2013/02/ 003.html.

143. Valchand P. Kothari, *The Law of Non-Violence(Ahimsa) and its Relevance For All Times*, Lalchand Hirachand, Sholapur, India, 1975. Page 46.

144. Ibid. Pages 46-47.

145. Eknath Easwaran, *Gandhi the Man*. Page 138.

146. Edward O. Wilson, *The Future of Life*. Page 10.

147. Edward O. Wilson, 'The Biological Diversity Crisis', BioScience, Vol. 35 No.1, Dec 1985.

148. Edward O. Wilson, *The Meaning of Human Existence*, Liveright Publishing Corp, New York, New York. 2014

149. Edward O. Wilson, *Half-Earth, Our Planet's Fight for Life*, Liveright Publication, New York, New York. 2016.

Notes

150. Ruth Patrick, 'Biodiversity: Why Is It Important?', in Biodiversity II, Understanding and Protecting Our Biological Resources, John Henry Press, Washington, D.C., 1997. Pages 18-19.

151. 'Dimethyl sulfide generated by the algae alone is believed to be an important factor regulating cloud formation.' Edward O. Wilson, *The Future of Life*. Page 11.

152. Jessica Saunders, Layla Parast, Susan H. Babey, Jeremy V. Miles, 'Exploring the differences between pet and non-pet owners: Implications for human-animal interaction research and policy', June 23, 2017, https://doi.org/10.1371/journal.pone.0179494

153. Sri Swami Sivananda, Practice of Karma Yoga, Page 89

154. *Cayce on Reincarnation*, Page 254.

155. *Cayce on Reincarnation*, Page 122.

156. Helena P. Blavatsky, *The Key to Theosophy*, An Abridgement;, 1992. Pages 122-123.

157. Wink, Walter; *Engaging the Powers, Discernment and Resistance in a World of Domination*; Fortress Press, Minneapolis, MN, 1992, Page 89.

158. John Dear, 'Walter Wink, our best teacher of Christian nonviolence', National Catholic Reporter, May 29, 2012

159. 'Radical Saul Alinsky: Prophet of Power', Time Magazine, March 2, 1970. http://content.time.com/time/subscriber/article/0,33009,904228,00.html.

160. Saul Alinsky, *Rules for Radicals, A Pragmatic Prime for Realistic Radicals*, Random House, New York, New York, 1971. Page 125.

161. The Nobel Peace Prize for 1986, www.nobelprize.org/prizes/peace/1986/press-release/

162. Elie Wiesel –Acceptance Speech,/www.nobelprize.org/prizes/peace/1986/wiesel/26054-elie-wiesel-acceptance-speech-1986/

163. Rose Kumar M.D., The Power of Bearing Witness', Huffington Post,THE BLOG, 11/25/2013 Updated January 25, 2014.

164. Richard Deats, 'Walter Wink, Presente!', May 11, 2012, Fellowship of Reconciliation, http://forusa.org/blogs/richard-deats/walter-wink-presente/10545

165. Gray J. Cox, Bearing Witness: Quaker Process and a Culture of Peace, Pendle Hill Pamphlet 262 Pendle Hill Publications; Wallingford, Pa, 1985. Page 15.

166. E.P. Clapp, 'Selma 's Missing Rabbi', 01/17/2015, Dec 06, 2017. www. huffingtonpost. com/peter-dreier/selmas-missing-rabbi_b_6491368.html. and
Susannah Heschel, 'Two Friends, Two Prophets, Abraham Joshua Heschel and Martin Luther King Jr',. Plough Quarterly.www. plough. com/en/topics/community/leadership/two-friends-two-prophets
167. Abraham J. Heschel, *The Prophets*, Perennial Classics, HarperCollins, New York, New York. 2001. 1962C. Page 19.

Chapter 10 Take a Break With a Mystical Experience

168. Nicholas Murray, *Aldous Huxley, A Biography*, Thomas Dunne Books, New York, New York, 2002.
169. Aldous Huxley, *The Doors of Perception*, HarperPerennial ModernClassics, New York, New York, C1954, 2009
170. Ibid. Page 26.
171. Ibid. Page 24.
172. Ibid. Page 24.
173. Ibid. Page 56.
174. www. stanislavgrof. com/page-6/
175. Stanislav Grof, Hall Zina Bennett, *The Holotropic Mind, The Three Levels of Human Consciousness and How They Shape Our Lives*, HarperSanFrancisco, San Francisco, California, 1990. Page 204.
176. Ibid. Page 206.
177. Laura Mansnerus, 'Timothy Leary, Pied Piper Of Psychedelic 60's, Dies at 75,' New York Times, June 1, 1996.
178. Don Lattin, *The Harvard Psychedelic Club, How Timothy Leary, Ram Dass, Huston Smith and Andrew Weil Killed the Fifities and Ushered in the New Age for America*, HaperOne, New York, New York, 2010.
179. Huston Smith, *Cleansing the Doors of Perception*. Page 15.
180. R. R. Griffiths & W. A. Richards & U. McCann & R. Jesse, 'Psilocybin can occasion mystical-type experiences having substantial and sustained personal meaning and spiritual significance', Psychopharmacology, August 2006, Volume 187, Issue 3, Pages 268–283 |smith
181. https: //iands. org/ndes/about-ndes/what-is-an-nde.html.

182. Kenneth Ring, Ph.D., 'Editorial: Paradise is Paradise: Reflections on Psychedelic Drugs, Mystical Experience, and The Near-Death Experience', The Journal for Near-Death Studies, Vol. 6, No. 3.

183. Craig R. Lundahl, Ph.D., 'Guest Editorial: Lessons From Near-Death Experiences for Humanity', The Journal for Near-Death Studies, Vol. 12, No. 1.

184. PMH Atwater, *Beyond the Light*. Page 134.

185. William James, *The Varieties of Religious Experience, A Study in Human Nature*, Barnes & Noble Classics, New York, New York, 2004, 1902C. Page 360.

186. W. T. Stace, *Mysticism and Philosphy*, Jeremy P. Tarcher, Los Angeles, California, 1960. Page 79.

187. John A. Derr, Michael Persinger, 'Geophysical Variables and Behavior: LIV. Zeitoun (Egypt) Apparitions of the Virgin Mary as Tectonic Strain-Induced Luminosities', First Published February 1, 1989 Research Article https:// doi. org/10.2466 /pms.1989.68.1.123

188. Huston Smith, Cleansing the Doors of Perception. Page 4.

189. Michael Pollan, *How to Change Your Mind, What the New Science of Psychedelics Teaches Us About Consciousness, Dying, Addiction, Depression and Transcendence*, Penguin Press, New York, New York, 2018. Page 58-59.

190. Ibid. Page 59.

191. Irving Janis, *Victims of Group Think—A Psychological Study of Foreign Policy Decisions and Fiascoes*; Houghton Mifflin & Co.; Boston, Mass., 1972. Page 5.

192. *Four Chapters on Freedom*. Page 219.

Chapter 11 Working with Samskaras

193. 'Loving God: The Practical Teachings of Baba Virsa Singh' www. gobindsadan. org/loving-god-the-practical-teachings-of-baba-virsa-singh/

194. Ibid.

195. Eknath Easwaran, *Gandhi the Man*. Page 138.

196. Mahatma Gandhi, *The Mind of Mahatma Gandhi*. Page 80.

197. Anonymous, *The Way of the Pilgrim and The Pilgrim Continues His Way*..

198. Ibid. Page 15.

199. Ibid. Page 82.

200. Richard Hanson, *Hardwiring Happiness, The New BrainScience of Contentment, Calm and Confidence*, Harmony Books, New York, New York, 2013.

201. Richard Deats retired editor of The Fellowship of Reconciliation's Fellowship magazine told me he looked hard for the quote when he wrote his biography of Gandhi and never found it. Brian Morton in 'Falser Words Were Never Spoken", The New York Times (opinion and Editorial) Aug. 30, 2011 notes that Gandhi never said such. He tells what Gandhi did say, "If we could change ourselves, the tendencies in the world would also change. As a man changes his own nature, so does the attitude of the world change towards him. ... We need not wait to see what others do."

202. The Mother, Mirra Alfassa, The Mother Collected Works Volume 9, Questions and Answers 1957-58, Centenary Edition, Sri Aurobindo Ashram Trust, Pondicherry, India, 1977. Page 417.

203. Ibid. Page 414.

204. Ibid. Page 416.

205. Matthew Fox and Rupert Sheldrake, *Natural Grace*. Pages 166-167.

206. Arthur C. Parker, *Seneca Myths and Legends*, University of Nebraska Press, Lincoln, Nebraska. 1989. Page XXXI.

207. Ibid. Page 55.

208. The 100th Congress 1987-1988 passed H.Con.Res.331 - A concurrent resolution to acknowledge the contribution of the Iroquois Confederacy of Nations to the development of the United States Constitution and to reaffirm the continuing government-to-government relationship between Indian tribes and the United States established in the Constitution.

209. https:// mediawiki.middlebury. edu/MIDDMedia/Marshall_McLuhan

210. Marshall McLuhan, *Understanding Media, The Extension of Man*, McGraw-Hill, New , New York, 1964. Page 9.

Notes

211. Ibid. Page 8.
212. Ibid. Page 18.
213. Joseph Campbell & Bill Moyers, *The Power of Myth, Betty Sue Flowers, Editor*, Doubleday, New York, New York. Pages 6, 7.
214. www. taosinstitute. net/alexandra-asseily
215. 'The Power of Forgiveness', A film by Martin Doblmeier, www. firstrunfeatures.com
216. Martin Luther King, Jr.; *Strength to Love*, Phoenix Press, 1984, 1963C. Page 51.
217. Ibid. Page 73.
218. 'Strength to Love', Martin Luther King, Jr. Research and Education Center, Stanford. https:// kinginstitute.stanford. edu/ encyclopedia/strength-love

Chapter 12 Drink Living Water

219. Frantisek Kozisek, 'RISKS FROM DRINKING DEMINERALISED WATER' in 'Nutrients in Drinking Water', World Health Organization, 2005, www. who.int/water_ sanitationhealth/dwq/nutrientsindw. Pdf.
220. Zoltan P. Rona MD MSc, 'Early Death Comes From Drinking Distilled Water', www. mercola. com/article /water/distilled _water.htm
221. Dr. Joseph Mercola, 'Distilled Water: Avoid This Type of Water Purification', December 18, 2010. https:// articles.mercola. com/sites/articles/ archive/2010/12/18/ distilled-water-interview.aspx
222. Andrew Weil. 'Water, The Essential Nutrient', www. drweil. com/health-wellness/balanced-living/healthy-home/water-the-essential-nutrient/
223. Michael Jacobi, Wolfram Schwenk, Andreas Wilhelm, Understanding Water: Developments from the Work of Theodor Schwenk, Floris Books, Edinburgh, Scotland. 2005. C 1995. Page 44.
224. https://stroemungsinstitut.de/institute/
225. Email correspondence with Dr. Manfred Schleyer of the Institute of Flow Sciences (Institut für Strömungswissenschaften)

https:// stroemungsinstitut. de/water/. Thanks to the guidance of Dr. Schleyer I was able to look at some images and table in "Entwicklung von Verfahren zur Qualitätsverbesserung von gefiltertembzw. gereinigtem Trinkwasser" put out by the Institute of Flow Sciences.

226. Callum Coats, *Living Energies: An Exposition of Concepts Related to the Theories of Viktor Schauberger*, Gill & MacMillan, Dublin, Ireland, 2001. Page 107.

227. Alick Bartholomew, *Hidden Nature*. Page 32.

228. Viktor Schauberger, *Living Water, Viktor Schauberger and the Secrets of Natural Energy*, by Olof Alexandersson, Translated by Kit and Charles Zweigbergk, Gateway Publishing, Dublin Ireland, 1990, Page 145.

229. Ibid. Page 77.

230. Ibid. Page 77.

231. Ibid. Page 77, 78.

232. Stephan Ernest Riess www. geni. com/people/Stephan-Riess/6000000004360867476

233. Becky Oskin, 'Rare Diamond Confirms That Earth's Mantle Holds an Ocean's Worth of Water', Scientific American, LiveScience, March 12, 2014. www. scientificamerican. com/article/rare-diamond-confirms-that-earths-mantle-holds-an-oceans-worth-of-water/

234. Andy Coghlan, 'Planet Earth makes its own water from scratch deep in the mantle', NewScientist, 1/27/17. www. newscientist. com/article/2119475-planet-earth-makes-its-own-water-from-scratch-deep-in-the-mantle/

235. For more information about Steve Herbert and his work go to the Earth Water Alliance webpage, www.earthwateralliance. Org.

236. Jacques Benveniste, Davenas E, Beauvais F, Amara J, et al. (June 1988). "Human basophil degranulation triggered by very dilute antiserum against IgE". Nature. 333 (6176): 816–8.

237. "High Dilution" Experiments a delusion", Nature Vol 334. July 1988. John Maddox.

238. Bernard Poitevin, 'Jacques Benveniste: a personal tribute', Homeopathy, Vol. 94, No. 2, April 2005. https://doi.org/10.1016/j.homp.2005.02.004

239. 'Thanks for the memory', Lionel Milgrom, The Guardian, May 14, 2001, www.theguardian.com/science/2001/mar/15/technology2. "Experiments have backed what was once a scientific 'heresy', says Lionel Milgrom."

240. 'Electromagnetic signals are produced by aqueous nanostructures derived from bacterial DNA sequences', June 2009. PMID: 20640822 https://doi.org/10.1007/s12539-009-0036-7

241. Martin Enserink, 'French Nobelist Escapes "Intellectual Terror" to Pursue Radical Ideas in China', Science Dec 24, 2010: Vol. 330, http://science.sciencemag.org/content/330/6012/1732

242. Andrew Lockie, *Encyclopedia of Homeopathy*, DK Publishing, New York, New York. 2006, 2000C. Pages 14-15.

243. 'Making Mother Tinctures', the Bach Centre, www.bachcentre.com/centre/tincture.Htm

Chapter 13 Earth Magic

244. Clinton Ober, Stephen Sinatra (M.D.) and Martin Zucker. *Earthing, The Most Important Health Discovery Ever?*. Basic Health Publications: Laguna Beach, California, 2010 Page 13.

245. My YouTube channel MotherEarthPrayers has two video's on a transcending time experience I had meditating in a Natuarl Vortex in a vortex on a 2000+ year old stone structures. 'Transcending Time with an Energy Vortex--The 4 Tiered Stone Mound Part 1', www.youtube.com/watch?v=LS8WPg27rlw&t=1s

Part 2, www.youtube.com/watch?v=JLtN-KPLcuE&t=9s

246. John Michell, *The New View Over Atlantis*, Thames and Hudson, New York, New York, 1983, 1969C. Page 50.

247. Ibid. Page 50.

248. Swami Vivekananda; *Raja Yoga*, Ramakrishna-Vivekananda Center, New York, 1973. Page 32.

Chapter 14 Blown Away

249. Kitty Dukakis and Larry Tye; *Shock, The Healing Power of Electroconvulsive Therapy*, Penguin Group, New York, New York, 2006.
250. 'What is Electroconvulsive therapy (ECT)?', www. psychiatry. org/patients-families/ect
251. Robert Whitaker; *Mad in America—Bad Science, Bad Medicine, and the Enduring Mistreatment o the Mentally Ill*, Persues Publishing, Cambridge, Massachusetts, 2001. Page 106.
252. Ibid. Page 102.
253. Kitty Dukakis and Larry Tye; *Shock*. Pages 120-121.
254. 'Chapter IV Adverse Effects of ECT', Electroconvulsive Therapy, Task Force Report 14, American Psychiatric Association, Washington DC. 1978. Available online.
255. Kitty Dukakis and Larry Tye; *Shock*. Pages 136-137.
256. Sri Swami Sivananda, *Mind—Its Mysteries and Control*, The Divine Life Society, Himalayas, India. 2011, C 1935. Pages 245-246.
257. Joseph Eppes Brown, *The Sacred Pipe, Black Elk's Account of the Seven Rites of the Oglala Sioux*, Norman, University of Oklahoma Press, Oklahoma, . 1967, 1953 C. Page 32.
258. As my training manual I used books from the Bihar School of Yoga (www. biharyoga. net) from their Yoga Publications Trust. In particular *Yoga Prana, Pranayama Prana Vidya* by Niranjanananda Swami and Swami Niranjanananda Saraswati; and *Sri Vijnana Bhairava Tantra: The Ascent* by Satyasangananda Saraswati. They struck me as incredibly knowledgeable about the techniques and specifics.

Chapter 15 The Great Cleansing

259. Saint John of the Cross, Dark Night of the Soul, in *The Complete Works of Saint John of the Cross*, The Newman Press, Westminster, Maryland 1964. Book I, Ch I.i.
260. Ibid.
261. Thomas Moore, *Dark Night of the Soul, A Guide to Finding Your Way Through Life's Ordeals*, Gotham Books, New York, New York, 2004. Page XIV.
262. Ibid. Page 5.

Notes

263. Thomas Moore, *Care Of The Soul - A Guide For Cultivating Depth And Sacredness In Everyday Life*, HarperPerennial, New York, New York, 1994. 1995 C. Page 4.

264. The Clinical and Affective Neuroscience Laboratory (CLANlab) website, www. brown. edu/research/labs/britton/home, 'Meditation is Touted as a Cure for Mental instability But it Actually be Bad for You', Miguel Farias, The Independent, UK, May 21, 2015. www. independent. co. uk/life-style/health-and-families/features/meditation-is-touted-as-a-cure-for-mental-instability-but-can-it-actually-be-bad-for-you-10268291. html

265. 'Teresa of Avila', The New Advent, www. newadvent. org/cathen/14515b.htm

266. R. A. Herrera, *Silent Music, The Life Work, and Thought of John of the Cross*, William B. Eerdmans Publishing Company, Grand Rapids, Michigan, 2004. Pages 40-47.

267. Gillian T. W. Ahlgren, *Teresa of Avila and the Politics of Sanctity*, Cornell University Press, Ithaca, New York. 1996. Page 33.

268. Ibid. Page 56.

269. Gerald G. May, *The Dark Night of the Soul, A Psychiatrist Explores the Connection Between Darkness and Spiritual Growth*, HarperSanFrancisco, San Francisco, California, 2003. Pages 34- 35.

270. Patrick Woodhouse, Etty Hillesum, A Life Transformed, Continuum, New York, New York, 2009. Page 5.

271. Etty Hillesum, *An Interrupted Life, The Diaries of Etty Hillesum 1941-1943*, Translated by Arno Pemoerans, Pantheon Books, New York, New York, 1983. Page 1.

272. Ibid. Page 54.

273. Ibid. Page 58.

274. Ibid. Page 62.

275. Etty Hillesum, Letters from Westerbork, translated by Arnold J. Pomerans, Random House, New York, New York. 1946.

276. Joseph Campbell, Reflections on the Art of Living, A Joseph Campbell Companion, Edited by Diane K. Osbon, HarperCollinsPublishers, New York, New York, 1991. Page 24.

277. Gopi Krishna, *Kundalini, The Evolutionary Energy in Man, With a Psychological Commentary by James Hillman*, Shambhala Publications, Boston, Massachusetts, 1997, 1967c.
278. Ibid. Pages 16-17.
279. Ibid. Page 69.
280. Ibid. Page 132.
281. Ibid. Page 251.
282. Sri Ramakrishna, *Sri Ramakrishna, Prophet of New India, Abridged from The Gospel of Sri Ramakrishna,* Translated into English by Swami Nikhilananda, Harper and Brothers and Publishers, New York, New York, 1951. Pages 104-105.
283. Carl Jung, *Memories, Dreams, Reflections*, Page 277.

Index

A

Ahimsa, 133, 134, 141
Alinsky, Saul, 143
Archetypal phenomenon of vortex formation, 37
Archetypes, 74–75
Atwater, PMH, 157
Aura, 41, 89, 90, 109, 207, 216

B

Baba Virsa Singh, 275
Baba Virsa Singh Ji, ix
Baba, Meher, 24
  On samskaras, 24–26
Babaji, 167, 168, 169, 173, 175
Bear Witness
  Speak Truth to Power, 142–44
  Spiritual experience, 144–45
  To your thoughts, 92–94
  Victims speak, 144–45
Benveniste, Jacques, 203
Biodiversity, 135, 136, 273
Black Elk, 226
Britton, Dr. Willoughby, 234
Brunton, Paul, 66

C

Campbell, Joseph
  Myth, 182–83
  On the abyss, 242
Cayce, Edgar, 58, 60, 87, 138–39, 188
  Reincarnation as Teacher, 58
  Tether to others, 60–61

Cellular memories, 1–2
Chief Jake Swamp, 181
Chief Red Jacket, 179
Circle, 35–36
  Big Circle of Reality, 151, 153, 154
  Consciousness quotient, 46–51
  Corrupted, 120–23
  Embracing, 110–11
  Merging, 40–42
  New circles influence, 51–52
  Soup Theory of, 44–46
Collective unconscious, 73–74
Connecting circle, 35
In Nature, 37–38
Consciousness, 16
  Devolution of, 19–21
  Karma attaches to, 18
  Morality of, 46
  Quotient, measure, 46–51
  Sea of, 17–18
  Soup theory of, 44–46
  Unity Principle of, 42–44
Consciousness quotient, 46–51
Cosmic Prana
  About, 108

D

Dark night of the soul, 231–50
  Buddha's and Jesus', 242–43
  Helpful tools, 240–41
  John of the Cross, 231
Desert Hermits, 79–80, 79, 236, 245
Drop Picture Method, 198
Dukakis, Kitty, 221, 222

E

Earth Mysteries, 211
Easwaran, Eknath, 13, 95, 134
Electroconvulsive therapy (ECT), 221–23
Emoto, Masaru, 202
Energy healing, 107, 215
Energy Vortex
    Forms by, 129
    Merging with, 51–52
Evolving soul. *See* Psychic being

F

Fellowship of Reconciliation, 143, 147
Forgiveness
    Failure leads to rebirth, 58
    Get by forgiving, 177
    Grace, 65
    Lesson to learn, 186–89

G

Gandhi, Mahatma, 13, 176
    Ahimsa, 134
    Dispossess, 191–92
    Lifting others, 127–28
    On Mantra, 170
    Renouncing, 95
Geopathic stress, 193
Gobind Sadan, ix, x, 167, 168
Grace, 65–66
Grof, Stanislav, 154, 155, 163
Group karma, 42, 106, 137, 138, 139

H

Hahnemann, Samuel, 205
Hanson, Rick, 32
Haudenosaunee, xi, 181, 212
Hermetic Tradition, 40
Heschel, Rabbi Abraham Joshua, 148, 149
Hillesum, Etty, 238–40
Hillman, James, 244, 245, 246,
Homeopathy, 204, 260, 279
Hubbard, Elbert, 57
Huxley, Aldous, 151, 152, 153, 155, 245
    Reducing Valve, 153

I

iGen, 120

J

Jesus prayer, 170, 171
John of the Cross, 231, 235, 236, 237
Jung, Carl, 62, 73, 99, 238, 244, 250
    Collective unconscious, 73–74
    Karma Influence, 74
    On facing our passions, 250
    Synchronicity, 62–64

K

Karma, 2
    Attaches to consciousness, 18
    Be the change, 176–77
    Distributive karma, 42, 139
    Expanded view, 9–10
    Group, 137–39
    In heart transplants, 3–5
    Influence on Jung, 74
    Know by fruit, 98–99
    Law of Attraction, 29
    Levels of, 33–34
    Loving boomerangs, 189–91
    Purpose, 56
    Taking on, 40–42
    Tether to others, 60–61
    Timing of, 61–62
    Traditional View, 2–3
    Water's picks up, 196–98
Karma Yoga, 94

Index

King, Dr. Martin Luther Jr, 146, 149, 189
    Forgiveness, 189
Krishna, Gopi, 243, 244, 245, 246
Krishnamurti, Jiddu, 89, 90, 91, 124, 151
Kundalini, 244

L

Land memories, 6–8
Lanier, Jaron, 88
Law of Attraction, 28–29
    Agent of Change, 60
Leadbeater, Charles, 89
Leary, Timothy, 155, 156
Leininger, James, 53
Lethbridge, T.C., 7
Living water, xii, 198, 199, 201
    Spiral dance, 200

M

Madame Blavatsky, 28, 42
    Group karma, 137–39
Maddox, John, 69, 203, 268, 278
Mainline Religion, 110
Mantra
    As Meditation, 172–73
    Gandhi, 170
    Nam, xii, 149, 167, 168, 169, 173, 175
    Russian Pilgrim, 170–72
McLuhan, Marshall, 182–84
Meditation
    As samskara, 172–73
    Burn off samskaras, 223–25
    Dark night troubles, 235
    Group, benefits, 229–30
    In Natural Vortex, 207–10
    Influences, 114–15
    Sportsman's cushion as meditation cushion, 219–20

Medium is the Message, 182–84
Merton, Thomas, 79, 80
Mescaline, 152, 153, 154, 245
Michell, John, 210, 211
Milarepa, 77--79
Mirra Alfassa. *See* The Mother
Moore, Thomas, 233, 234, 241
Morphic field, 70
Morphic Resonance, 67–68
    Scope of, 70
    Transcend time, 178–79
Mother Earth
    Bondingg with, 215–17
    Nourishes your soul, 109
    Relationship humankind, 213–14
Mystical experience, 151, 154, 156, 157, 158, 159, 160, 161, 162, 163, 165, 167, 207, 227, 243
    Aldous Huxley's, 152
    Benefits, 154–56
    Consciousness raising, 160–62
    Defined, 158–59
    Huston Smith's, 156
    Turn to Mother Earth, 207

N

Nam, 167
Natural Vortex, 105, 106, 109, 129, 207, 208, 209, 210, 213, 214, 218, 219
    About, 207–10
    Responds to, 129
Near Death Experience, 156–58
Neuroplasticity, 32
New Thought Movement, 28, 32

P

Parker, Arthur Caswell, 181
Patanjali, 26, 27, 30, 48, 61, 134, 164, 172, 227, 261
Pearsall, Dr. Paul, 2, 3

Persinger, Michael, 159
Pranayama, 57, 91, 227, 228, 229, 246
Pratyahara, 164, 165
Psychic being, 47
   Consciousness quotient, meaure of progress, 46–51
Pumpkin Hollow Retreat, 215

R

Reducing valve, 153
Reiki, 122, 123
Reincarnation, 56–57
   Lessons to learn, 58–59
Resistance training, 130–31
Riess, Stephen, 201
Ritual, 83, 178–80
Russian Pilgrim, 170–72

S

Sacred site
   Benefits, 211–12
Sacred space
   Creating, 217–18
Saint Teresa of Ávila, 236, 237, 238
Samadhi, 27, 28, 30, 48, 160, 169, 172, 244, 246, 248, 249, 250
Samskara, 23
   As Meditation, 172–73
   Big dose of spiritual nutrtion burns off, 229–30
   Loving boomerangs, 189–91
   Meditation burns off, 223–25
   Meher Baba on, 24–26
   Properties, 23–26
   Ritual, 178–80
   Some to embrace, 173–75
   Sportsman's cushion imprint attaches to, 219–20
   Swami Vivekananda on, 30
   Transcend time, 178–79

Schauberger, Viktor, 198, 199, 200, 201, 202
Schwenk, Theodor, 36, 198
Shankara, Adi, 19
Sheldrake, Rupert, 67, 68, 69, 70, 71, 72, 73, 75, 76, 145, 178, 203, 253
   Morphic Resonance, 67–68
   Ritual, 178–79
Siddhis, 78
Sin eating, 8
Singh, Ralph, xii, 167
Smith, Huston, 86, 127, 129, 130, 155, 156, 162, 260,
Solitude, 78, 79
   Empowerment, 80–85
Soul group, 60–61
soup theory, 45
Soup Theory of Sacred Space, 104
Speak Truth to Power, 142–44
Spiritual nutrition, 12, 107, 109, 110, 112, 113, 114, 115, 117, 184, 207, 212, 214, 216, 219, 223, 225, 229, 232, 235, 246, 247, 255
   About, 106–9
   Big dose burns off samskaras, 229–30
   Blocked, 109–10
   Needed for Soul development, 107–8
Sportsman's cushion
   Importance, 219–20
Sri Aurobindo, 16
   On consciousness, 17–18
   Spiritual transformation, 176
Sri Ramakrishna, 27, 30, 250,
   on Samadhi, 250
Steiner, Rudolf, 36, 90
Story mantra, 48
   Creating, 184–86
   Listeners Influence, 103–5
   Oral tradtion, 180–82
Swami Satyananda Saraswati, 26, 27, 48, 61, 95, 165
Swami Vivekananda, 30, 51, 100, 218

Index

sweat lodge, 225, 226, 227
Sylvia, Claire, 1
Synchronicity, 62–64

T

Technology kills, 115–20
The Mother, 17
    Be the change, 176–77
    Psychic Being, 47
Theosophy, 28, 36, 257, 266, 273
Thoreau, Henry David, 84, 85, 89
Thoughts, 26
    Morphing, 31
    Seed Thoughts, 32
Transcend time, 34, 66, 70, 169, 179, 178–79, 210
Twenge, Jean, 119

U

Ultimate reality, 15–16
Unity Principle, 42–44

V

Vasanas, 30
Vedanta, 23, 30, 40, 151 264
Vortex Test, 105–6
Vrittis, 23

W

Water ceremony, 206
Weiss, Dr. Brian, 53–56
Wiesel, Elie, 144, 273
Wilson, E. O., 135, 136, 262, 272, 273
Wink, Walter, 142, 143, 147, 262, 273
    Jesus' Third Way, 142–43
Wisdom's Golden Rod, 66, 215

To Learn More

Books by Madis

Sacred Sites in North Star Country: Places in Greater New York State (PA,OH,NJ,CT,MA,VT,ONT) That Changed the World

Vortices and Spirals, Unlocking the Mystery of Our Dynamic Relationship With Mother Earth

The Way Home, Making Heaven on Earth

Japanese Euroderivatives

See, www. motherearthpress. net

Madis' Blogs

http:// motherearthprayers.blogspot. com

http:// clarksgully.blogspot. com Mother Earth Prayers

YouTube

MotherEarthPrayers

www.ingramcontent.com/pod-product-compliance
Lightning Source LLC
Chambersburg PA
CBHW071620170426
43195CB00038B/1501